NUNS

NUNS

A History of Convent Life
1450–1700

SILVIA EVANGELISTI

OXFORD
UNIVERSITY PRESS

OXFORD

UNIVERSITY PRESS

Great Clarendon Street, Oxford OX2 6DP

Oxford University Press is a department of the University of Oxford.

It furthers the University's objective of excellence in research, scholarship,
and education by publishing worldwide in

Oxford New York

Auckland Cape Town Dar es Salaam Hong Kong Karachi
Kuala Lumpur Madrid Melbourne Mexico City Nairobi
New Delhi Shanghai Taipei Toronto

With offices in

Argentina Austria Brazil Chile Czech Republic France Greece
Guatemala Hungary Italy Japan Poland Portugal Singapore
South Korea Switzerland Thailand Turkey Ukraine Vietnam

Oxford is a registered trade mark of Oxford University Press
in the UK and in certain other countries

Published in the United States
by Oxford University Press Inc., New York

© Silvia Evangelisti 2007

The moral rights of the author have been asserted
Database right Oxford University Press (maker)

First published 2007

British Library Cataloguing in Publication Data

Data available

Library of Congress Cataloging in Publication Data

Data available

Typeset by SPI Publisher Services, Pondicherry, India
Printed in Great Britain
on acid-free paper by
Biddles Ltd., King's Lynn, Norfolk

ISBN 978–0–19–280435–8

1 3 5 7 9 10 8 6 4 2

CONTENTS

ACKNOWLEDGEMENTS

This book owes much to a number of people. First of all I would like to thank Olwen Hufton and Gianna Pomata whose more than inspiring intellectual example and invaluable help have been immensely important for me. Many friends and fellow historians have contributed, in different ways, to my research in these years, in particular Ulrike Strasser, Sharon Strocchia, Raffaella Sarti, and Concha Torres who also read the nearly final version of the manuscript. Part of this book was written during one year at 'I Tatti', in Florence, where I had the opportunity to enjoy not only the beauty of the place and richness of its library but also many conversations with other fellows and staff, amongst them Molly Bourne, Roberta Morosini, Bronwen Wilson, Pedro Memelsdorff who helped me to decipher a German article on early music, and Katy Bosi who provided me with access to music databases. While this project was on its way I spent two fruitful months at Newberry Library, where I benefited from stimulating talks with Dale Kent, and the warm welcoming of Sara Austin and Jim Grossman. At the University of Birmingham, Monica Borg and Franco D'Intino, gave their sensible and witty opinions on this project when it first started to take shape, while Gerry Slowey was a really wonderful colleague. At UEA, Jim Casey read a part of this book offering his very straight forward and reassuring view, and Margit Thøfner gave me very good tips on the selection of images for the book while patiently listening to my quite naïve questions on the matter. At UEA, I also had the pleasure to engage in exciting and at times very random discussions with the components of the Gender Reading Group, run with impeccable determination by Nicola Pratt. My OUP editors Luciana O'Flaherty and Matthew Cotton helped me to bring this project to completion, while their two predecessors, Catherine Clarke and Katharine Reeve, saw the very beginning of it. Some non-historian friends, and my mother, added to this work. Claire Kilpatrick and Sylvaine Laulom have witnessed and amused themselves with my research on 'the nuns'. Angela Evangelisti, Corinna Rinaldi, Valerio Cocchi, and later Paola Lopilato, also expressed genuine interest in my work, alternated with sane boredom. My deep gratitude goes to all my baby-sitters and child minders too, in particular Emma Draper, Valentina Cardo, and Lucia Paliotta. Finally, Jonathan Hopkin threatened to leave me many times had I dared to dismiss his help with a simple 'thanks for polishing my English'; it is therefore with the greatest pleasure that I would like to thank him indeed for polishing my English and much more than this. I dedicate this book to my young daughter Giulia, though I doubt she will ever want to read it.

LIST OF FIGURES

Introduction

For many of us, nuns are a remote reality, detached from the world. But we are all more or less familiar with the sight of convents. Convents are part of both the urban setting and the rural landscape of a number of Western countries. Some still exist, while others have been turned into museums and become part of the national heritage, or have been transformed into schools, university departments, hotels, or—less happily—into hospitals, prisons, and army quarters. We are also familiar with the inside of these places: small rooms, internal cloisters, corridors, austere and imposing refectories, all spaces that often boast an impressive range of frescos, paintings, and architectural features. We may have visited these buildings or stayed in them, or simply learnt about them in novels, specialized publications, paintings, and films. This book deals with the women who lived in such places before they became what they are now. It invites the readers to go back a few centuries to discover what life was like in these communities, and to see how nuns, despite their small numbers, took on crucial social roles. Hopefully the following pages will persuade them that nuns' lives were not at all remote from those of their contemporaries. Their history is as remote from us as any other part of the past can often be—a faraway land, inexplicable but partly accessible.

Nuns have recently attracted many fans.[1] Female monastic communities, as well as individual nuns, have been the object of careful scrutiny by scholars seeking to explore their ecstatic visions, intellectual aspirations, and creativity in the domains of the visual arts, music, and the theatre.[2]

Many books have described their excursions outside their convents and their journeys outside Europe to participate in the colonial enterprise, inviting discussion on cultural encounters and new worlds.[3] This interest in convents has thrown light on political and religious changes and the ways in which these changes were experienced at grass-roots level, and the responses of different social groups to the State- and Church-sponsored policies that aimed to shape their lives.[4] The lives of nuns have also been reconstructed to explore the links between religion and ideology about gender and sexuality.[5] Convents have provided useful case studies of the dynamics of local economies.[6] Part of the reason for this success is that the history of nuns offers multiple insights into different spheres of knowledge, making convent life a truly multidisciplinary field of study.

Drawing on the many questions that this very fertile literature has proposed, this book looks at the history of convent by focusing on the period from roughly the late fifteenth century to the early eighteenth century. These two chronological markers are, like all chronological limits, rather arbitrary. The history of nuns begins in the early centuries of the Christian era, with the first sporadic groups of men and women who opted for spiritual life, alone or in communities. These communities then evolved into the more and more formal institutions of the Middle Ages, and underwent sometimes major redefinitions following the reorganization of the confessional map of Europe triggered by the outbreak of the Protestant Reformation in the sixteenth century and the French Revolution in the eighteenth, and continue to exist in the present day. It is not easy to establish meaningful cut-off points within such a long period. Furthermore this book draws on a secondary literature which, as far as the early modern period is concerned, has recently benefited from some wonderful additions focusing on the sixteenth and seventeenth centuries. I have therefore tried to identify a manageable period for this study that, while fitting in with my own research interest, can draw on recent thought-provoking research on female religious lives. The period covered by the book allows us to look at some much-discussed aspects of European history from the gendered perspective of female monastic communities. These include the growing call for spiritual renewal in the second half of the fifteenth century, the major reform programme launched by the

Catholic Church with the Council of Trent in the middle of the sixteenth century, and the slow implementation of this reform whose directives were ratified by some states as late as the early seventeenth century. We can also use the study of convents to understand the flourishing of the arts and literary activities in the Renaissance and Baroque age, the launch of colonial enterprise in America, and the establishment, in the seventeenth century, of socially oriented forms of spiritual commitment, such as charitable and teaching organizations and new religious orders.

The geographical context explored in this book is Catholic Europe—a Europe which extends to the New World and its Spanish and French American colonies, but which at the same time barely extends eastwards at all. Indeed, the existing and abundant literature on convents in Eastern European countries is not available to this author since it is rarely translated. Such focus on a specific type of institution within a broad geographical space and a time-span of over two centuries has some implications worth noting. Convents were highly regulated institutions, subject to one normative model which to a certain extent was designed to be international and universal. But the Catholic world in which nuns were present was geographically vast, and culturally, socially, and politically very heterogeneous.[7] We are therefore presented with a variety of pictures of convent life as we move between countries and continents. This inevitably complicates the task of the book and it has not always been possible to draw connections between the different geographical contexts, identify differences and similarities, and meaningfully elaborate on them.

One crucial issue that arises wherever we approach the study of nuns is the reason why these women entered convents. What did convents offer to those who joined them? The life of the nun entailed a total spiritual experience in the service of God, based on prayer, silent contemplation, and an unconditional commitment to the religious community, according to the ideal and rules of the early monasticism. Entering the convent required a radical change in lifestyle, the acquisition of a new name and a monastic habit, and the abandonment of all worldly goods and values. In the convent, nuns were to live enclosed and pray for the worldly community of men and women, invoke God's protection for them, and interact with the Divine on their behalf. But on entering the convent women gained spiritual fulfilment as well as something else: a perfectly acceptable social identity outside marriage. They became part of an all-female group organized like a spiritual family while escaping family duties, motherhood, the possible dangers associated with childbearing, the uncertainties of widowhood, and—not least—marital authority. In the hagiographical literature and lives of saints that proliferated in the Middle Ages and early modern period, this idea of religious commitment as an alternative to family is described through the examples of holy women who rejected marriage in favour of the 'heavenly groom'. We read of women escaping from home in order to join a monastic community, and even throwing themselves into boiling water, so that their scarred bodies and faces would be unappealing for the prospective husbands their families were determined to impose on them.[8] This literary representation drew on the gender ideology of the time, which allowed women only two acceptable paths: religious life in the cloister, or marriage and family commitments.

Convents provided more practical opportunities too, for women and in particular for their families. First of all, convents were places of female education. The spiritual teachings imparted to novices and girl boarders not only placed great emphasis on morality but also taught them very basic reading and writing, as well as more practical and domestic skills. This education would eventually turn them into either good nuns, or good wives and mothers. Because of this, convents became popular for families whose daughters, sisters, and sometimes widowed mothers could be accommodated and educated in a safe environment, where their honour was protected by the exclusion of outsiders, the vigilance of other holy women committed to chastity, and the supervision of father superiors.

Female monastic houses also provided an option for families who wished to place their female offspring in monastic retreat instead of marrying them off. This choice could be made on the grounds of piety and the desire to support religious institutions, or for economic reasons. Indeed, convents were vital to the patrimonial needs and marriage strategies of the elites and rich middling sorts. The case of Italy has been widely studied in this respect and reveals a good deal about the logic of these family decisions. The cost of placing a daughter in a convent often was far lower than a marriage dowry. Aristocratic and mercantile families therefore pushed some of their women into nunneries in order to protect their wealth from the constantly increasing cost of these dowries. In some periods, dowries far exceeded the value of the sums—the so-called spiritual dowries—families were required to pay to convents for their women who became nuns. For instance, between the fifteenth and the sixteenth centuries in a number of Italian cities, convent dowries—although subject to inflation themselves—were between one-third and one-tenth of marriage dowries.[9] This resulted in a boom of female monastic professions: in Florence, between 1500 and 1799, 46 per cent of the women of the female elite—for a sample of twenty-one patrician families—entered religious institutions. In Milan three-quarters of the daughters of the aristocracy lived in convents.[10] Female monastic professions were therefore in part explained by the inflation of marriage dowries, and by elite families' attempts to ensure their women did not marry outside their rank and status. A similar trend can be observed also in Spain. However, such a pattern was not entirely typical. In England, where women could enter convents until the Reformation, the picture was different. Since families tended to allow their daughters to marry outside their rank with cheaper dowries and less damage to their patrimonies, the demographic pressure on convents was less intense and fewer women ended up in religious retreat.[11]

Convents also offered a response to the social problems created by families' weaknesses and disfunctions. Although they mostly recruited amongst the elites, convents also opened their doors to women from less privileged social backgrounds. Women from humble origins often entered as servant nuns, and performed domestic services and manual work. Convents could also serve as a refuge for single women. Widows and women with troubled pasts, such as abandoned and battered women or ex-prostitutes willing to reform, could find protection and a degree of economic stability within the cloister walls.

Seen from the perspective of family strategies, monastic life could be a paternal imposition as much as a choice, as a number of authors—from nuns to enlightened thinkers such as Voltaire—described. This book touches on this by looking at the words of the talented seventeenth-century Venetian nun

Arcangela Tarabotti, a woman who had been placed in the convent against her will, and who denounced the pressures from fathers who forced women into the convent, thus turning their life into 'hell'.[12] But women could also suffer the exact opposite of this fate. Following the advent of the Protestant Reformation, many convents were closed and nuns were sent back to their families, sometimes against their will. In England convents were suppressed by Henry VIII in 1536 and nuns forced to flee the country. In Germany nunneries were abolished too—though a few survived in hybrid forms as Protestant nunneries. In cities that turned Protestant, such as Strasburg, the majority of nuns left, and only a few of them resisted, vehemently opposing their families' decision to take them out of the cloisters.[13]

The Council of Trent (1545–63), the major reform programme launched by the Catholic Church to pursue spiritual renewal and respond to the Protestant threat, crops up in many pages of this book. Trent outlined an articulate reform programme addressed to the regular clergy, and most notably reasserted strict cloister rules in female monastic communities. Although there has been much debate on the impact of Trent on female communities, and the extent to which enclosure was successfully or unsuccessfully introduced in them, two important aspects still deserve attention. On the one hand, it is true that enclosure was not strictly observed in many communities before Trent. When Tridentine orders were implemented, many nuns—in Germany, Italy, and Spain—rejected it on the grounds that it would have irremediably jeopardized their traditions and way of life, subjecting them to conditions stricter than those they had subscribed to on joining religious life. On the other hand it is also undeniable that the impact of Trent on nunneries has been overestimated and that the history of nuns seems to have been characterized by a kind of continuous tension between enclosure and the push towards a more open model of religious life. Nuns continued to live unenclosed well after Trent, and in some cases practised flexible and relaxed forms of enclosure. External circumstances also deeply clashed with enclosure. In times of war, such as during the Thirty Years War in Germany, convents were attacked and sometimes destroyed, obliging nuns to escape and find shelter elsewhere. When communities were re-established after the war enclosure was not always strictly observed.

In the Bavarian convent of Mariastein, close to Eichstatt, the nuns had to leave; when they returned, in the early 1630s, they had to work in the fields in order to regain their economic stability.[14]

The application of rigid enclosure was questioned in some religious orders in the context of discussion over their internal organization. The case of the Ursulines is particularly interesting. Deeply engaged in teaching and educational work, Ursuline houses—although mostly enclosed—ran convent schools in seventeenth-century France and Italy, where communities negotiated specific permission from Rome for this educational enterprise. In France some communities devised a system of enclosure that allowed female students inside their convent building, whilst minimizing direct contact with them through a resourceful re-organization of the rooms and doors. Additionally, in France, the order was divided over the issue of enclosure. In a number of communities young nuns supported it against the older generations who instead opposed it.[15] It seems, therefore, that nuns had different understanding and practices of enclosure, and for some of them it was not a barrier denying them access to the world, but instead something which liberated them from restrictions imposed by the outside world. Similarly, enclosure acquired a positive meaning for nuns who faced the closure of the convents as a result of the Reformation. The *Petite Chronique* by Jeanne de Jussie, the abbess of the Poor Clare convent in Geneva, reports how in 1535 the nuns were forced out of their cloister, and describes the violation of enclosure perpetrated by a group of armed citizens. In this case, nuns saw enclosure as the means of guaranteeing the very existence of their community, whilst the violation of enclosure was the symbol of its dissolution.[16] So we are presented with two different narratives of enclosure, reflecting either resistance or acceptance according to how best nuns could keep control over their religious community. In both cases what the nuns demanded—through their actions and writings—was the right to decide for themselves how to organize and govern their collective life.

It is also evident that enclosure, when enforced, did not necessarily imply the isolation of convents or the breaking-off of all contact with the world. True, enclosure initially had significant economic effects, making convents poorer in many cases. Enclosure undermined nuns' direct contacts with the external market, making it difficult for them to trade and halting the charitable works they performed for the benefit of the community. Nuns were now banned from going out and begging alms, and became completely reliant on dowries and donations from their benefactors. Still, despite this economic strain they found ways to adapt their remunerative activities to enclosure and reach the outside market, as Claire Walker shows for the English convents in seventeenth century.[17]

Enclosed or not, convents appear to have been, ever since the Middle Ages, sources of female creativity and intellectual production. In aristocratic convents in particular, artistic and writing activities flourished. Nuns copied manuscripts and were active in writing an extraordinary variety of texts, as well as engaging in the visual and musical arts, and in the production of textile works such as embroidery and tapestries. Nuns commissioned frescos and paintings for their convents, and hired well-known and popular artists. They were also the recipients of works of art commissioned by wealthy patrons and displayed in their convent public church, which explains why convents possessed masterpieces of Renaissance and Baroque art, and precious objects and musical instruments such as organs.[18] When we look at the works of the nuns who wrote, painted, sculpted, organized theatrical performances, sang, and played music, the convent appears to have been more of a catalyst for female cultural production than an impediment. This seems to have been a continuous tradition that bloomed in the late Middle Ages—embodied by icons of female creativity like Roswitha of Gandersheim (935–73) and Hildegard of Bingen (1098–1179)—and survived through the following centuries. Such activities received additional input from the emphasis the Catholic reformers placed on education and piety. The example of convent theatre shows how performances on the cloister stage, in which the nuns participated as authors, actors, and spectators, were educational tools for delivering messages about female perfection, chastity, and obedience, the same messages conveyed by devotional literature and hagiographical texts. Theatre could be a very direct and effective medium, more effective than books read loudly in the communal rooms. This is particularly important if we consider that, even though nuns received basic education, many of them may still have been illiterate.[19]

But when examining convent arts and culture, we have to consider a key factor: the nuns art often had a deep devotional meaning and function outside the literary and artistic canons of the time, and was primarily addressed to the restricted audience of the convent. Nuns wrote for and about their sisters, organized theatrical performances with music and dance, and painted sacred images on the walls of their cloister and churches to aid them in their prayers and contemplative moments. In rare cases, this artistic activity reached people outside. In the seventeenth century, the Mexican poet and writer Sor Juana Inés de la Cruz, published her works with the help of the vicereine who was one of her strongest supporters, and won acclaim. Similarly, artist nuns—many of whom have just begun to be identified—sometimes exhibited their works outside the walls. In the sixteenth century Plautilla Nelli, in Florence, was one nun—though not the only one as we will see—who reached the city's art market. She painted for her convent, received commissions for works to be exhibited in public churches, and completed a few works for patrician Florentines.[20]

According to a tradition dating back to the origin of monasticism, the religious community acted as a 'spiritual family' and called on its members to fulfil typical family roles. Nuns were 'sisters' who should love each other equally. They were the 'daughters' of the 'mother' abbess, whom they had to obey, and were governed by the 'father' superior. Spiritual ties, as opposed to blood ties, were eternal and therefore indivisible. Spiritual sisters were united by divine grace. As families outside the family, convents gave women permanent membership of the spiritual community, contrasting with the merely transitory membership of the worldly community. Once in the convent, women also acquired an entirely new set of symbolic 'relatives' that reached beyond the boundaries of kinship, although not necessarily those of class.

Spiritual communities though they were, convents also reproduced the dynamics of the society within which they were placed and nuns were a group tightly linked to the outside world. Convents contained many siblings and other relatives such as aunts, nieces, and sometimes mothers, and were run by father superiors who often had relatives among the nuns.[21] Cloistered buildings were sometimes built in close proximity to family palaces, or even attached to them, a proximity which accentuated in bricks and mortar nuns' connections with their origins. Nuns also maintained links with their relatives, acquaintances, and patrons outside the walls through letters and conversations in the parlour. Convents were places of civic sociability.

The global perspective adopted by this book allows us to focus on the nuns' osmotic links with the larger social environment from a particular angle: the expansion of female monasticism in the sixteenth and seventeenth centuries in both Europe and the New World, and the conditions that made it possible. For example, the book examines two specific contexts: the new Discalced foundations in Europe, and the first establishment of convents in New France and New Spain. The Discalced departed from Spain and began—following the example of their holy founder, Saint Teresa of Avila—the systematic foundation of new houses, moving from Portugal to Poland and from Italy to the English Channel. In little more than half a century they extended the female branch of their order throughout Catholic Europe. Their mission was sponsored by the Catholic elites, in particular the archdukes of Flanders, who saw in these cloistered and travelling nuns a weapon to fight against the Protestants and to reinvigorate Catholicism. At the same time as the Discalced were founding convents, the Ursulines began to join the American missions. The story of the French nun Marie de l'Incantation, and her work in Canada where she set up a convent to educate Amerindian girls, shows the active participation of cloistered women in the making of the new colonial society. We learn a similar lesson from looking at female religious houses in Spanish America. These were not only repositories for surplus women whose families did not want to marry them off, but also a focus for the reproduction of the new American culture, in part similar to that of the old world, but also imbued with the values of the new one.

Finally this book looks beyond the enclosed version of female monastic life and the purely contemplative spiritual experience, to consider the different expectations and ambitions of religious women. Many new orders and congregations were founded in the seventeenth century, most of them in France. These new orders promoted new social roles for religious women, in the service of the community. Indeed, at least some of them were founded with the precise intent of placing women in charge of teaching, care work, and charitable activities in hospitals, asylums, and prisons.[22] This active form of religious commitment opened up the possibility of women embracing a socially oriented apostolate. This was a development that would have changed women's place in religion. More important still, it forwarded the opportunity for them to follow a life-path as single women, out of the binary divide of either marriage or the cloister.

ONE

On Nuns and Nunneries

One day in April 1575, the citizens of Florence witnessed a great ceremony: seven young novices made their solemn profession of vows in the convent of San Giovannino of the military order of the Knights of Malta. A large female community located along Via San Gallo, not far from the Duomo, San Giovannino mainly hosted the daughters of the aristocracy, some of whom came from the ruling Medici family. The seven girls walked into the church in pairs while singers and musicians performed the traditional 'Come Thou Brides of Christ', and then headed toward the altar of the church where they received the black veil and habit before the father superior of the convent. Great numbers of patrician men and women, as well as the girls' families and the local clergy, participated in these splendid celebrations, orchestrated by the nuns as memorable occasions which maximized their public visibility and presence in the city. Indeed, as reported in the convent chronicle, written by a nun towards the 1740s, the nuns would

> make a great feast in the church inviting noble men and women and all the knights of Malta who were in Florence at the time. The novices who professed gave a certain number of pounds of wax for the sacristy, and on this occasion they gave 80 pounds of wax; the expenses for the profession were covered by the families; and the convent gave each novice 7 lire for the banquet of the ladies who accompanied them.[1]

For these sumptuous feasts, knights and dames, and the Medici duchesses, would invite women from noble families to join them in their carriages to arrive at the convent, and these aristocratic women joined in the party organized inside the parlour reserved for visitors, staying until it ended, sometimes late at night. This was the conclusion of the rite of passage marking the women's definitive abandonment of the world and the beginning of their new holy life, and consigning them to their eternal heavenly groom. This ritual also had a political meaning as it celebrated, through the passage of women from lay society to the religious institution, the alliance between the political elites and the Catholic Church so crucial to public life.

Analogous scenes were played out, on the occasion of a nun's profession, over a long period of time in convents across the Catholic world. Two centuries later, in very different surroundings, the citizens of Mexico witnessed a similar ceremony. This time, in the role of 'Bride of Christ', an Indian princess entered the convent of Corpus Domini to become a nun. 'Sister Maria Magdalena'—the religious name she took—paraded through the streets of the city escorted by an armed group of Indians:

> The news that the Indian woman had at last achieved the opportunity to enter the religious state was celebrated not only among her family but also throughout the whole city;...Her father made the arrangements for the journey, and as he was rich in worldly goods, he wished his daughter to be transported [to Mexico] with every pomp and in complete safety, fulfilling what he thought to be his obligation to display his nobility and estate, and at the same time assuring that the young girl would cross those vast and desert lands without the dangers posed by the proximity of wild Indians. He hired a competent party of tamed Meco Indians who, armed with bow and arrow, served as a defensive escort, at the same time attracting attention and curiosity regarding the motive for that strange cavalcade, so strange that while it looked like a guard for protection, it had all appearance of a triumphal procession.[2]

Maria Magdalena's entrance into the cloister inaugurated a new era. Founded that same year, 1724, the Corpus Domini of Mexico city was the first of a series of institutions created in New Spain to allow Indian women to profess the solemn vows. Foundations of this kind, which allowed Indians officially to become part of the body of the Church, aimed at consolidating the image of the new Christian and Mexican religiosity, as well as reaffirming the importance of class and race issues within the colonial world. At the same time they also imposed a puzzling reverse of the principle of purity of blood. Aspiring nuns were allowed to take the veil only if they could prove that they had noble origins and no European ancestors whatsoever—not an easy test to pass in the ethnically mixed world of the colonies.[3]

But if monastic profession generated public rituals across the globe, what happened once the celebrations were over, the doors of the convent were closed, and quiet descended? What brought women to the convent? What kind of life did they live in the monastic community? How easily did they fit into their new religious 'family'? And what was the geography of convents, particularly in light of the great changes and religious reforms that swept Europe at the beginning of the early modern era?

Marriage or the Cloister

From the very origins of Christianity, women joined the Church and pursued an intense religious existence in imitation of Christ and the Apostles. They practised acts of self-denial and mortification, embraced chastity in order to be purified and to attain sanctity, and served society by performing charitable services.[4] Female religious communities bloomed rather early, often following the advice and spiritual guidance of charismatic men or women. Their history, from antiquity to modern times, reveals a multiplicity of associative forms, which progressively developed into ever more institutionalized communities under the control of the Church.

Strictly speaking, nuns were devoted to a contemplative life of prayer, and bound by the three solemn vows of poverty, chastity, and obedience, professed before their ecclesiastic superiors, either the bishop or the leaders of the religious order. These vows were irreversible: to be released from them and leave the convent involved a complicated and difficult legal procedure. But the profession of these strict vows was not the only way to pursue religious existence within a group. Women also joined communities under more flexible conditions. These women, known as Tertiaries, could join a religious order and adhere to monastic regulations, embracing a life of sexual abstinence and penance, without the solemn vows, instead professing simple and private vows. Known only to God, simple vows were reversible and left them free to maintain their secular status and return, if they wanted, to the world.[5]

'A husband or a wall': for many pious women, whether taking solemn or simple vows, life in a convent appeared an attractive alternative to marriage, or even a good way of avoiding it. Since the Middle Ages, a flourishing tradition of biographies of saints described many examples of how religious life could sometimes enter into conflict with family duties, or maternal care for children. The devout daughter of the count of Anjou, Ermengarde, entered the abbey of Fontevraud—located in the west Loire valley and known for its observance of rather strict enclosure—in part to escape a second marriage.[6] The visionary Christina of Markgate (d. 1160) suffered persecution from her family, who wanted her to marry, in spite of the private vow of virginity she had made when she was still a child.[7] Forced to marry, she fought not have her union consummated, in the face of psychological pressures and physical violence from her parents. Determined not to break her vow, she ran away from home and took refuge in a hermitage where she was able to dedicate herself to ascetic life, praying and fasting locked up in her cell, and becoming known for her penance and piety. She then abandoned hermitic life to be named prioress of a nunnery in Markgate. The mystic Angela of Foligno (1248–1309) devoted herself to a holy life of penitence and extreme poverty. But her family duties clashed with her powerful desire to reach divine perfection. As her confessor and earliest biographer reported, Angela felt so constrained by family life that she prayed for the death of her mother, husband, and children, so that she could completely dedicate herself to the search for true faith, and ultimately God. Eventually her hopes were realised: 'In that period,' she told the confessor,

> by God's wish my mother, a great hindrance to me, died, and soon after, so too did my husband and all my children. Since I had ... prayed to God that they should die, it was a great consolation to me and I thought that, after these divine gifts, my heart should always be in God's and His in mine.[8]

Once alone, she sold all her possessions and donated the money to the poor, finally free from worldly ties to embrace the life that she had longed for. Less extreme than Angela, but still quite radical, was Caterina Benincasa (1347–80). The future saint from Siena corresponded with popes and many members of European royalty, as well as travelling to Avignon—during the Pope's captivity in this city—as a peace negotiator to intercede on behalf of Florence. Accustomed to extraordinary and self-inflicted physical mortifications, her biographer tells us that when she was still very young she threw herself into the boiling waters of a spa near her home town, in order to burn the skin on her body and face. Strongly opposed to the marriage plans of her parents, and of her mother in particular, she deliberately disfigured herself so as to repel potential husbands, leaving her free to serve God. Catherine lived as a Tertiary in her father's home. For her part, Margery Kempe (c.1373–1438) begged her husband to free her from wifely duties: 'Sir, if it please you, . . . grant me that ye will not come into my bed . . . Make my body free to God so that ye never make challenge to me, by asking any debt of matrimony.'[9] Conflicts between parents and children over religious vocation appear to have increased towards the end of the Middle Ages. Unwanted husbands were therefore not an exception, and avoiding marriage was not easy, even on the grounds of following a superior spiritual calling.

Echoes of these stories can be heard in the experiences of early modern nuns for whom the convent offered the perfect way to live outside marriage and the family. Before she become an influential mystic, and one of the founders of the Visitandines, the widow Jeanne de Chantal (1572–1641) longed for a spiritual existence that would inevitably subtract her from motherly duties. Soon after the death of her husband, and on her father-in-law's insistence, she abandoned the castle of Bourbilly and went to live with him, after he had threatened to disinherit her children had she not obliged. She spent there seven painful years until she finally entered the first community of the Visitation, not without the strong opposition of her youngest child who vehemently disagreed with her plans. In order to be completely free from worldly matters, as all religious persons should be, she settled her affairs and estate, and divided the family wealth amongst her sons. One of her daughters also followed her example and boarded in the convent, though she soon left and married. In opting for religious life Jeanne was following both her desire, as well as the advice of her spiritual director, François de Sales (1567–1622), the bishop of Geneva: 'One day'—he had once told her—'I will advise you to leave everything. I say everything.'[10]

The convent might be seen as an option also by those who wanted to live as lay unmarried women, and did not necessarily desire religious life. The extraordinarily well-documented case of the Mantuan Camilla Faá (1599–1662) illustrates this clearly. A lady-in-waiting at this splendid northern Italian court, Camilla became first the lover, then the secret wife, of Duke Ferdinando Gonzaga, and the mother of his only child. Marriage was not, however, in the best interests of the court and political pressures obliged the weak and less than devoted Ferdinando to reject her, and marry Catherine de' Medici. Sent away from Mantua and separated from her son, Camilla was presented with the option of either finding a new husband or becoming a nun, in spite of her clearly stated wish to live in a convent in Piedmont, without taking vows, as a laywoman. 'In these times I was always being pushed to marry, but I resisted', she wrote, and indeed her resistance lasted some five years before she finally gave in and was persuaded to enter the Corpus Domini convent of Ferrara. Here she wrote her memoir at the request of the abbess, in order to narrate the events that had turned her life upside down and led her to sacrifice her 'freedom on the altar of obedience'.[11] Freedom, for Camilla, consisted in living unmarried as well as uncloistered, though finally she took the vows.

Interestingly, monasticism and the spiritual marriage that women might prefer to the carnal one, did not entirely exclude them from their families, and indeed they could remain in quite close touch. Entire female clans lived within the same walls: siblings, aunts and nieces, and even—though perhaps more rarely—mother and daughters. The siblings and parents of the seventeenth-century mystic from Spain, Maria de Agreda (1602–65), ended up in two different institutions. In 1618 Maria entered the Franciscan convent founded by her mother in one part of the family house, in the company of her sister, while her father and two brothers themselves joined the Franciscan order. Convents were erected and built by noble families in the wings of their imposing palaces, so that the newly consecrated nuns might maintain a close physical proximity to their family throughout their lives, surrounded by the rooms, alleyways, and the spaces in which they had grown up and which evoked images and words from their childhood.[12]

But membership of a convent could afford nuns distinctive spiritual benefits as well. The condition of chastity was particularly praised in Christian society as superior to any other state and essential for religious life. Nuns committed themselves to virginity and perpetual dedication to God in order to serve the civic community and intercede between heaven and earth. They prayed and performed rituals for the benefit of pious male and female acquaintances, sought grace from saints on behalf of their patrons and devout supporters, and invoked divine protection for the city, the ruling family, their own relatives, and their spiritual sisters. Charismatic holy and visionary nuns could win the favour and support of political leaders, such as princes and kings and high-powered ecclesiastical figures. This brought them visibility and prestige. Indeed, convents, and in particular the older and wealthier ones, became crucial devotional centres and poles for civic life, the sites of many public celebrations and feasts. Obviously, the more they succeeded in attracting powerful patrons the more prominent they would become within the city. Finally, convents allowed women to cover a whole range of monastic administrative and leadership positions, from abbess down to the many other lesser functions which nuns were called on to perform. The 'wall' offered women roles and responsibilities they would rarely experience outside.

Family Strategies and Nuns without Vocation

It would be misleading, however, to think that all women entered the convent in order to fulfil their spiritual aspirations, or to avoid marriage. Indeed, many women took the vows also as a result of family pressures and patrimonial strategies.

One tradition dating back to medieval times was for kings and queens, as well as lay wealthy aristocrats, to establish and support churches and religious institutions in the hope of obtaining divine protection and ultimately salvation. Queen Christina of Sweden, a fervent supporter of the Franciscans, founded a convent of Poor Clares in Copenaghen in 1497, which hosted mainly burgher classes and some poorer women. A few years later, she opened another Franciscan house in Odense.[13] Similarly, Queen D. Leonor of Portugal founded in 1509 the Clarissan convent of Madre de Deus de Xabregas, located just outside Lisbon on the river Tajo.[14] In the sixteenth and seventeenth centuries, the Habsburgs threw themselves into the development of convents. In Madrid they built at least three female religious houses in just fifty-seven years: Princess Juana of Portugal founded Las Descalzas Reales in 1554; Alonso Orozco, the preacher of King Philip II, built La Visitación in 1589; Philip III and Margaret of Austria started La Encarnación in 1611. They followed the same policy in their transatlantic possessions. In Cuzco, Peru, they set up three religious houses between 1558 and 1673, vital institutions for implanting European society in the colonies.[15]

These 'gated' communities served multiple purposes, and were particularly attractive and convenient locations for hosting the daughters of the elites. Aristocratic and emerging mercantile families established their power and social status on the basis of financial wealth and property. Nunneries offered them a safe, honourable, and economically attractive alternative to marriage, a means to soften the onerous impact of supporting female offspring. The convent dowry, or 'spiritual dowry'—the sum of money required to place a woman in monastic retreat—was usually lower than a marriage dowry, allowing families to compensate for the dispersal of family patrimonies inevitably caused by the high costs of marriage. Furthermore, convents provided the kind of basic education that parents sought for their daughters, and—like colleges and schools—represented an invaluable opportunity for networking, helping families to reinforce ties within their social rank, and opening up paths for social mobility.

This mechanism generated a growth in female professions, and induced patterns of gentrification. According to a trend that has been observed in many European countries, a high number of patrician women dwelled in monastic houses.[16] In Madrid, for instance, in 1674, there was a queue of up to 160 women waiting to enter one of the city's convents. Favouritism was not infrequent as the girls from noble houses were likely to be preferred to their less prosperous or less noble peers. A member of the German guard, who petitioned to the Council of Castile—the Camara de Castilla—in order to obtain a place for his daughter, received a negative reply. He was told that future vacancies would be reserved to women of a higher status.[17] In some areas, such as Italy, this trend seems particularly clear when marriage dowries reached their peak.[18]

Unsurprisingly, forced monastic professions were not infrequent, as families did not hesitate to sacrifice their daughters for economic convenience. The result of this was that many nuns lived in religious houses against their will:

> two thousand or more noble women...in this city live locked up in monasteries as if they were a public store...they are confined within those walls not for spirit of devotion but because of their families, making their freedom, so dear even to those lacking the use of reason, a gift not only to God, but also to their city, the world, and their closest relatives.[19]

According to the Venetian nun who wrote these lines, the extraordinarily incisive Arcangela Tarabotti (1604–52), it was politics rather than devotion that brought women to the cloister. Tarabotti bravely denounced the role assigned to women in family politics, who were treated by their ruthless fathers as goods to be bought and sold:

> They do not give as brides for Christ the most beautiful and virtuous, but instead the ugly and deformed, and if there are daughters who are lame, hunchbacked, or have any other crippling torment, as if the defect of nature was a defect of theirs, they are condemned to spend the rest of their lives in prison.[20]

Tarabotti was referring here to her own situation: she was disabled and the oldest of five daughters, and therefore unappealing to the marriage market. She was the only one of the five that her father destined to the cloister. Tarabotti was one of the many voices against forced monasticism. When we listen to early modern scholars, playwrights, or authors of travel literature, we learn of the troubles of miserable women who had been sent to the cloister without vocation by cruel parents who therefore deprived them of their freedom, and condemned them to eternal unhappiness, with great offence to God. Uncommon though it was for these women to escape and be released from their vows, it was not completely impossible and some of them were married off: 'Don Francisco de Luzón', reads a Spanish document, 'married one sister of *señor* Conde de la Puebla del Maestre, who had been a professed nun in Saint Clare for fourteen years, and had managed to escape from her convent.'[21]

If forced monasticism became a favourite subject for many authors, and for nuns' and monks' claims before ecclesiastical courts, the best portrait of an unwilling nun can be found in the pages of Diderot's novel *The Nun*. Probably inspired by a real court case involving a forced nun, it told the tragic story of Suzanne Simonin, a nun without vocation who experienced first her parents' violence, then the unsolicited sexual attentions and harassment of the mother abbess. 'No, Sir,' she replied to the question whether she, already a novice living in the cloister, wished to profess the sacred vows. This was only the beginning of her unhappy existence:

> 'Marie-Suzanne Simonin, do you promise God chastity, poverty and obedience?' I answered in a louder voice: 'No, Sir, no.' He stopped and said 'My child pull yourself together and listen.' 'Monsignor,' I said, 'you are asking whether I promise God chastity, poverty and obedience. I heard what you said and my answer is no.' And turning round to face the people, among whom a loud murmur had arisen, I made a sign that I wished to speak. The murmur died down and I said: 'Gentlemen, and you especially, my own father and mother, I call you all to witness...' At these words one of the sisters let the curtain fall over the grille and I realized it was useless to go on.[22]

A careful observer of his own times, Diderot was determined to attack the constraints of religion. His work vividly recreated the unbearable pressures, as well as the complicity between the family and the monastic institution, that could determine the entrance of women into religious life. Diderot's heroine experienced injustice and violence, both psychological and physical. Unable to make her voice heard—if not through the author's pen—her tragedy lay in the vows she took against her will, as much as in her awareness of her hopeless situation. Diderot's scenario recalled the case of Arcangela Tarabotti. But Tarabotti, unlike Suzanne, was not a character in a novel. She was made of flesh and blood, just like the many other women who remained cloistered for life, without having much of a true inclination to be so.

Leaving aside these extreme cases—and we have no precise idea how many they were[23]—we encounter a variety of women who entered the doors of the convent with neither great satisfaction nor true vocation. As we have seen, this was probably the case of the Indian girl described at the beginning of this chapter, for whom the convent could be a vehicle for the social integration of her group as much as a means to spiritual fulfilment. But this was also the case of different confessional groups in Catholic Europe, such as, for instance, the Jews. In the sixteenth century, when the Roman Church approved a series of disciplinary measures to contain heretical doctrines and convert the unbelievers, the conversion of Jews was a primary concern. The Jesuits were at the forefront of this operation and contributed to several initiatives to instruct Jews in the Catholic credo and prepare them for baptism. In Rome, Pope Paul III authorized the foundation of specific houses for male and female Jews, and of 'a convent for Jewish women and girls who had been baptized or wished to be baptized'. Jewish women, who because of their origins were prohibited access to monastic institutions, were allowed to remain in this convent until they had found a suitable Christian prospective husband, and—with the financial support of some Roman charitable confraternities—were given the opportunity to put together a dowry enabling them to get married. Those who did not marry could be initiated into religious life as nuns, living in a separate section of the building. Thus, under the missionary label, the Church removed women from the Jewish marriage market by offering them a choice which could win their soul for the Catholic cause: a Catholic marriage, or a life in the religious institution.[24] All this happened at a time when the Jewish community in Rome was under great strain because of the approval of anti-Jewish ordinances, and because of poverty which obliged the administrators of the ghetto to place restrictions on marriage dowries, making marriage more difficult for poor Jewish brides. There is no evidence that these converted women were coerced into becoming nuns. Still, some Jewish fathers would probably push their daughters though the door of the convent, whether they were willing or not, in order to gain relief from material difficulties and poverty.

Married Women and Ex-Prostitutes

In many ways, convents also appealed to women as places of retreat and refuge. Many female patrons paid regular visits to convents, building their own private quarters in which to spend varying periods of time, thus maintaining influence over the institution they promoted. Marie de' Medici—one of the pious queens of France—was very devoted to Carmelite foundations. At least 'once or twice a week', she visited the nuns in the convent of the Incarnation, in Paris:

> From her chateau, close to the Luxembourg Gardens, Marie de' Medici could reach her Carmelite pavilion in just a few minutes. She was often accompanied by her daughters the princesses. On the eve of her departure for England, Marie-Henriette, already married off to Charles I, visited the Great Convent with her mother and spent the whole day there... After Marie de' Medici's exile, Anne of Austria frequently made use of her privileged access to the monastery. She had her coat of arms placed in the various rooms of the pavillion that her mother-in-law had had built.[25]

Another royal woman, the Spanish Infanta Anne of Austria, since her childhood was a frequent guest of the convent of Las Descalzas Reales in Madrid, where she had often stayed during her father's numerous absences from the court. A number of noble and patrician women of less prestigious status did the same and retired to a convent for brief periods, or in the later years of their life. The illegitimate daughter of Duke Alessandro de' Medici, Giulia, was a faithful guest, in the company of other ladies, of Santa Maria of Regina Coeli in Florence, where she often ate and slept, requesting entertainment at Carnival and feast times. After her unhappy marriage to Bernardetto de' Medici Giulia's visits became less frequent, although the nuns continued to welcome her to their convent, and even prepared an entire set of clothes and linens for her newborn baby. Overall however, they found her presence quite demanding and very expensive, since she almost never paid or contributed to her expenses there:

> [1560] Signora [Giulia] has come here almost every day and often has been lodged and for Carnival the lamentation of David was performed on her commission [...] we paid 12 scudi for the stage and scenery and the meals

eaten by the ladies who came with her every day and . . . stayed . . . here for two days with some or all of her entourage . . . and she still has not given us anything.[26]

Lay guests sometimes included married women as well as widows looking for a place to stay, other than their family home, and for paths to a better life. They were admitted under certain conditions: they had to obtain their husband's consent, behave according to the discipline, and observe enclosure. Were they to exit the convent, they were never to be allowed back again. These rigid conditions—made even tougher after the disciplinary restrictions introduced by the Council of Trent—also applied to any servants that they might want to take with them. In 1616, Doña María de Albion received permission to live, with her servant, in a convent in Zaragoza, Spain. Her request was accepted, provided that the servant was a virgin, dressed decently, and respected strict cloister rules. In Spain, like in France, Italy, the Low Countries, and Russia, widows often were a regular presence in convents.[27] The English Sepulchrines of Liège took in respectable widows of means who wanted to live in religious observance. They lived in separate rooms, but were able to converse and dine with the nuns, and their servants were expected to be 'peaceful and modest'.[28] Of course, only a few wealthy women could afford monastic retirement. Indeed, in order to be admitted they had to pay full board and lodging, in lieu of a dowry, or donate part of their wealth to the religious community. Furthermore, they needed to win the nuns' acceptance and this was not to be taken for granted. The coexistence of laywomen and nuns created much friction which might sometimes be disruptive for the collective order. Not only did the integration of laywomen into the disciplinary monastic existence prove difficult, but their economic negotiations with the nuns did not always go smoothly and often gave rise to endless conflicts. One Florentine nun wrote in her convent chronicle: 'no more widows in our convent and remember that our rule prohibits it'.[29]

So far we have placed emphasis on the significant number of convents which recruited amongst the wealthy elites. These houses owed their wealth to substantial nuns' dowries, as well as large endowments—lands with houses and rents—acquired at the time of their foundation or soon after, from their generous patrons: emperors, kings, queens, and other members of the ruling classes. But there were also poorer communities with more limited incomes, which survived on charitable legacies and the nuns' own work, and naturally hosted the less wealthy classes. When we leave the rarefied life of the privileged groups and head down to the lower social ranks, we are faced with quite a different picture, and the reasons for entering the convent were often related to the need to find a refuge from poverty and social exclusion.

From the twelfth century onward, Europe saw a proliferation of charitable residential institutions specifically intended to shelter vulnerable women who had experienced poverty, family disintegration, and violence: abandoned wives, battered women, widows, ex-prostitutes, or women 'in danger' of losing their honour and good reputation. Founded with public and private wealth, and in certain cases co-sponsored by State and Church, these multiform communities had 'both logistical and normative functions' preventing women from falling into sin.[30]

Given that prostitution—a basic resource for the female poor—was considered one of the greatest 'crimes' committed by women, great emphasis was placed on the spiritual conquest of prostitutes, or 'fallen women' as they were known. Men were encouraged to marry women of dubious reputation in order to take them away from brothels, inns, and the city streets. The Church, for its part, did not fail to target this particular female group. In 1227 Pope Gregory IX founded the order of Saint Mary Magdalene dedicated to the prostitute that Jesus helped to redeem, and promoted the creation of 'Magdalenes': convents for ex-prostitutes willing to abandon their supposedly sinful existence. In serving Christ as nuns these women would purify themselves and gain salvation. Inside the walls, it was hoped, they would find relief from economic uncertainty, and perhaps see the attraction of a new spiritual path to guide them towards a socially acceptable 'normality'. Still, for these women there was a price to pay: discipline, work, and ultimately, physical segregation.

Convents for ex-prostitutes offered a social solution to a gendered problem of long-standing concern in both Catholic and Protestant countries. In Britain, a group of philanthropists founded houses for women adapting this Catholic model in their homeland. The London Magdalene House opened in 1758, following the initiative of Jonas Hanway. Observing the example of Italy, Hanway was particularly interested in the variety of retreats that existed: [...] that existed in almost every city of this country. He described three types of them, each of which catered for a different category of female member: 'one of St. Magdalene, who makes vows; one of St. Martha, who are not admitted to make vows; and one of St. Lazarus, who are detained by force'.[31] In describing his short typology of institutions, Hanway had probably captured what each had in common with the others: their corrective nature, which gave the Magdalene houses a certain resemblance to female asylums and penitential institutions. Comfortable refuges for aristocratic ladies and patrician women, convents could also act as rather inhospitable places for the less fortunate.

Rules and Roles

Whatever convent or religious order women joined, and whatever their reasons for joining, all had to subscribe to a highly disciplined life, under the guidance and authority of male superiors. This way of life was modelled on the long and robust tradition originating in early forms of Western monasticism, and codified in a set of regulations specifically devised for nuns. Written by influential ecclesiastics, and addressed to those in charge of governing convents, these regulations would be read periodically to the nuns in order to instruct them on the main principles of communal life, their spiritual duties and monastic offices, and the basics of their everyday living. Although not always fully observed—as we will see in the following chapters—they are particularly revealing, amongst other things, of how the spiritual dimension of the nuns' existence related to the material one.

The rules were quite detailed. A cyclical routine of praying, penitence, and work shaped days in the convent. Bells pealed at specific times, giving the cue for prayer, work, and all the other activities of the day. Prayer began early in the morning, as soon as they nuns woke, with the reciting of the hours in the choir, and ended with night prayers before going to bed.

Nuns worked in order to avoid idleness, gossip, and vain thoughts. Keeping silent throughout the day, and during working time, allowed every thought to be reserved for God. Nuns carried out their assigned offices taking care of convent management, administration, and finances, and performed those practical tasks that kept the community going. This routine was broken by times for eating and resting. Communal meals were served in the refectory, where food would be provided for every sister, and eaten while listening to edifying texts read aloud. A brief rest was allowed after lunch before everyone returned to their mansions. At the end of the day nuns retired to the dormitory where they slept, or to their individual cells. On Sundays and holy days they were required to sing mass and take communion.[32]

'The chief motivation for your sharing life together is to live harmoniously in the house and to have one heart and one soul seeking God,' taught Saint Augustine.[33] Communal life was based on material deprivation and self-inflicted poverty—the poverty of Christ. Nuns were to reject all material goods and free themselves from worldly ties in order the better to serve God. They were required to give up all individual property rights, and all possessions were held in common with the other members of their community. Their existence was inspired by the notion of 'basic living'. In practice, this meant they were only allowed a restricted range of objects and furniture in their cells: a bed, a crucifix, a small altar, and a kneeling stool for individual prayer, a breviary, and a chest or cabinet. In the course of the year the mother abbess would inspect each cell in order to make sure that each nun had no more than was needed. Nuns were also obliged to hand in everything they possessed at the moment in which they entered the convent, and anything given to them after their profession would be immediately appropriated by the convent. Those who failed to obey were punished severely.[34]

For sure, the impact of such restrictions on the lives of nuns much depended on their community's disciplinary traditions, effective wealth, and the nuns' own private incomes. Indeed, those who came from wealthy backgrounds—as many of the early modern inhabitants of convents did—regularly received support from families, friends, and patrons, in the form of yearly allowances and gifts of money, food, and objects of various sorts such as clothing, books, paintings, or devotional images. These material contributions mitigated the restrictions imposed by monastic discipline, enabling them to lead a life that was not too dissimilar to the one they had been used to before taking the veil. Women who came from more humble backgrounds enjoyed far less—sometimes virtually non-existent—external support, and were therefore more heavily dependent on the convent. For women from very poor families, the convent could even offer an improvement of their material condition, providing a degree of economic stability they could not aspire to otherwise.

Attention was paid to both the quantity and the quality of the things used by nuns, and their symbolic implications. This applied for instance to clothing and to the objects that might be found in the nuns' cells. Nuns were required to wear the religious habit of their order. The habit, as well as the veil and cloak, was the sign of their definitive departure from the world, and their inclusion in the spiritual family of the monastic community. Like everything else in the convent, the habit reflected the nuns' virginal status and integrity. It had to cover the whole body from head to toes, and to be made of rough and unrefined fabric of bare colours. Together with the habit, their short hair—'not to take any time combing it'—marked their condition of eternal chastity as brides of Christ. Consequently, any other outfit was prohibited. Similarly, many objects were deemed inappropriate for the sacred space of the cloister, such as the kind of things that furnished the patrician domestic interiors familiar to many nuns. Mirrors were absolutely forbidden, as were decorations on the walls, or luxury objects such as tapestries and sumptuous pillows. Lay and elegant clothes were also prohibited, and nuns were told to avoid ribbons on the habit, perfumed gloves, jewels, badges, and other similar gadgets. These objects and clothing might evoke lust and the worldly existence the nuns had left behind, therefore undermining monastic values and inducing them into sin. Colours should be particularly rejected, since they evoked the idea of pleasure and contrasted with the bare tones of the monastic environment. Only bright tapestries in the convent church were welcomed as embellishing items and tributes to God.[35]

The point of these regulations was to create a protected environment in which even the faintest desire for the world and its dangerous temptations was to be removed. For this reason, visitors had to conform to the monastic spirit. Female visitors who came to the parlour were to be simply dressed in order to avoid reminding nuns, who had left 'the sea of the world never to return', of 'what they had once left to please God'.[36] At the same time, nuns should not trigger desire in their visitors by appearing unchaste, and were not be seen without their habit or veil, exceptions to be made only for their 'father or mother', or for a few other trusted people. Restrictions of this sort, however, aimed not only at keeping the nuns pure but also at reducing the influence of families and external groups associated with them. Titles of social distinction, like Lady or Madame, and family coats of arms, were not to be tolerated inside the cloister. And embroidered decorations displaying the nuns' names to be hung or painted on the walls were to be banned.

A life of total sharing in the name of God, which broke with the materiality of the world outside the walls—as outlined here—did not necessarily mean strict equality. Nuns may have eaten from the same table and worn the same religious habit, but they certainly did not enjoy the same opportunities. Indeed, two groups of nuns—technically defined 'classes'—inhabited the convent: choir nuns, also called veiled nuns, and servant nuns or *conversae*, not to be confused with the lay servants who worked for the convent. Choir nuns usually came from noble and wealthy families, and those sections of society that could afford to meet the convent's economic requirements. They were expected to run the community and to occupy the highest and most important offices in convent governance and administration, such as the abbess, her vicar, the sacristan, the *procuratrix*, the sister-bursar, the cellarer. Other relevant roles reserved to choir sisters were those of advisers of the abbess, the so called discreet nuns—the teacher of novices, infirmary-attendant, and gatekeeper—whose task of regulating outside contacts was extremely important. Unlike choir nuns, servant nuns often came from rural or lower class families. They did not necessarily profess the solemn vows, and often paid a smaller dowry than the choir nuns.[37] Their status, monastic career, and access to monastic offices were deeply different from those of choir nuns. Indeed, they were admitted to the convent not to run it but to serve. They did all the humble domestic jobs, confining them to the kitchen and service areas: cleaning, washing, cooking, baking the bread, and tending the animals. On top of this they were engaged in heavy duties which brought them directly in contact with illness and death, such as taking care of choir sisters in the infirmary, feeding them and washing them.[38] Interestingly servant nuns formed a significant portion of the community, often representing up to 20 or even 30 per cent of its members in the case of some Italian and Spanish communities.[39] In the light of the social composition of female monastic houses this is hardly surprising. It is not difficult to imagine that the wealthy and aristocratic daughters of the urban elites, who filled many convents of the Catholic world, were used to the presence of servants as part of their family life, and were keen to try to maintain their old habits and comfortable life once they had settled into the convent, expecting to be dutifully served by other sisters.

The distinction between these two classes was a formal feature of monastic life. Regulations defined the precedence of choir nuns over servant nuns, and the subordinate position of the latter. Choir nuns were physically unable to do the heavy jobs. 'Because they are noble and used to spiritual exercise,' stated the Roman Congregation of Bishops and Regular Orders in 1627, if they were obliged to work 'they would contract some sort of infirmity'. Servant nuns, on the contrary, were accepted on the assumption that they were strong enough to do these jobs. 'In receiving servant nuns the abbess will have to make sure that they are able to carry the weight of the works which they will be destined to.' Therefore they 'should not be above forty years old, nor below twenty; they should be physical healthy, and of obedient nature'. Since no nun could be paid for her work, and all income went to the convent, in line with the idea of communal property, servant nuns could not be given any money either, and received no compensation at all for their efforts. They had to 'serve without salary, with charity and with the merit of holy obedience'. It is important to note that servant nuns did not simply happen to belong to the wrong group of nuns. Indeed they were deliberately kept in a subordinate position by being denied access to education and literacy. Learning to read would have diverted their attention from working duties, and would be useless and even 'damaging' for them. Serving was their only function in the community. On top of this, servant nuns suffered open discrimination in the form of their exclusion from any participation in collective decisions or representation in the chapter, i.e. the general assembly of all professed nuns. Indeed, they were allowed to join all the others in the chapter room, but without the right to vote.[40]

Such hierarchical dynamics found expression in many other aspects of everyday collective existence. For instance, the servant nuns' clothing bore the signs of their particular identity and status within the community. Their veil was white, as opposed to the black veil of the choir nuns, and sometimes the decorations on their cloak also pointed to their subordinate condition. In Florence, in the convent of the military order of Malta, choir nuns had a full cross of Malta on their cloak, while servant nuns had only the half-cross.[41] Sometimes, the use of communal spaces and the size and shape of the cells also signalled the status of nuns. Some regulations recommended that servant and choir nuns should lead quite separate lives. Servant nuns slept in separate dormitories, ate in the communal refectory but only after all the other sisters had finished, and, if they were given individual cells, they were usually the smallest and less desirable ones. The best cells were reserved for the 'Mothers' and senior nuns; more average cells were for ordinary choir nuns, and those remaining, the 'infamous' cells were for the servant nuns.[42]

We might think that this profound inequality ended with the end of the nuns' lives, but even this was not completely true. Although each nun who died was entitled to receive 'the extreme honours and burial with a wake and a mass'[43] before being buried within the convent perimeter, choir nuns might be afforded extra celebrations and honour. Exceptionally the most noble amongst them were granted public funerals, with masses and singing celebrations. Their catafalque was exposed in the church, and brought in procession through the nearby streets and then back to the convent again.[44]

The monastic community—despite all communal and almost egalitarian claims—was deeply anchored in a system of privilege and social exclusion. Nuns could have radically different experiences of life depending on their family background and class. The distinction between servant and choir nuns survived until very recently. Only as late as the 1960s, the Second Vatican Council addressed the issue by calling for the abolition of such discrimination, unifying the two groups of religious individuals into one.[45]

Changing Times: Convents and the Reformation

So far we have followed nuns on their journey towards abandoning the world and beginning a collective life based on established disciplinary principles. But even after they entered the cloister, nuns still maintained connections with the world beyond the walls, and could not remain immune to the events affecting the lives of men and women in outside society. If this is so, how did they experience the turmoil of political and religious conflicts characterizing the history of Europe in the sixteenth century? And in particular, how did they experience the advent of the Protestant Reformation, and what impact did the Reformation have on convents?

In those areas where the Protestant cause won support, Catholic institutions and religious orders came under threat. Protestants rejected contemplative life in monastic retreat, claiming that it was useless and no better way of life than any other. They regarded monks and nuns as men and women who devoted themselves to idleness, gluttony, and dubious sexual morality, and convents were often compared to brothels. Chastity, so important in the Catholic tradition, was regarded as being particularly bad for women as it prevented them from fulfilling their imperative role as mothers and wives. Luther himself had given a spectacular example of rejection of monasticism: he abandoned the Augustinian order and habit and married an ex-nun, Catherine von Bora, after she had also escaped from her convent in a wagon, together with eight other sisters.[46]

This famous couple apart, in Protestant Europe religious women who lived through the Reformation witnessed a time of change which in many cases led to major transformations of their lives. Indeed, while Catholics were eager to place their women in convents, in some cases by force, Protestants on the other hand were driving theirs *out* of them. One of the first institutional transformations to be set in motion in newly Protestant countries was to close down monasteries and convents, confiscate their buildings, lands, and properties, and order their inhabitants to move to Catholic areas. Nuns were pensioned off or their dowries returned, and were sent back to their families. Some were allowed to remain in the convent until their community—forbidden from accepting new members—died off. This happened in Germany, where a number of prince electors embraced Luther's teaching and introduced them into their states as early as the 1520s. More or less the same happened in the Netherlands, and also in the kingdoms of Denmark and Sweden, where the Reformation was completed by 1550 with the establishment of the Lutheran Church in Iceland. In England, in the 1530s, Henry VIII approved a series of reforms which aimed to dismantle Catholics, dissolving monasteries and convents, and making it impossible to enter a religious order. Nuns were forced to hide and then flee to the Continent.[47]

In some countries, nuns were the victims of religious persecution just like other Catholics. The first female English Catholic martyr was the visionary woman, and former domestic servant, Elizabeth Barton from Kent, also known as 'the Nun'. A nun with a reputation for holiness, Barton was a controversial character, mainly to due to the nature of her prophecies, some of which invoked opposition to the king's divorce. She became a target for detractors of Catholicism, and was executed without trial in 1534. Her example shows how nuns could assume a powerful public role and come to be identified with the Catholic cause.[48] Even symbolically, however, the physical destruction of nuns and nunneries represented a potent sign of Protestantism's success, and the crumbling of the old religion. Convents were turned into institutions catering for the entire community, such as hospitals or schools. Occasionally, stone and other materials from the closed monastic buildings and churches were used for constructing and extending royal palaces, as in the castle of Vadstena in Sweden.[49]

In the face of Protestant attacks, some nuns resisted and refused to abandon their religious houses even when their relatives ordered them to do so. 'Brother,' wrote Anna Wurm from the convent of St Nicholas-in-Undis, in Strasburg,

> I understand that you have written publicly and expressed that you want to remove me from the cloister...and yet you do not even know whether

I want that or not....I am in a good, pious, blessed, honourable, free, spiritual estate, wherein both my body and soul are well cared for... I want to stay here....I have never asked you to take me out of the cloister, and I am not asking you to do so now.[50]

Although Anna was not immediately removed, she did not remain for long. In 1525, during the Peasants' War, all the nuns were moved out of their community, for safety reasons. Some returned but Anna did not.

Like Anna, other nuns fought hard not for their own individual sake, but to prevent their communities being closed down. A well-known example of this is that of the aristocratic and learned Caritas Pirckheimer (1467–1532), abbess of the Poor Clares of Nuremberg and the sister of the humanist Willibald Pirckheimer. As the head of her community, Caritas was in the front line in the negotiations with the city fathers who, in 1525, approved a series of regulations which would dismantle her convent. These regulations, amongst other things, prohibited Caritas and her sisters from attending Catholic mass, receiving the sacraments or confession, or wearing their religious habits. Furthermore, the nuns were free to leave the convent, and their parents free to take them away. Only after Caritas's resistance against the fathers' ordinances, and the intervention of the Protestant preacher Melanchthon who opposed violence against the convent, were the nuns granted permission to remain in their community for the rest of their lives, although without admitting any new members. As Caritas reported in a written narrative, these events caused great sorrow to all of them, constituting an attack on their faith as well as on their way of life. Particularly disruptive was the departure of four sisters, who went back to their families. Three of them left against their will, and were physically dragged out of the cloister by their mothers and other relatives. The event gained the attention of the city, and it was witnessed by a large gathering of citizens packed outside the building. Before leaving, the three nuns were obliged to remove their Poor Clare habits, an act which almost amounted to an inversion of the clothing ceremony which had inaugurated their entrance into religious life. Caritas described how

with many tears, we took off their veils and belts and the white skirts, and put little shirts on them and worldly belts, and headdresses on their heads.

I led them with a few sisters into the chapel, where we waited probably an entire hour before the she-wolves [i.e. the nuns' mothers] rode up in two carriages...Meanwhile, cries came from among the common folk who gathered in a large crowd as when a wretched man is led to execution. All the streets and the churchyard were so full that the wives could scarcely enter the churchyard with their carriages. There, they [the relatives] were ashamed that so many of the people were present: they would have liked to have seen us come through the back gate into the garden.[51]

In Germany, other stories of female resistance to the Reformation, like that of Caritas Pirckheimer, included narratives of women defending their churches and religious houses in all manner of means. Nuns armed themselves with pitchforks, or took refuge in their convents locking all the doors, setting fire to their old slippers to keep the preachers away, and singing loudly so as to blot out the preachers' sermons, all because they did not want to leave or allow sermons in their convents. It appears that nuns fought harder than men to defend their institutions, some of which survived until the seventeenth century; their male counterparts vacated their religious houses and gave away their properties more rapidly. Neither was this gender difference a quirk of the Reformation; nearly three centuries after, in Revolutionary France, monasteries and convents were closed down, and nuns similarly proved more reluctant to abandon their houses than monks and friars.[52]

Exceptionally, convents won Protestant women over to the popish cause. These women converted and embraced Catholic faith, and subsequently entered religious life. The English and Protestant born Catherine Holland described her conversion and monastic profession in her spiritual autobiography. Although, convent life seemed to her 'a miserable Life' and 'a Prison' her spiritual evolution brought her to flee to Flanders where—penniless—she embarked on a completely new chapter of her existence, becoming an Augustinian canoness. As she later described, she did this 'even, as I may say, blindfold; for I was as ignorant as a Child, what a Religious Life was'.[53]

Class and social prestige aided resistance to the Reformation, and convents were able to survive in part because they suited elite interests and family strategies. Indeed, the Catholic aristocracy—including even some Lutheran families—were willing to maintain their unmarried daughters in the safe and prestigious monastic enclaves that they regarded as appropriate to their status. They contested the decision to sweep convents away on the grounds that their daughters and sisters would have been obliged to marry renegade monks, or men from lesser status than their own, instead of living in honourable religious retreat consistent with their social class.[54] This is one of the reasons why the convents that fought the Reformation, or which flourished during this period, were often those associated with wealthy families and endowed with lands and properties, such as the canonesses' house in Germany, or the convents opened in France and Flanders to provide for the young daughters of the English aristocracy seeking Catholic education abroad after the English Reformation.[55] By defending convents, elites could defend their privileged and exclusive way of life as much as their faith.

Moreover, nuns' resistance can also be understood in terms of the traditional lack of opportunities for women. Whilst former priests, monks, and friars might obtain ecclesiastical promotion and become pastors in the new Protestant Church, no such option was available to women who had no institutional role in it, and whose only option was to go back to family life. Lack of opportunities might also mean economic uncertainty, in particular for those ex-nuns who did not marry. In England, for instance, the Reformation clearly had harsher consequences for religious women than men. In the dioceses of Lincoln, monks obtained ecclesiastical promotion, and a number of ex-nuns were married off. But those ex-nuns who were pensioned off received meagre compensations of as little as £2, condemning them to poverty.[56]

It is important to remember, however, that the sterling defence of the monastic model was not the only response women offered to Protestant reformation. On the contrary, many of them were willing to profess the new faith, and they left the convent to begin a new life outside. In Strasburg, for example, the vast majority of nuns left their cloisters, and ten out of sixteen convents were dissolved by 1538 because of the departure of their residents.[57] The words of those who left the cloister provide a clear indication of the various reasons which might lie behind their action. 'High honourable and beloved mother', wrote Martha Elisabeth Zitter in

1678, to explain her decision to leave the French Ursuline convent in Erfurt,

> [I know] that you were very afflicted by and spoke strongly about the news of my leaving the convent and changing from the papist religion—which happened through the undoubted prompting of the Holy Spirit—and that you disinherited me with nothing because of this. . . . I realize I am obligated to indicate the reasons that I had to leave the order and this form of religion. . . . I did not enter into this of free choice, but was sent into the convent by you eight years ago when I was fourteen years old, in order to learn the French language and all sorts of maidenly virtues as well as respectable work. Very shortly after I had begun to become somewhat comfortable with such things, and not yet a month gone by, some of the Ursuline nuns began to try to influence me through all types of means and ways to want to put on their habit.[58]

Relying on the Old and New Testaments, Zitter explained to her mother not only that she entered under 'coercion', but that the Catholic under-standing of holiness resulted in the nuns 'chattering the monastic hours in Latin at certain times in the choir', and pronouncing sentences that they did not understand, whipping themselves once a week until the blood flowed, wearing little silver barbs, brass belts with points, and horsehair belts on their bare bodies, fasting on bread and water, confessing their sins before the whole community or, secretly, to their confessor, and other similar 'human inventions'.[59] Following the Protestant line—and employ-ing anti-Catholic arguments—she questioned the superiority of monastic life, and the existence of the solemn vows, as a restriction on free choice, and hinted at the laxity, material comfort, and worldly goods available to nuns in spite of the voluntary poverty they claimed to observe. To this she preferred 'Christian good works, in accordance with the commandments, through which we show true faith and love toward God and our neigh-bour'.[60] She also rejected Catholic teachings in matters of salvation and the doctrine of purgatory. She chose, in short, to embrace a credo different from the Catholic one, and one that she personally found more congenial.

Finally, irrespective of religious beliefs, convents remained a possible model for women—Catholic as well as Protestant—to pursue. In Protestant Germany, forms of female religious associative life did not die out, but instead survived in the shape of Protestant convents. Theses could be governed by a Lutheran abbess, and inhabited by Lutheran nuns in religious habits who claimed membership of a monastic order, paradoxical though this may seem. Luther had condemned the Catholic faith, but allowed Protestant men and women to retain forms of collective life under a rule. He had argued that if people 'of outstanding character, capable of living under a rule, feel a desire to pass their lives in the cloister, we do not wish to forbid them, so long as their doctrine and worship remain pure'.[61] A few Protestant convents flourished and were rather successful, like the canonesses' house of Quedlinburg, which became Protestant in the 1540s, was turned into an elementary school, and managed to retain papal privileges. Others experienced major difficulties and eventually failed. In Denmark, where the crown granted a number of formerly Catholic convents permission to survive as Protestant institutions, the convent of Maribo was devastated by internal conflicts amongst opposing factions of nuns, and some of them were suspected of still practising the Catholic faith. After new statutes were imposed in order to regain order and peace, it was closed in 1612.[62]

But even if these somewhat hybrid communities were the product of complex dynamics, in which religious ideology and the local family factions played an important part, rather than an idyllic compromise between Catholic and Protestant forms of religious life, they stood as proof that the convent continued to appeal to women. In the seventeenth century, the English educator and writer Mary Astell (1668–1731) envisaged a monastic retreat where unmarried women, like herself, could live and freely dedicate themselves to study. Her retreat for women was modelled on the idea of a convent or, as she put it, a 'Protestant monastery'. Thus women in different confessions, both religious and lay, claimed their right to a kind of unmarried community life, religious or not, as an alternative to the family. The convent, or a revisited version of it, was their model.

TWO

Cloistered Spaces

Stendhal's novel *The Abbess of Castro* tells the story of two young aristocrats, Hélène and Jules, in sixteenth-century Naples. After falling in love
and encountering the disapproval of their families, they are separated
from each other and Hélène is obliged to enter a convent and become a
nun. In a desperate attempt to see his beloved again, Jules goes to the
convent of the Visitation—now her new home—in the nearby city of
Castro:

> The day after, just before dawn, he entered the walls of the small city
> of Castro;...even before entering the city, Jules saw the convent of the
> Visitation, a vast building circumscribed by black walls, and very similar to
> an army quarter. He ran into the church; it was marvellous. The women
> religious, most of them nobles from wealthy families, would fight amongst
> themselves to enrich this church, the only part of the convent exposed to the
> public gaze...but his glance disdained the richness of the altar, addressing
> instead a golden grate, about forty feet high, divided into three parts by
> two marble columns. That grille, whose huge size gave it an imposing
> appearance, stood behind the major altar, and separated the choir of the
> nuns from the open church that was accessible to all the faithful....It is
> true that an immense black veil garnished the interior side of the grate...
> Jules chose a very visible seat facing the left part of the grate, in the lightest
> place; there he spent his life hearing mass.[1]

An impressive but austere building with dark and thick walls: viewed from
outside the convent could almost be mistaken for army quarters,
protected from incursions by formidable defences. The only part of it

open to thepublic was the church, with its huge golden grate covered by a black veil, beyond which stood the nuns' inaccessible choir. All these features together created an extremely powerful scene, providing an aura of drama.

Stendhal's imaginative narration captures perfectly a typical feature of early modern convents: they were separated from the world but also closely connected to it. A complicated system of gates and grilles made it possible for the nuns to come into contact with the public outside, although this contact was difficult and mostly indirect. Convents were closed spaces that also functioned as centres of devotional, social, and even political life. This intriguing contrast invites us to leave Stendhal and take a look at convents and their inhabitants to discover what life was like for women living under such restrictive conditions, and how enclosure was understood in early modern times.

Cloistering Religious Women

Enclosure has a long history. A recognized element of Western monasticism from the earliest times, enclosure fostered an atmosphere of prayer and collective work, away from worldly distractions. Monks and nuns were thus free to completely dedicate themselves to God, while finding in their spiritual retreat the basics for living. There was no need for them to leave. 'The monastery', said Saint Benedict 'ought if possible to be so constructed as to contain within it all necessaries, that is water, mill, garden and the various crafts which are exercised within a monastery, so that there be no occasion for monks to wander abroad, since this is in no wise expedient for their souls.'[2]

Since the very beginning, however, strict physical segregation was particularly a women's affair. Although early prescriptions were rather similar for monks and nuns, they invariably placed more emphasis on strict cloistering in female religious houses than in male ones.[3] Monks were to spend their time praying and working, and were allowed outside only when strictly necessary for spiritual or economic purposes. They were to stay clear of certain kinds of behaviour typically attributed to men. They could not frequent taverns, enter hostels, go to banquets, take part in worldly festivities, wander from place to place, occupy themselves with temporal affairs, embrace a woman, serve as godfathers, or do anything involving monetary gain. Like their male counterparts, nuns too were required to spend their lives praying and working, detaching themselves from worldly matters. But they were more radically exhorted never to leave their convent and to practise full, unbroken, enclosure.

This gendered discrepancy relied on a long-standing Christian tradition that associated female chastity with the protection of a closed environment, whether this was a domestic one or a monastic one. Nuns were the brides of Christ and had to maintain their virginity intact as a gift for their celestial spouse. Only if they died intact could their sacred marriage be consummated. Enclosure ensured that their immaculate bodies would be preserved for ever. Saint Jerome (c.347–c.420), for instance, had advised the Roman matron and nun-to-be Eustochium that it would have been dangerous for a virgin to leave the protected environment and venture outdoors: 'Go not out from home, nor wish to behold the daughters of a strange country... Diana went out and was ravished. I would not have you seek a bridegroom in the highways, I would not have you go about the corners of the city... Narrow and strait is the way that leadeth to life.'[4] One century later, the bishop Caesarius of Arles (470–542) reformulated this idea and for the first time gave specific prescriptions on full enclosure for female religious communities. In his *Rule for Nuns* written in 513 for the convent of Saint John, which was headed by his sister Caesaria, he exhorted nuns to refrain from any contact with the world. 'A soul chaste and consecrated to God', he contended, 'should not have constant association with externs, even with her relatives, either they coming to her or she going to them; lest she hear what is not proper, or say what is not fitting, or see what could be injurious to chastity.'[5]

To a certain extent medieval cloister rules were intended to provide protection. In times of barbarian invasion, political instability, and local violence, enclosure guaranteed the permanence of an inviolable space which would insulate nuns from the dangers of the outside world. But in the course of the Middle Ages, the notion of enclosure underwent a subtle shift. Physical segregation increasingly began to be conceived not so much as a means of protecting nuns from the dangers of the world outside, but rather as a response to a more serious danger that nuns posed to themselves. Like all women, they were frail and naturally inclined toward sin, easily exposed to the temptations of the Devil, lust of the flesh, and frivolous inquisitiveness. Enclosure and the restriction of nuns' uncontrolled contacts with outsiders served to eliminate all opportunities for sinful and scandalous behaviour.[6] Nuns would avoid exposing themselves to the public gaze, and keep at a safe distance from situations that could trigger their sexual desire, and spoil their virginity. From his monastery in Cluny, the monk Peter Abelard (1079–1142) wrote to his former lover Héloïse, now herself a nun in the convent of the Paraclete: 'solitude is more necessary for your fragile femininity than for our concern, we are less prone to the conflicts of the temptation of flesh, and less susceptible to the things of the flesh'.[7] 'Because the feminine sex is weak, it needs greater protection and stricter enclosure', echoed the German Cistercian monk Idung of Prufening in the same period. This was why enclosure was more necessary for nuns than for monks.[8] The gender-biased understanding of the world which made enclosure a must for nuns was deeply rooted in the most traditional and misogynist ideas about women.

But there was more than this. This notion of female nature had practical political implications for religious women living in communities. The ease with which women naturally fell into sin and were unable to govern themselves, was not simply a threat to their purity; it also rendered them incapable of governing their communities. As Caesarius remarked, it was 'not expedient for that sex to enjoy the freedom of having its own governance—because of its natural fickleness and also because of outside temptations which womanly weakness is not strong enough to resist'.[9]

These opinions regarding female nature deeply influenced ecclesiastical legislation regarding the discipline of nuns from the Middle Ages onward. As early as the eighth and ninth centuries, a number of Carolingian councils invoked a general reform of male and female monastic houses, submitting them to the authority of the bishop, and establishing the imperative obligation of strict active enclosure for nuns.[10] Towards the end of the thirteenth century the first universal legislation was launched, when in 1298 Pope Boniface VIII published a bull that made enclosure a

compulsory requirement for all nuns in the Catholic world. Known as
Periculoso—the first word of the Latin text—Boniface's law claimed that
physical segregation would enable nuns 'to serve God more freely,
wholly separated from the public and worldly gaze, and, occasions for
lasciviousness having been removed, may most diligently safeguard their
hearts and bodies in complete chastity'.[11] Three centuries after Boniface, in
1563, the Council of Trent promoted a disciplinary reform of monastic
institutions which reaffirmed *Periculoso*, and emphasized enclosure as 'the
primary obligation for nuns'.[12] Building on an entrenched tradition,
Tridentine decrees were uncompromisingly gender-specific, and no
similar legislation existed for the male clergy. Furthermore, soon after
Trent, new restrictions were to come, introduced by popes eager to
strengthen the new guidelines of the Council, as well as responding to
the Protestant attacks against the appropriateness of monastic life.[13]
Enclosure was extended to all female religious, including Tertiaries, who
often lived uncloistered and performed care work in the service of the civic
community, assisting the poor and the dying. Inevitably, this restriction
undermined their active social role, obliging them to switch to a
radically different form of collective life, in which their active religious
commitment was transformed into a closed and mainly contemplative
one.[14]

Although it did not invent enclosure *ex-novo*, Trent did represent a
watershed in the history of nuns. Enclosure assumed a new relevance. First
of all, by making enclosure an unavoidable requirement for female religious life *tout court*, Trent turned it into a fundamental and intrinsic step
in the global reform of the Church, and of Catholic society as a whole.[15]
Secondly, Trent played a major role in creating an apparatus for
the implementation of enclosure. Tridentine decrees won acceptance in
Catholic countries, and enclosure laws were passed on to the local bishops
and princes. Slowly, sometimes through difficult negotiations within local
communities, involving the nuns and their families, enclosure was
brought into practical effect, and became an obsession for many Catholic
rulers as never before. In Spain, Philip II made the letter of Trent the law of
the land.[16] All the Italian states introduced strict cloister policies, and in
some towns—like Genoa, Venice, and Florence—boards of lay officers and

ecclesiastical men were appointed to take charge of the nunneries, and collaborated with the bishops in applying the discipline of enclosure.[17] Similar developments could be observed in Catholic German states, such as Bavaria; here Maximillian I—determined to turn Munich into the model of a Catholic city—made sure that the city's female monastic establishments conformed to the Tridentine parameters.[18] Tridentine dispositions were accepted in France too.[19]

It should be noted, however, that the powerful momentum of the Catholic reformation had its limits. Although in theory enclosure was imposed universally, the extent to which this really happened is still unclear and the impact of Tridentine legislation on female monastic communities is still an under-explored topic. There were undoubtedly exceptions to this rule. Some communities of uncloistered women, who participated in forms of active apostolate and charitable work outside the cloister, still persisted after Trent, in particular in some areas, such as in the Low Countries.[20] The dynamism of the Tridentine Church did not succeed in creating a completely homogeneous map of female religious life in the early modern world.

Walls, Doors, Grilles, and Curtains

'Confession shall be the chapter house, because it tells the truth. Preaching shall be the refectory, because it feeds souls. Prayer shall be the chapel, which must be high according to contemplation and beyond all worldly cares. Compassion shall be the infirmary; devotion, the store-room; meditation, the grange.'[21] As in this medieval devotional compendium, monastic architecture contributed to shaping nuns' lives, liturgical experiences, and schedules. Indeed, according to monastic regulations each area of the convent building was to host specific activities, time and space in the daily routine being strictly bound together. But what exactly did this circumscribed monastic space look like? What use did the nuns make of it, and what was its symbolic meaning?

The walls, the church, the internal cloister, and a sequence of rooms and passages, formed the stage for the collective and individual routine of monastic life. In the French Cistercian convent of Coyroux—founded in 1142 and built according to Cistercian ideals that were shared by other religious houses—the nuns inhabited a vast building, which surrounded a square cloister. Their monastic complex included the church, where they prayed and held the chapter, the gatehouse, the heated parlour, and living quarters formed by the dormitory, the refectory, and the rooms for boarders (girls who had entered the convent for educational purposes, without taking vows). The building also comprised working spaces, an infirmary, and a series of service rooms such as the kitchen with annexes, the storehouse, the bathroom, and a latrine. Some of these medieval features proved durable and were still in place in the early modern period, in spite of the many changes to which the convent was subjected through-out the centuries.[22] Spaces with similar functions were to be found elsewhere, for instance in Santa Giulia of Brescia, one of the most ancient and powerful Italian Benedictine convents of the Middle Ages. Founded between 753 and 759 by the Lombard Queen Ansa and King Desiderius, Santa Giulia was endowed with land and income. By the early seventeenth century, over 150 nuns lived in this huge complex made up of three churches and their respective cloisters, two large separate dormitories (one for the nuns and another for the boarders), the infirmary, and the service areas, including a kitchen with an adjoining baking-room containing a large oven, and an extended garden bordering part of the convent.[23]

The Tridentine reform brought about a significant emphasis on the restructuring of convent architecture. After the Council, ecclesiastical authorities approved very precise norms concerning the shape and functions of convent buildings. In 1599 the archbishop of Milan, Carlo Borromeo—one of the most active supporters of the Catholic reformation—published his *Instructions on Ecclesiastical Buildings*. His political influence and prestige among the elites—as well as the general need for proper architectural guidance regarding the physical construction of enclosure—rapidly transformed the *Instructions* into a model for the enclosure of convents in Catholic countries.[24]

When we look inside female monastic communities in the period following Trent, we often get a picture of meticulous inspections of convent buildings by bishops—including Borromeo—and apostolic visitors, and feverish construction activity. To the eyes of reformers, convents looked ill-equipped for the new requirements. As enclosure was to be both active and passive, nuns would not be allowed to set foot outside the cloister, nor would unlicensed outsiders be allowed inside. Furthermore, enclosure required visual as well as physical separation, whereby nuns would neither see the world, nor be seen by it.[25] In order to match these requirements, new walls were built, and existing ones were raised so as to close off any outside view of the community within. All existing windows, gates, grilles, or holes facing the public street were to be walled up, including the doors connecting the convent to the church. Fixed windows with tinted glass let in the daylight, but obscured views of the outside world. Parlours were remodelled by providing them with grilles, heavy curtains, and lockers. These works were often paid for by the nuns and their families. Some Florentine nuns, for instance, had to build solid 'enclosure walls . . . and the sisters contributed with all they could and with what their families sent them: wine, or wheat, or money'.[26] Not only did nuns face great expense, but they also had to make sure that architectural changes did not interfere with, or impede the fulfilment of, all fundamental spiritual functions: celebrating masses, holding processions dedicated to their protector saints, or other vital religious services which took place inside the convent, such as the monastic profession of nuns and their funerals. 'I remember', wrote another Florentine nun from the Dominican convent of Santa Caterina da Siena, that

> on 14 May 1587 we divided the room behind the confessional and we built a wall . . . and we did this in order to create a place for the room of the father confessor in the sacristy in the church and to allow him to stay there and be able to give Holy Sacraments to the dying nun; a new order prohibited confessors to sleep where there were confessionals, turnstiles or grilles.[27]

The Tridentine idea of the convent emphasized in particular three architectural features: the gate, the parlour, and the church. These three places represented a threshold between the sacred and the secular worlds. Here the closed convent space finished, and the open, public one began. Here nuns made contact, materially and symbolically, with outside society. Access to these places therefore needed to be controlled and restricted, for nuns as well as for outsiders. Indeed the real problem in constructing enclosure was to shape the nuns' complex and subtle interaction with society, making them part of the world without being in it.

The gate had always represented the nuns' main point of contact with the world. All material needs were satisfied through the gate, sometimes with rather elaborate arrangements. In the medieval Cistercian abbey of Coyroux the nuns had always received goods and chattels from the monks of the nearby monastery of Orbazine, who were also charged with performing all the necessary ecclesiastical duties for them. For receiving supplies the sisters used a gatehouse consisting of two main gates facing each other and situated between the church and the storehouse. The prioress kept the key of the inner gate, while one of the monks kept the key to the external one, and supervised all dealings. In order to provide the nuns with all they needed, he would gather various goods between the two doors, such as bread, wine, herbs, wood, vegetables, and meat, and everything required in case of illness. Then he would bang on the door with a stick, and then lock himself out of the external door. The porter nun, thus notified of the delivery, opened the door and collected the supplies. We do not know if this medieval tradition was still in place in the early modern period, but the Coyroux gatehouse remained in use until the early seventeenth century.[28]

Tridentine directives followed a similar pattern in order to ensure that the door would not become a meeting point between nuns and outsiders. Each convent was allowed up to two gates only, one for carriages and goods deliveries, the other for visitors. The male superior of the convent was responsible for locking both doors from the outside. Through the gate passed all the goods and work produced by the nuns, and all their written correspondence, which was subjected to strict control like everything else. Nuns could not send or receive letters unless they had previously been read by the abbess. Doorkeeper nuns administered the arrival and postage of letters by handing incoming mail to the abbess and taking from her hands the outgoing mail.[29] The ideal of perpetual enclosure, as formulated in Trent, meant that nuns crossed the threshold of the convent door, took the solemn vows, and never went out again. The only exceptions that could spare them this prohibition were wars, invasions, fire, and epidemics that were lethal for the entire community like leprosy or the plague. Tough penalties were prescribed for all those who transgressed the strict cloister rules: excommunication for outsiders, and suspensions from the offices, or even prison, for nuns. The enclosed convent was designed as a hermetically sealed micro-community where nothing was missing: not even, paradoxically, a place of corrective reclusion *within* this monastic reclusion.

The convent gate also acquired specific meaning in the ritual celebrations associated with the nuns' entrance into religious life, as the symbol of their definitive departure from the world. It was by walking through the gate that nuns left their family and were consigned to their heavenly groom. They would never again pass through it, not even as corpses, as nuns were usually buried within the cloister. It was also at the gate that their relatives and acquaintances gathered in order to bid farewell to the future nuns. A seventeenth-century French traveller through the Italian city of Bologna described the ceremony to enter the Corpus Domini convent, which involved the nuns-to-be following a ritual walk to see 'the city for the last time'. They were completely dressed in white veils as 'brides of Christ', and wore a flowered crown on their heads: '[they] are made to walk in front of the house of their parents so they can be withdrawn if they are not sure of the idea of becoming nuns. They are invited to enter, the fathers and mothers stand by the door and pray the nuns not to abandon them'.[30] Then they would ring the bell of the convent and step inside the hall, where the procession of relatives and friends could enter. When they finally walked into the church they were welcomed by all their future sisters singing the hymn 'Come thou Bride of Christ'. After this ceremony and the traditional distribution of food and gifts made to the convent by the nuns' families, everybody left, the door was closed, and religious life began.

Like the gate, the parlour also fulfilled a key function in the nuns' links with worldly society. Tridentine restrictions envisaged strict control over the direct contacts that nuns maintained with outsiders, during their time spent in the parlour. A rigid system of licences limited access for visitors.

The bishop, and no one else, could grant these licences, and only to very few people, such as the nuns' relatives and acquaintances, doctors, friars, and convent workers. Parlours had to be a safely enclosed area. The gatherings and conversations which took place in them were to be minimal, and would be witnessed by the listener nun. All parlour windows were to be equipped with thick double grilles, and if possible with dark veils. The Benedictine constitutions for the nuns of San Benito in Valladolid specified, for instance, that the iron-made grilles should be cut in such a way that neither an arm nor a hand could pass through them.[31] But in spite of the rules, parlours were not the silent and austere spaces that the authorities would have liked them to be.[32] In these rooms, sometimes furnished with stools to sit comfortably and often decorated with paintings, nuns received their lay or ecclesiastical visitors, and kept up to date with city news. They delivered in exchange stories and gossip about their enclosed life, distributed spiritual advice to relatives and faithful friends, commissioned works, negotiated the purchase or sale of lands and properties, and dealt with all the other collective business of the community. Judging by the number of seats and grilled windows (sometimes up to ten), parlours could resemble places for entertainment and conversation, as we see in the eighteenth-century Venetian painting *The Parlour* (see Fig. 15). The nuns stand behind large grilled windows with drawn curtains, while a group of men and women, dressed up for the occasion, are gathering on the other side of these windows, in the external part of the parlour. We see also a lapdog and two children watching a puppet show. A beggar in a corner, and a woman coming from outside and handing in a basket of what was probably food, emphasize the openness of the place. The idea suggested by the artist—G. B. Guardi—is that cloistered convents allowed society to be part of them. Although Guardi offers an idealized image of monastic places, his image finds support in written sources, which provide evidence on how, well after Trent, nuns played harps and guitars in the parlour, sang profane songs, or even danced in their habits in front of the visitors, who did the same on the other side of the windows.[33] At least to some extent, nuns attempted to use the parlour as a space where they could recreate the lay world they had left, and which at least some of them still wanted to belong to.

Of the three places connecting the inner and outer worlds, the convent church represented, more than the other two, the key focus of religious devotion, both for nuns and outsiders. Because nuns had to be separated from the public, a wall divided the convent church into two halves, or two churches. Each of the two churches was equipped with an altar and together they formed the so-called 'double church', an architectural solution already found in the Middle Ages.[34] While the public church was easily accessible to all outsiders, the nuns' church—their choir—was part of the internal, cloistered, space. It was connected to the public church by one wide window, with grilles, sometimes placed right above the altar, so that the nuns could hear the mass. Two other small windows enabled contacts with the external space, and allowed nuns to confess and take Holy Communion.[35] Different iconographic motives might decorate the two sides of the separating wall: for example, in the church of San Maurizio in Milan—beautifully frescoed by Lombard artists including the sixteenth-century painter Bernardino Luini—on the internal side the nuns looked at scenes from the life of Christ, and images of male and female saints which were depicted on the walls and the vaults. On the other side of the wall, men and women gathering in the public church looked at a wider variety of holy scenes, some of which included the effigies of donors and patrons.[36] Notwithstanding its architectural separation from the public church, the choir was an obvious link for the nuns, which allowed for their spiritual reconnection with the world. From their choir, through the window that opened into the external church, they followed religious ceremonies. They heard the words of the priest, and joined the public in simultaneous singing, or watched the elevation of the Eucharistic bread and body of Christ. Both the nuns and the public could see the Eucharist as it was placed on the altar, without seeing each other and in full respect of enclosure. When the priest turned his back to the nave and elevated the host, both groups were presented with the view of the most important moment of its consecration.[37] By participating in the same religious rituals the two groups became part of the same community of the faithful.

This combination of separation and connection within the convent church expressed the integrity of the female contemplative experience, conveying a sense of isolation from society as well as continuity with it. The convent church epitomized the ambiguity of the nuns' position in society: they were a group apart, but remained linked to the outside world. Many examples of convent architecture attest to the nuns' social presence and inclusion in social events.[38] Take for instance Clarissan architecture, the product of an early tradition of strict enclosure pre-dating Trent. In the Neapolitan convent of Santa Maria della Sapienza, designed by the architect and Theatine father G. B. Grimaldi, the choir's arch, located above the altar in the public church, was open and visible. Grimaldi's architectural solution underlined that, although separated from the public and trapped inside enclosure, the choir was still accessible for the people outside, though only visually. In other words, nuns were enclosed, yet integrated.

Other areas of the convent attested to the continuity between the secluded female religious community and outside society. In order to know more, we need to look at other parts of the building inhabited by the nuns, areas associated with more private and domestic functions. Indeed, nuns did not confine their existence to communal and liturgical spaces only and their convents also contained living spaces, both internal and external, that gave the monastic interior some resemblance to the domestic interiors of family houses and palaces. Gardens of varying sizes could be found in monastic houses, together with patios adorned with flowers, fountains spilling fresh water, and orchards, like those which were found for instance in some convents in sixteenth-century colonial Cuzco.[39] Nuns kept herb gardens, where they grew plants and flowers for the medical lotions they sold outside the walls. Additionally, according to widespread custom, nuns enjoyed the use of personal cells, which they used as their own private quarters, sharing them with their relatives, circles of friends, allies, servants, or slaves. Sometimes built over multiple floors, the cells comprised several fully furnished rooms, separate kitchens and fireplaces, and restrooms. In upper-class convents, cells' furnishings consisted of all sorts of valuable objects, mainly received from their families and friends, comfortable furniture and furnishing, like rugs and tapestries, embroidered pieces of fabric, and pillows, together with pictures, crucifixes, *agnus dei*, and various devotional objects.

Post-mortem inventories of nuns' possessions also list entire sets of linen, beddings, kitchen utensils, and clothing such as sumptuous dresses, mantels, scented gloves, and macramé. In Naples, amongst the possessions of some late sixteenth- and seventeenth-century nuns, were books, paintings, crystal objects and china, faience plates, a crown, a clock, and a coffee mill. The cell of the noble Giulia Caracciolo—in 1577—contained furnishings in ebony and ivory, marble busts in black and white, a Persian carpet, a large mirror that reflected objects twice life-size, a guitar, and many other fine objects.[40] Furthermore, convent internal spaces were marked not simply by the material objects of the outside world, but also by multiple signs of the nuns' attachment to their families, and it was possible to find coats of arms triumphantly hanging on the door or the wall of the richest cells, turned into showcases for dynastic power.[41] Living domesticized spaces expanded well beyond the cells, and assimilated corridors and staircases where small altars, tabernacles, and sacred images could be found, so as to recreate what had been recently defined the 'domestic holy' dimension of convents.[42]

The recreation of a domestic environment within the walls stood in stark contrast to the ideal of monastic poverty evoked by rules and regulations. It spoke, once again, of the many links that nuns maintained with outside society and its power structure. These links probably helped bridge, at least in the eyes of the nuns, the sense of distance from the world they had come from. The same was probably true for the nuns' benefactors—i.e. the nuns' families and acquaintances—who provided many of the nuns' possessions, and saw the convent not only as a place of material deprivation for the sake of spiritual perfection, but also as an extension of their domestic and social domains. The effective recipients of the gifts received by the nuns were not just the nuns themselves but all those patrons and the social groups associated with the convent, who participated in its social events, and whose taste was reflected in the selection of objects that they had destined to the nuns. Of course these patrons remained outside the closed space of the cloister, and as visitors they were admitted only to the liminal area of the parlour or the church. But it remained that, in spite of enclosure, the segregation of nuns might be challenged.

Operating within Enclosure

Since a desire for withdrawal from the world was one of the motivations for women entering the convent, it is not surprising that at least some of them were keen to embrace enclosure and found themselves at ease in the cloistered space. In the centuries which preceded Trent, the Poor Clares had already sought an enclosed life from their very foundation in the thirteenth century. Their founder, Clare of Assisi—the future saint who gave the order its name—ran away from her patrician paternal home one night to a hill outside the city walls where she joined the young Francis, who was preaching in the public squares, emulating the poverty of Christ. Here Francis dressed her in a rough and grey religious habit. Clare, soon joined by her sister Agnes, founded the convent of San Damiano which it was quickly turned into an enclosed environment, with walls and partitions. For Clare, enclosure was the ideal monastic condition, and a path towards spiritual perfection.[43]

But what about other nuns, in particular those who lived under a Tridentine regime? How did they envisage their monastic life and relations with the world? Of all the nuns who lived through Tridentine reorganization, Teresa of Avila (1515–82) proposed perhaps the most original discourse on enclosure. Born into a wealthy Spanish family, with Jewish *converso* origins, Teresa initially joined the Carmelite community of La Encarnación in Avila where discipline was not too tight, and nuns were allowed to receive visitors and spend time with their families or acquaintances. She herself was absent from her community for long periods. As she would recall years later, in her *Life*, 'In the convent where I was a nun there was no vow of enclosure.'[44] Reaching the age of 40, and having spent twenty-five years at La Encarnación, she underwent a radical process of spiritual conversion, and found a deeper understanding of God that turned her into a rigorous religious reformer. Her conversion pushed her to leave her convent and establish a new one, bound to a stricter interpretation of the monastic ideal. 'I was thinking', she wrote 'about what I could do for God, and I thought that the first thing was to follow the call to the religious life, which His Majesty had given me, by keeping my rule as perfectly as I could'.[45] A well-disciplined female

religious community was the beginning of spiritual renewal. In 1562 she
entered the Discalced Carmelite convent of San José, with four other
women. Inspired by the clerical and ascetic movement active in her city
in the mid-sixteenth century, Teresa was concerned to ensure that in her
newly founded convent enclosure was respected. She recommended that
nuns should limit their contacts with relatives, friends, confessors, and
doctors, and refuse conversations about worldly matters: in talking to
anyone from outside the convent, 'even with near relatives, they should
observe great care; and, if these are not people who delight in speaking of
the things of God, they should see them very seldom and bring their visits
quickly to an end'.[46] Insistence on enclosure was easily justified. First of all,
it guaranteed the fulfilment of chastity—one of the pillars of nuns'
existence. Secondly, it guaranteed the most important form of freedom:
autonomy from social obligation and particular interests, which made it
possible to fully dedicate oneself to God. Cloistered nuns, therefore,
enjoyed more freedom that those who engaged with society. Enclosure,
in Teresa's interpretation, could have a liberating effect.[47]

Keeping nuns to a strict cloister regime was part of a monastic plan that
had a specific missionary goal. The Church needed the efforts of women if
it was to win peace and regain its unity. Aware of the attempted destruction of the Catholic Church by Protestants, Teresa was determined to fight
for her Church, and contended that nuns should do the same. Perfectly
equipped to participate in this mission, nuns should be 'fighting for Him
even though [they] are very cloistered' and they could do it with
their prayers for the Church and its members.[48] In the words of her
niece Teresita—herself a Discalced Carmelite—Teresa was 'determined
to ... make war on the heretics with her prayer and her life and with the
prayers and lives of her nuns and to help Catholics by means of spiritual
exercises and continued prayers'.[49] While secular clergymen engaged in
active apostolate, Discalced Carmelites dedicated themselves to a contemplative apostolate. Furthermore, praying, in full detachment from the
world, would turn nuns into models of virginal perfection, living proof
of how wrong Protestant criticisms of monastic life could be. Teresa's
advice to her nuns was to practise a particular form of contemplation,
that of mental prayer or recollection, which was non-discursive and relied

on silent meditation. This was the means of achieving complete union with God. Rejecting the widespread suspicions and fears of the potential dangers of mental prayer for women, Teresa believed that this was a safe exercise for nuns.[50]

In Teresa's understanding of monastic life, enclosure did not prevent nuns from connecting with the world, and cultivating spiritual friendships with their confessors and friends. According to the rules, all contacts with outsiders had to take place under the supervision of other sisters, the listener nuns. Nuns were permitted to seek guidance from laymen and clerics, who could provide edification and help, as well as spiritual consolation. They might even raise their veil in the presence of people who came to assist them with the practice of prayer. The ideal convent Teresa envisaged was physically enclosed, but spiritually permeable.[51] More importantly, enclosure did not prevent Discalced nuns from engaging in a determined expansion of their order, through the foundation of a number of new convents. Not surprisingly, given the emphasis Teresa placed on the missionary campaign against Protestants, the first Discalced convents outside Spain were founded in France and the Low Countries, Catholic areas where Protestant movements had attracted supporters.

Teresa probably knew only too well that, in Tridentine times, sponsoring enclosure was the only way to success. Operating within this restrictive context, she turned enclosure from an instrument of control and the guardianship of women into a condition that might guarantee their spiritual liberty and enhance their position and influence in the world, ultimately affording them a special role in the defence of faith.[52]

However, notwithstanding Teresa's speculations, one undeniable fact remained: enclosure challenged the economic status of convents, representing a real practical problem for nuns' lives.[53] The loss of direct contact with society led to a dramatic fall in all activities, economic as well as religious. Nuns were forbidden from going out to beg, or doing charitable work in hospitals. The drastic reduction in communication brought by enclosure automatically affected the circulation of goods between the convent and the city, stopping secular people entering the convent to work or buy products made by the nuns. Outsiders wishing to enter the convent to purchase the nuns' products needed a licence from the bishop, slowing down convent business. Trapped by this package of restrictions, nuns became more and more dependent on dowries, boarders fees, private incomes from families, and the generosity of rich and powerful patrons and patronesses who provided them with alms. Preaching, teaching, the celebration of religious festivities (such as the feast of the convent's saint protector), and charitable works became almost the sole means to raise funds.

The troubled experience of the English nuns who fled to France and the Low Countries after the dissolution of the monasteries ordered by Henry VIII illustrates the material difficulties caused by enclosure. Leaving their homeland, and setting up new houses far away from their families and supporters, required a massive effort. The narratives reporting this forced female 'exodus' tell a sad tale of harshness and deprivation, in particular the very beginning of their life abroad: suppers of eggs and bread, old linen and kitchen utensils donated by their old convent, few liturgical books and church objects, and barely enough money to transport their baggage.[54] Opportunities for setting up new religious houses depended mainly on the generous bequests of devout Catholic families on the Continent and in England. Indeed, English monastic communities, which flourished in France and Flanders in the late sixteenth and seventeenth centuries, ensured the preservation of the female Catholic elite, as well as making a general contribution to the Catholic faith, since some initially believed Catholicism could be restored in countries like England, where it had been banned. In this context, raising money became a key priority for nuns and spiritual assistance was one of their most effective tools. As well as opening schools for girls, engaging in needle- and craftwork, and sometimes in other remunerative industries such as malt-making, brewery, laundry, or watch-making,[55] nuns would also pray for their families, founders, and benefactors. In exchange for their prayers they received money in the form of alms, rents, yearly incomes, and gifts such as icons, artworks, and household goods. This kind of spiritual labour was both a response to laypeoples' demand for the intercessory power of nuns, and an effective way of meeting their own material needs, providing a basis for the endowment of their cloisters. In 1658, some Franciscan nuns from

Nieuport settled down in Paris and opened a new convent. There they were fortunate enough to find pious patronesses who gave them food and fuel. Owing their survival to these French women, they offered, in return, their spiritual assistance. The abbess decided that a *Te Deum* and *Salve Regina* were to be regularly recited by all the sisters in order to honour and recompense their patrons.[56] Spiritual intercession for benevolent givers guaranteed nuns' collective survival within the limits of their segregated life.

Resistance

A sixteenth-century Peruvian chronicle tells the story of a nun who, just before entering the convent, waved at her mother through the grilles and said: 'Be it, mother, for the love of God.' Conversely, on the day of her profession, a novice was asked about her last desire: 'What would you like to have?' was the question. Her answer was a straight one: 'I want the keys of the convent in order to leave.'[57] A sought-after location for some women, enclosed convents also represented the horror of unwanted segregation for others. In the literary tradition these two recurrent and opposite visions were metaphorically captured by the two images of the convent as a paradise and the convent as hell.

As we are reminded here, while some nuns accepted and even demanded enclosure, others dissented and resisted it. They expressed their dissent though words as well as deeds. Some attempted to found communities free from the obligation of enclosure. Others claimed before ecclesiastical authorities to have entered religion under pressure and against their will, demanding to be relieved from solemn vows and to return to their families, though families were not always willing to take them back.[58] Others even tried to escape, maybe with the help of some relative, or by setting fire to their convent. In some cases, nuns really resisted enclosure with all possible means available to them. In 1628 the nuns of Santa Cristina, in Bologna, repeatedly refused to obey episcopal orders and let stonemasons wall up their building, greeting them with stones and tiles. One day, they literally assaulted the archbishop's notary who had come to their convent to make them see reason.

When he approached the courtyard asking to see 'the mother abbess' they
politely invited him to come closer, beneath a high window. By the time he
realized he was in danger it was almost too late: the nuns 'let fall from the
window a great piece of marble, with the words, "Here is the mother
abbess". And if the poor man had not quickly jumped backward, he would
have been overwhelmed and crushed by that blow.'[59]

Various reasons lay behind this insubordination. Enclosure naturally
presented nuns with alarming visions of imprisonment, stirring up their
fear of reclusion. Strict cloister meant the loss of the freedom to go out: 'It
is not the grilles that make enclosure but the prohibition to exit without
permission', the Cistercian nuns of Liège and Namur pointed out in 1699
in a collective letter to their superior general, the abbot of Citeaux.[60]
Moreover, enclosure could have grim consequences: the documented
cases of fights between nuns involving physical violence and threats, as
well as sexual scandals and even poisoning attempts, reveal how segregation could seriously affect personal and power relations, and suffocate the
nuns' sociability by constraining it to monastic community.

But enclosure hid other equally insidious dangers. It was an obligation
imposed on all female religious communities by the Church authorities.
Alongside it went the establishment of a more articulated male authority,
required by Tridentine ordinances, which subjected nuns, as well as
Tertiaries, to the authority of the bishop, or the male superiors of their
order. Enclosure therefore challenged not only the freedom of women to
choose the form of life that they wanted, and whether they wanted to live
in a cloistered or an open community, but also their own ability to govern
their communities.[61] No wonder that nuns fought all this, some of them—
like the thirteenth-century Italian religious reformer Santuccia Carabotti
of Gubbio who opposed cloister rules—arguing that in matters of
governance female communities should be no more constrained than
male ones.[62]

The Florentine convent of Santa Caterina da Siena offers interesting
evidence on this matter. The convent had been founded at the end of the
fifteenth century, in the wake of Gerolamo Savonarola's call for religious
renewal. Starting out as a community of Tertiaries living together according to monastic observance, the nuns progressively turned towards a more

formal model of community life. They obtained specific rules and constitutions, and finally acquired the status of professed nuns. Keen to involve
themselves in pious and charitable activities outside their cloister, the
nuns had asked for and obtained papal exemption from enclosure, and
had been able to live an 'open' form of reclusion. This meant that their
presence in the city was restricted but not eliminated. They went out to
attend mass, confession, and the divine office, and to offer their charity to
poor and sick people.[63] As their rule stated, their chastity was guaranteed
by their will, self-control, and mutual support and guardianship, not by
walls or external male control. Inevitably, when the apostolic visitor
Alfonso Binarini came to the convent in 1575 to impose strict cloister
rules, the sisters rejected his orders. His visit was carefully recorded by
the prioress in a brief and untitled memoir written in the summer of
that year:

> I remember that His Sanctity sent a visitor from Rome who has to look at all
> convents and wants all of them to be cloistered... The visitor... came into
> the church and stood at the grate... then he visited the outer altar and
> sacristy. And then he came in through the door of the parlour and looking
> at the grates he said that they needed to be doubled... and he did not like
> the window either and we moved on. And while he was coming in front of
> the lodge, saying that he was coming to look at the cloister, the prioress
> addressed him kindly and said: *monsignor* and Reverend father, we are not
> living in claustration but we have our Rule and constitution, which have
> been approved by Pope Paul III and they do not oblige us to enclosure; we
> do not have it and we do not want it. Thus the said Reverend Bishop became
> so furious that he addressed the prioress and told her that she was being
> arrogant... and that he was going to give her the punishment that she
> deserved.[64]

The prioress's description of the visit, during which the apostolic visitor
had looked around their church and checked all the grates and doors,
emphasized that these barriers already marked a clear separation between
the convent's inner space and the outer world. As far as the nuns were
concerned, their convent was already a closed building even though they
were not observing the rule of strict enclosure, as they were sometimes
going out. Her description also underlined that they did not want to
accept enclosure, as intended by Trent, because it was incompatible with

the original nature of their community. Maybe even more important was
the fact that the visitor and his orders undermined their power to choose
and their legitimate right to decide in matters concerning their own
community and life. To the nuns' eyes this visit was an act of intrusion
into their convent's protected sphere by a male outsider.

The nuns' determination to stick to their traditions was not enough and
in the end they lost their battle. On 21 August 1575 a bull by Pope Gregory
XIII calling for excommunication of anyone entering the convents was
published in the Duomo of Florence; nine days later the nuns of Santa
Caterina were locked in: 'the day 29 [August 1575] we were ordered by the
Reverend Father Prior of San Marco . . . on behalf of the vicarious [of the
archbishop] of Florence to wall up the door of the church in five days or
he was going to give us excommunication; and thus it was walled up that
day . . . and we were the first [to be cloistered] to our great sorrow'.[65]

A general look at the dynamics associated with enclosure reveals yet a
further outcome of it. If the women's—albeit unsuccessful—resistance
originated in the need to maintain control over the circumscribed world
of their community, it also had broader goals, extending well beyond the
walls. Indeed while enclosure was expected to erase religious women from
the public scene by turning them into an invisible presence, they tried very
hard to claim their right to a place within it, to remain visible and even
influential. Sometimes they succeeded in doing this, sometimes they did
not. Most often, however, they did so behind the scenes through indirect
influence, interacting with members of the elite and weaving webs of
political support.

In seventeenth-century Moscow, nuns seldom disregarded strict cloister
rules and left the convent, but they did maintain close links with the ruling
family, to the point that Princess Sophia, the sister of Peter I, was accused
of instigating an uprising in Novodevichij convent.[66] In Rome, in the same
century, the young aristocrat Fabrizio Spada, eager to pursue a political
career, was advised to work on his family's friendship with the Carmelites,
who enjoyed the confidence of the queen of France. A similar story
emerges from Vienna. The countess of Lambergh, who wanted to place
her husband as ambassador in Rome, spent a lot of her time lobbying
ministers, friars, and Carmelite nuns who acted as intermediaries.[67]

The nuns of the most prestigious and aristocratic convents in Madrid, saw their communities as places for networking, and conducting family and other business. In the Carmelite convent of Las Descalzas Reales powerful Habsburg women negotiated important political decisions.[68] Piety maintained an important political resource for these women, and through their pious activities they could exercise power and influence in ruling circles. During the reign of Philip III (1598–1621), the empress Maria, Margaret of Austria, and the nun Margaret of the Cross, gained a reputation for their charity, piety, and sanctity. They were believed to spend most of their time in spiritual contemplation and prayer. All three, in different ways, were closely linked to the Descalzas. Margaret of the Cross spent forty-eight years of her life in this convent before her death. She professed the Franciscan rule and became a cloistered nun, thereby avoiding a marriage to her uncle Philip II, who was fifty years her senior. The empress Maria lived in separate quarters adjacent to the convent, but went inside on a daily basis to join the nuns in their prayers, masses, and sometimes for meals. To seal her ties with the Descalzas convent, she had her portrait, made-dressed in the garb of a Franciscan nun holding a rosary and standing beside a symbol of the imperial crown. Margaret of Austria also visited convents daily, wherever she happened to be. Whenever Philip III needed to leave the court, she often moved into the Descalzas, bringing her children with her. Monarchs, state councillors, papal nuncios, and foreign ambassadors were all regular visitors; the Austrian ambassador in particular, who served as the empress's personal attendant, was a constant presence. Needless to say, the presence and proximity of royal women, and in particular of the empress, made the Descalzas a very special place. The nuns strategically exploited their close relations with the court to request support and financial aid, or to score political points by sponsoring the publication of manuscripts of an openly political nature. The Descalzas functioned as an extension of the court, and as a female centre of the Austrian Habsburg diplomatic network, partially independent from Madrid.[69] The nuns sought to gain public presence, in some cases successfully, by exploiting the overlap between the religious and the political realms.

But perhaps one of the best examples of how enclosure raised issues concerning women's quest for a place in the city's public life is the

Bavarian convent of Putrich in Munich. This was a community of
Franciscan Tertiaries with a traditionally active participation in civic life
through charitable works, which in the beginning of the seventeenth
century had been transformed into a closed convent by the implementation of Tridentine dispositions. In 1662, the nuns became involved in a
battle with their male superiors over the corpse of the early Christian
martyr Saint Dorothea that they had recently acquired from Rome.[70]
Disputes over relics were not infrequent in convents. Possessing
holy remains brought the benefit of their supernatural power, and the
protection of the saint, as well as fame and prestige for the community.[71]
For the Putrich sisters the display of Dorothea's bones was the perfect
occasion to celebrate the convent's status as a cornerstone of civic religious
life. Exhibited in their church, the saint's body could become a great
attraction for all citizens, thus enhancing the public visibility of their
convent. The nuns had purchased Dorothea's relics almost secretly, behind
the back of their father superior. They had supervised each stage of the trip
from Rome to Munich, and instructed—by letter—a Capuchin father
hired for the occasion. Dorothea's remains had been transported, locked
in a trunk. After numerous misadventures—including the temporary loss
of the trunk on its way to Bologna—Dorothea finally arrived in Munich.
The nuns' plan was to have 'the holy martyr [. . .] approved by the bishop
in Freising and put in our church for public veneration with his licence'.[72]
They were to have decorated the body, dressing it with precious clothing
and a veil, and adorning it with jewellery and gems. But when their
convent father superior found out what had happened, sparks flew. By
dealing with outsiders and acting outside his control, the nuns had
violated enclosure and challenged his authority. Furthermore, if the
nuns wanted to keep Dorothea in their convent, it would be in their
cloistered church and for their private veneration only, and not for display
in the public church, as the nuns had hoped. According to the superior,
and his strict interpretation of enclosure, nothing associated with
cloistered women, including the body of a female saint, could be seen or
venerated in the public space which was out of bounds to them, even
if this space was the convent church. The nuns, in contrast, demanded
precisely this, as they saw the convent public church as a part of

their community's space which was open to the public, and extended to the city, although it was inaccessible to them. The battle over the possession and display of the relics quickly turned into something completely different: a battle for nuns' place in the public sphere. For the father superior, nuns needed to be kept out of public view. For the nuns the exhibition of Dorothea would have placed them, once again, in contact with the city, enabling them to reconnect with their not-so-faraway past.

How did this story end? After they had spent many days preparing and decorating Saint Dorothea's body, they had to hand it to the father superiors. When finally the Franciscan fathers carried Dorothea in procession through the streets of Munich and back to the convent church again, the nuns remained locked in their choir, while the Franciscans outside played the leading role in this event. The message of the ceremony was clear: the only public role allowed to religious women was an invisible one, and men would take their place as public representatives. Still, precisely the exhibition of the martyr and its very visible decorations, which made it an attraction before the citizens, amounted to a public representation of the nuns, which allowed them, in a sense, to reappropriate their presence in the city.[73] Neither could their close association with Dorothea's remains, displayed in their convent church, be ignored. By venerating Dorothea, looking after her body, and offering intercessory prayers to the saint in order to invoke her protection over their community and the dead, the nuns were able to leave a mark on the wider world.

Whatever nuns' attitude towards enclosure, whether convents were experienced as a paradise or a prison, monastic communities were places for female agency, and 'women's creation of religious and social meaning'.[74] Nuns may have wished to play by the rules and be obedient brides of Christ, understanding enclosure as the most appropriate condition for contemplative retreat but at the same time, they did not wish to see their liberties or their public role curtailed. While enclosed, they still found ways to participate 'from within'.

THREE

Voices from the Cloister

'No institution in Europe has ever won for the lady the freedom of development that she enjoyed in the convent...The impulse toward leadership which kept the men in the world sent women out of it.'[1] Writing at the beginning of the twentieth century, the American historian Emily James Putnam described in these powerful terms the impact of convents on the history of women. Removed from society, convents acted as catalysts for female freedom and individual development. No other institution could be compared to them. They were unique. Putnam's forthright view may have drawn on her own personal, professional experience. A distinguished scholar, she worked in some of the most prestigious academic institutions in her country, including Barnard College, and the New School for Social Research. She probably had a clear understanding of what it meant for a woman to pursue an intellectual career in a predominantly male world, and how attractive a separated place, free from the challenges and constraints of this world, could be.[2]

A century after Putnam, our greater knowledge of convents complicates the picture, though confirming her early insights. Female monastic communities offered women opportunities for spiritual leadership roles, and favourable conditions to develop their education, creativity, intellectual, and writing skills. From the late Middle Ages until the early eighteenth century nuns have been abundantly represented amongst women writers all over Catholic Europe and the New World.[3] Nor were nuns' efforts limited to writing: many women musicians, singers, painters, and sculptors of the past were to be found inside the cloister. Let us trace the lives of these women, beginning with the writers. What prompted them to write, which audience were they addressing, and how did they projected onto the printed page their individual and collective sense of self?

Silences and Words

Those nuns who took up the pen in order to write did so in defiance of the long-standing assumption that women should be silent: 'Let the woman learn in silence with all subjection. But I suffer not a woman to teach, nor to usurp authority over the man but to be in silence. For Adam was first formed, then Eve. And Adam was not deceived, but the woman being deceived was in the transgression.'[4] Created after Adam, and out of his body, women were spiritually weak, they easily felt victim to deception and sin, and were more prone to transgress the order of things than their male counterparts. If they were to learn they should do so under male supervision, and they were not to teach or speak in public. Early modern intellectuals distanced themselves only partially from Saint Paul's assertions. Humanists, such as Leonardo Bruni, Thomas More, and Juan de Vives, maintained that women might be encouraged to learn and develop their intellectual talent. They discussed the possibility of women studying in order to acquire basic literacy, or even an education which, for some of them, might include the study of Latin and the classics. All of them agreed that Christian readings were to be given preference over all other texts, and that learning should be foremost addressed to religion and devotion, devoid of practical purpose. Women did not need to be trained for public offices, political responsibilities, or university positions, because they were excluded from all of these roles. The main purpose of their lives was marriage, childbearing, and family responsibilities. Education served to improve them spiritually, and enabled them to teach their children to read and write, and maybe also help out with family business affairs when their husbands were not around. This discrimination was applied to all women including-to a certain extent-queens and princesses, whose political authority was perceived to be unnatural, a 'monstrous regimen...the subversion of good order'.[5] Like politics, intellectual activity was an exclusively male domain.

Of all women, nuns had a further reason for keeping the Pauline silence. Silence was required by monastic regulation as it fostered contemplation and full dedication to God. It was therefore the natural condition for religious women whose main task was to pray and interact with God on behalf of all human beings. Precisely in these silent and cloistered environments, however, nuns found the means to write. Female religious communities, in particular older convents serving the aristocratic and wealthy classes, provided education for boarders and nuns: reading, in some cases writing, sewing, good manners and behaviour.[6] Particular emphasis was placed on moral and spiritual education but also literary knowledge. Collected in the libraries of some aristocratic and wealthy convents, were books of prayers and devotional texts of various kinds, lives of saints, as well as handbooks for learning how to read and write. Nuns copied and illuminated manuscripts, and some of them wrote a remarkable variety of works of their own. They wrote spiritual tracts and letters describing their own mystical experiences and inner conversations with God, and those of their sisters. Some turned their prophetic abilities into advice for kings and princes, to whom they offered their thoughts and political ideas. Others wrote about the foundation and history of their communities, and chronicled the lives of exceptionally pious or learned nuns. Very few of them contributed to the *Querelle des femmes*, the major polemic on the nature of the sexes. Inevitably, they often faced obstacles in gaining access to material for their writings, but managed to cope with such difficulties.[7] Unlike monks, nuns could not travel to other convent libraries or archives, and they mostly relied on the books and documents owned by their own religious houses. Their contacts with outsiders were tightly controlled by the doorkeeper or the abbess. Notwithstanding these limitations, they were able to acquire books and materials from relatives and patrons that gathered in their parlour, and they learned about the world though conversations with their visitors. Most importantly, they found a major source of information about the spiritual and material dimensions of their individual and collective life inside their convent, through their own direct experiences and those they witnessed, or from the oral tradition preserved by the oldest sisters, which survived though generations of nuns. Being part of a monastic community, therefore, might work to the advantage of women: they gained education and a spiritual identity, as well as the authority to break the silence and engage with the written word. Whether their works were published or not—and most of them were not—their writings represented an extraordinary testimony of their inner and social world, as well as a tangible sign of their intellectual aspirations and familiarity with written culture.

Messengers of God

> While I was beseeching Our Lord to-day that He would speak through me, since I could find nothing to say and had no idea how to begin to carry out the obligation laid upon me by obedience, a thought occurred to me which I will now set down, in order to have some foundation on which to build. I began to think of the soul as if it were a castle made of a single diamond or of very clear crystal, in which there are many rooms, just as in Heaven there are many mansions.[8]

In 1577 Teresa of Avila began work on *The Interior Castle*, a presentation of her spiritual experience and relationship with God. Considered as one of her masterpieces, the *Castle* was an act of obedience to her confessor, Jeronimo Gracian, who had 'commanded' her to put on paper her extraordinary inner life and her way of praying, for the benefit of other nuns. As Teresa explained, 'the nuns of these convents of Our Lady of Carmel need someone to solve their difficulties concerning prayer, and as . . . women best understand each other's language, . . . anything I might say would be particularly useful to them'.[9]

Teresa is perhaps one of the best-known figures in the female Western intellectual tradition, and in particular in the female mystical tradition. Her charismatic gifts, leadership, and incursions into the dangerous territory of religion and theological meditations, gained her fame as well as controversy. Backed by aristocratic families, influential ecclesiastics, and other eminent men, including King Philip II, she nevertheless faced direct attacks on her ideas about monastic reforms, spirituality, and forms of contemplative prayer, which were seen as too close to Protestant practices and heterodoxy. She was placed under scrutiny, the Inquisition examined her works, and seven years after her death theologians urged all her writings to be burnt. In spite of all this she was canonized—not without debate—in 1622, and more recently proclaimed Doctor of the Church (1969). An eclectic spirit, Teresa composed a number of mystical works including the *Castle*, *The Way to Perfection*, *The Book of her Life*, the *Meditations on the Songs of Songs*, the *Book of Foundations* of the Discalced Carmelite convents, and a vast corpus of letters, all of them published inside and outside Spain. The first Spanish edition of her complete works was printed in 1588, only six years after her death, and thirteen further editions came out between 1588 and 1636 in Spain, Italy, and France. This amounted to an extraordinary level of public impact for the work of a cloistered nun.

Admittedly, Teresa was an exceptional woman, who lived an unusual existence in comparison to that of other nuns of her time. But she was certainly not the only one to describe her spiritual life and make it available to those around her. Indeed drawing on the tradition of their late medieval predecessors—such as Mechtilde of Magdeburg, Brigid of Sweden, Catherine of Siena[10]—many early modern nuns, and some Tertiaries, wrote spiritual autobiographies and mystic tracts, and exchanged spiritual letters with male and female acquaintances outside the cloister. These literary nuns came from a variety of different religious orders, such as Poor Clares, Capuchins, Carmelites, Dominicans, but also Ursulines and Visitandines, and often contributed to the spiritual and learned tradition of their order or community. They were particularly active in the most Catholic countries such as Italy, Spain, Portugal, France, and the New World, though a few of them came from religiously divided areas like Germany or the Low Countries. Given the extraordinary nature of the mystical experience, it is hardly surprising that these exceptional women were sometimes venerated as saints. They were also religious reformers, or the founders and mother superiors of convents. Their numbers should not be underestimated. In Spain—one of the most studied cases—113 nuns wrote spiritual autobiographies in the period between the end of the sixteenth and the middle of the seventeenth century.[11]

Some female mystics were laywomen who lived in the family home or in communities of Tertiaries. The Spanish Dominican Tertiary Maria de Santo Domingo (c.1470–1524) from Piedrahita, near Avila, dictated her book of prayers to her confessor and other clergymen she knew. Agnes van Heilsbach (1597–1640) and Joanna van Randenraedt (1610–84), both from the Dutch city of Roermond, were *kloppen*—pious laywomen who dedicated their life to the service of God. They lived outside the convent, under the guidance of the local Jesuit fathers, and left thousand of pages of notes written on their confessors' orders, in which they described their mystical dreams, visions, and voices. Although these lay mystics continued a well-established medieval tradition of spiritual writers, the nuns proper were the great protagonists of early modern mysticism, and a distinctive feature of female creativity.[12]

As Isabelle Poutrin has suggested, early modern convents were 'ateliers of autobiographical writing'.[13] Within these monastic ateliers writing could become a collective act, it developed as collaborative work, and the notion of the individual author blended with that of collective author-ship. The Spanish Tertiary Juana de la Cruz (1481–1534) dictated her revelations to one of the sisters of the Franciscan convent where she lived; the result was the *Libro del Conorte* containing her sermons of the year 1509.[14] Similarly the Carmelite saint Maria Maddalena de Pazzi (1566–1607) engaged in an elaborate writing process. This aristocratic nun from Florence was blessed by almost daily mystical raptures that could last several hours. During these raptures she was able to work, sew, and paint, and her physical behaviour verged on the bizarre: strange gestures, great agility, and rapid movement alternating with complete immobility. While she was in this ecstatic state she talked to an invisible interlocutor. Her fellow sisters put her words on paper as soon as she pronounced them, some repeating her words, others transcri-bing them. When the ecstasy was over the nuns would compare their written texts, edit them, and the saint would clarify the most obscure points.[15] The five manuscript books collected in her convent archive, containing her visions and her advice to her sisters, are the result of this curious 'division of labour'. Her works were published in 1611, soon after her death.

One of the most interesting aspects of female mystic writing is that it was the expression of the complex spiritual relationship between women and their confessors.[16] Claiming to be inspired by God, women wrote their spiritual autobiographies in response to requests or even orders from their confessors or other clergymen in their circles of acquaintance. They narrated their visions, divine favours, doubts, battles with the Devil, and turmoil in their souls, sometimes openly calling for the confessors' help in interpreting their extraordinary experiences. They found in their directors a male authority that guided them in their spiritual travels and search for a complete union with God. 'My most reverend . . . Father', wrote the Italian Camilla Battista Varano (1458–1524), in her autobiography, 'I am letting you know that all of this month of February I have been in great agony and mental turmoil, and the reason is this, that I have had a vehement . . . and fervent inspiration, to which I have opposed great resistance, as if it were the temptation of the Devil'.[17] Camilla—who also composed a spiritual tract published in 1490, and other spiritual works in verse and prose— would indeed consult her confessor and tell him about her spiritual life, in the hope of discovering—amongst other things—whether her mystical 'inspiration' was a manifestation of the Devil or the will of God.

The confessors, in turn, by guiding their 'spiritual friends' also submitted them to their control, vouching for the authenticity of their mystic experience and their religious orthodoxy. In extreme cases, confessors assumed the role of vehemently repressive censors.[18] The confessor of Maria de Agreda, claimed that 'writing is not women's work' and ordered her to burn the only copy of her spiritual and intellectual masterpiece, *The Mystical City of God*. Maria did as she was told and destroyed her manuscript. Years later, a subsequent confessor ordered her to rewrite it. Again she obeyed, and her work was finally completed. It was published in 1670, five years after her death. In spite of her vicissitudes with her different confessors, this visionary nun was amazingly prolific. On top of the *City of God* she wrote a variety of texts including her autobiography, some spiritual works, and a collection of correspondence with Philip IV of Spain over twenty-two years. The confessor of Maria de San José (1656–1719) from Puebla, Mexico, subjected her to an exhausting writing discipline. As she reported, '[My confessor] commanded me to write during every minute of the time I had at my disposal, taking no more than one hour at night and sleeping only for that hour'. He repeatedly tormented her, first ordering her to stop writing, and then to start again; secondly demanding she give up all the books in her cell; thirdly taking away the papers she had written, leaving her aghast: 'he determined that he could neither read nor know what was written in the papers I delivered to him, and he sealed as they were when he received them, as he took them to his confessor, a priest of the Society [of Jesus]. I do not know what has become of those papers'.[19] Ruthless confessors could do even worse, as in the case of the Italian Capuchin Clare, Maria Maddalena Martinengo (1687–1737). The author of a tract on humility, poetry, letters, and advice for her sisters, Maria Maddalena had her autobiography burnt directly by her confessor. A few years later, she manifested her intention to replicate the fire herself, allegedly 'because she took care not to leave memory of herself in the world'.[20] Narratives of self-censorship such as this, attest to the tensions nuns faced between submission to authority and the desire to exert their control over their writings by destroying them.

The spiritual demand made by their superiors made nuns acutely aware of their lack of appropriate training and their inadequate resources for textual creation. Some of them suffered crippling insecurity and begged their confessors to let them stop writing. Veronica Giuliani (1660–1716) perfectly illustrates this condition. Locked up in the Capuchin Clares' convent of Città di Castello, Veronica had daily visions, which she was told to report on paper. Soon her writing became a very stressful duty that she fulfilled under strict supervision. Veronica was illiterate, and had barely learned to write when she began to fill pages and pages of notes that she handed in to her superiors, without any opportunity to revise or correct them. She was not allowed to see any of this work again. She wrote in quite punitive conditions, usually at night, sitting uncomfortably on the bed in her cell using a small wooden surface placed on her knees. During her life she endured heavy penitence and, suspected of heresy, was denounced to the Holy Office, put on trial, and subjected to invasive physical examinations. Finally she was rehabilitated and declared a saint in 1839. Against all odds, she remained one of the most productive authors in the whole history of female mysticism, her autobiographical essays amounting to around 6,000 printed pages.[21]

This is, however, only one side of the story. Whilst nuns often celebrated in their works exemplary piety, chastity, and austerity, they also explicitly asserted their spiritual authority and privileged role as interlocutors with God. In recording their life they embarked on an adventure that implied the possibility to address an audience, inside and also outside the convent, made up of their sisters, confessors, and other devout associates, who in turn—in listening to their words and hearing of their visions—found a means to reach the Divine.

If we look closely at convent mysticism, we are presented with a multitude of examples that point at the different empowering opportunities of spiritual writing for nuns. Thus we encounter Caterina Vigri (1413–63), one of the protagonists of the religious Observant reform of convents in northern Italy. Born to a patrician family, she grew up and was educated at the court of Ferrara as a lady-in-waiting of Margherita d'Este. Deeply influenced by Franciscan spirituality, Caterina embraced religious life at the age of 13 as a lay nun. She was then involved with other women in the founding of a Poor Clare convent in Ferrara, where she professed the solemn vows and lived until she was 43. Subsequently she moved to the nearby city of Bologna to found the new convent of the Corpus Domini, becoming, despite her humble resistance, its first abbess. Throughout her life, Caterina had visions and ecstasies, and was venerated as a living saint. One of the few mystics to take up her pen freely without the insistence of her confessor, she composed spiritual lauds, letters, a breviary in Latin and Italian, and in 1438 her best-known work, the spiritual tract *The Seven Spiritual Weapons*. For Caterina, writing was not only a means of reaching God herself, but also a way of teaching her sisters how to do so, thus asserting her influence over her community. Indeed, she wrote *The Weapons* whilst acting as mistress of novices, in order to share her spiritual experience with her sisters: 'I write, with my own hand, only for the fear of divine reprehension if I would keep silent about all the things that might improve other people,'[22] she declared before spelling out her teachings and recommendations: to be diligent, to mistrust oneself, to trust God and imitate him, to study the Gospel, and to resist the temptations of the Devil. Based on her own life, which she intended to be an example for all sisters, her work was an act of self-celebration, in which she described her own piety and perfection thus enhancing her role as spiritual leader. Although she claimed to have kept her written work secret, she gave precise instructions for multiple copies to be produced after her death, revealing how keen she was for her teachings to circulate among her sisters. As she wrote 'I by myself have written for divine inspiration this little book in the convent of the Corpus Christi in the cell where I was living . . . and in my life I have never manifested it to anyone', adding that

> Any person who will come to possess this book should give it to our father confessor and he should copy it, or have it copied by somebody else . . . and then he should give it to . . . my mothers and sisters of the Corpus Domini in Ferrara and the above said book should remain in [the convent] where I will end my pilgrimage. . . . The father confessor should do this as soon as possible. I impose this on behalf of our Lord, for the consolation . . . of all the poor and devoted sisters who willingly incarcerated themselves for him.[23]

Her prayers were heard. *The Weapons* circulated amongst the Poor Clares in manuscript form, and the text was published in 1475. Caterina's work became widely known some time after her death, cementing her posthumous fame and spiritual authority. She was canonized in the eighteenth century.

Surely, the claim for spiritual authority asserted by many nuns found its supporters above all, amongst their sisters and within their community. The closest companions of Teresa de Avila wrote to her and about her, contributing to spreading the fame of the saint, and her authority within their convent and religious order, although their relationship with her was not without its contradictions. Ana de San Bartolomé (1549–1626), an illiterate Castilian peasant who learnt how to write in the convent of San José, founded by Teresa, became the saint's personal assistant, secretary, confidante, and nurse. She travelled and founded convents in France and Flanders, where she eventually died. Under Teresa's tutelage, she developed visions, foreseeing Francis Drake's defeat of the Spanish *Invincible Armada*. After the saint's death, she compiled a number of letters to clerics, regents, princesses, and commanders, and a spiritual autobiography which circulated in manuscript form in Spain, and was first published in Flemish six years after her death in 1632. She depicted Teresa as a trustworthy guide, more reliable than her own confessor, about whom she clearly had her doubts:

> when my confessor saw that my zeal and love for the other souls was lasting such a long time, he told me . . . : 'Beware, my child, for this charity is of the Devil, and he is trying to deceive you.' I went to our Saint [Teresa], to ask her if this were true, and I told her all that had happened. And she told me not to worry, that it was not the Devil, for she had gone through that same way of prayer, with confessors who did not understand it. With that I was comforted and I believed that just as the Saint told me, it was of God.[24]

Ana de San Bartolomé regarded Teresa as her spiritual mother, and saw herself as the only true heiress of the saint. She wrote the *Defence of the Teresian Legacy* in support of Teresa and her monastic ideas, a work that she completed in 1621–3. In the case of Saint Teresa and her faithful companions it was almost inevitable that female and male spiritual authority would enter into conflict. Teresa directed her teachings not only at her sisters, but also at her male superiors, whom she felt could benefit equally from her insights into God's will: 'There is one thing that I want to say', she wrote in her *Life* addressing her confessor, 'if Your Reverence thinks it well that I should do so, as in my opinion it is important. It will serve as what may be necessary advice.'[25]

Here we see how spiritual power, mediated through writing, served to legitimize the actions of a leader and a group, acquiring particular importance for reformed religious orders, as in the case of Teresa and the Carmelite nuns, and for new orders too. The example of the Visitandines reinforces this point. Founded by the mystic Jeanne de Chantal in the early seventeenth century, the order of the Visitation maintained a high profile in seventeenth-century France, mainly thanks to Jeanne's influence and her numerous and powerful friends outside the cloister. She entertained many 'spiritual relationships' with religious and laymen and -women, with whom she exchanged spiritual advice by letter. Another mystic writer of this order contributed to its visibility: Marguerite Mairie Alacoque (1647–90). 'I want you here', God had apparently told her when she visited the Visitation convent, in Paray, for the first time, at the age of 24. She went on to profess the solemn vows, and lived in monastic retreat for the rest of her life. She wrote her autobiography and letters describing her spiritual ascent and visions. Extremely devoted to the cult of the sacred heart of Jesus, a symbol of spiritual comfort and a talisman against physical danger, Marguerite recalled that she once saw it 'inside a throne of flames, blazing like a sun and clear as crystal ... And he showed me the ardent desire that he had to be loved by men and to lead them from the path of perdition'.[26] One of the great mystics of seventeenth-century France, she became a key figure in the establishment of this major cult, and her visions—publicized by her writings—later played an important part in the development of a French nationalistic, Catholic political culture.

Writing about their spiritual journeys offered religious women yet another opportunity: that of reaching an audience that transcended the cloistered space. Many of them exchanged letters with well-known protagonists of the religious and state affairs of their times: political rulers, important aristocratic men and women, and powerful ecclesiastics. In Italy we encounter a number of examples of this type. The Milanese Paola Antonia Negri (1508–55) acquired fame as a 'divine mother', within circles of devout men and women inspired by ideals of religious and spiritual renewal. Active as a religious reformer, she was involved in the foundation of the Angelic convent of San Paolo in Milan. Although she was unable to read and write she dictated her *Spiritual Letters*, addressed to her fellow Angelics and their associated Barnabite fathers, as well as to illustrious men and women of her times, such as Pope Julius III and the Venetian poet Gaspara Stampa. She was persecuted by the Church authorities for her actions, and sorely missed the pleasure of creative writing. Her letters were printed in Rome in 1576, under the name of one of her former supporters, Giovanni Pietro Besozzi, who was later to become one of her persecutors.[27] In Tuscany, Caterina Ricci (1522–90) from the Dominican convent of San Vincenzo in Prato, outside Florence, was a locally well-known mystic followed by many Medici women and powerful men. An energetic woman who reformed her convent, she provided charitable support to poor girls, and epistolary advice to her group of 'spiritual brothers'. In the turbulent years of the Council of Trent, she shared her opinions about the reform of the Church with high ecclesiastics such as Carlo Borromeo and Filippo Neri. A century later, the discalced Paola Maria di Gesù (1603–70) of Florence exchanged letters with her spiritual daughter outside the convent, Maria Maddalena Giacomini, the lady-in-waiting of the Great Duchess Vittoria della Rovere. An aspirant nun, Maria Maddalena needed someone to guide her in her vocation and introduce her to the joy of monastic life. The spiritual influence of Paola Maria inspired other female conversions in the Great Duchess's circle—something of which she was well aware: 'It is a good thing', she wrote, 'to see that in the court of our Most Serene [Great Duchess] there are many souls [who want] to be brides of Christ'.[28]

Besides, having a charismatic daughter, sister, aunt, or relative could also be useful for the prestige and position of the family, a particularly important consideration in elite circles. In Sicily, the ducal family of the Tomasi benefited from the raptures of Maria Crocefissa (1645–99). Enclosed in the Benedictine convent of SS. Rosario in Palma di Monte-chiaro, near Agrigento, which was founded by her brother in one wing of the family palace, this nun consigned her visions and prophecies to poster-ity through her own writings. From an early age Maria Crocefissa was devoted to long orations. Soon she also engaged in self-punitive actions including tough and dirty physical work, physical mortification, and the use of a hairshirt. At the age of 23 she experienced her first ecstasies. During these periods of trance—lasting well over a week—she regressed to a childlike state which left her completely paralysed, with empty eyes, pale skin, and grey lips. 'She could not speak, nor move, she looked at everybody without recognising anyone', narrated one of the sisters of her convent. She sometimes briefly recovered from this torpor, and would laugh and weep as if a child, unable to take food in her mouth, and 'the nun who fed her had to open her own mouth and pretend to chew, and she would look at her with great attention and do exactly what the other nun was doing'.[29] The doctors stared helplessly at each other without knowing what to do. The presence of Maria Crocefissa within the walls brought about a series of supernatural episodes which the nuns, and some of their associates, interpreted as diabolical manifestations: mysterious and invisible individ-uals knocking on the door of the convent in the middle of the night, ringing bells, a black stone thrown by- allegedly- the Devil, and a letter containing indecipherable signs which he dictated to her. It was her father who pressed the bishop of Agrigento to allow three Jesuit fathers to examine her 'interiors' and analyse her extraordinary revelations, in order to decide whether or not she was an impostor. While Maria Crocefissa was still alive her papers were widely copied. After her death, they became important documents for the process of canonization, carefully and actively pursued by her family, the Tomasi, new nobility anxious to climb the social ladder.

For some nuns, spiritual influence, and the social and political networks which came with it, opened the door to paths of social mobility. Since a large portion of the convent inhabitants came from privileged and wealthy social groups, it is reasonable to assume that a number of mystics had aristocratic or patrician origins. The few data available support this assumption. In Spain, for instance, between 1471 and 1770, three-quarters of the mystics—77 per cent—came from noble families.[30] However, for women from humble origins, charismatic fame won through mystical writings could contribute to redefining and reinforcing their social position. The visionary Caterina Paluzzi (1573–1645)—the daughter of a humble family from Morlupo, near Rome—brought together a group of followers in her paternal house, who lived under the Tertiary Dominican rule. With her companions she divided her life between textile work and contemplation. Initially illiterate, she learned to write and wrote her autobiography, as her confessor ordered. Her charisma brought her fame and put her in contact with very high-powered members of the Church, in particular Cardinal Federigo Borromeo. Always attracted by female sanctity, Federigo invited her to Rome, where apparently she was transported in a litter, and frequently exchanged epistles with her. Eventually, Caterina's Tertiary community became a proper convent, subject to strict enclosure, and Caterina became the prioress in 1610.[31] The life of Isabel de Jesús (1586–1648) followed a similar pattern. An illiterate peasant, who spent her childhood tending flocks on wild mountains, Isabel had always been driven by mystical enthusiasm and had early visions. Reluctantly married to an older man, she soon became a widow, and happily retired to the convent of San Juan Baptista in Arenas, as a servant nun. Here she dictated her life story and visions to a learned and richer sister, Inés del Santissimo Sacramento. The two provided each other with mutual assistance: the learned Inés transposed Isabel's extra-ordinary life and mystical experience onto paper, while the illiterate Isabel enlightened Inés with her spiritual teachings, prayed for her, and cared for her in illness. Isabel contributed to speeding up Inés's convent career, since the latter became abbess soon after having completed Isabel's *Life*. Isabel, for her part, was upgraded from humble servant nun and admitted to profession, Inés being in charge of the licences for professing.[32]

Finally, there is a further aspect of female monastic mysticism we need to consider. Nuns' spiritual influence extended not only within the Old Catholic world, but also to a much broader geographical context. Some of them were active travellers and founders of new religious houses in Europe. Others joined the colonial enterprise in faraway lands where Europeans exported Catholicism. Others were actually born in the New World. Indeed, nuns were well represented amongst early native writers in Mexico and Peru, the two viceregal centres though which Spain governed its colonies. Madre Maria Magdalena de Lorravaquio Mugnoz (1576–1636), a Hieronymite nun in Mexico, wrote the first mystical text to emerge from New Spain, describing her 'suspensions', or mystical raptures. Bedridden for forty-four years of her life, she became an adviser for lay and religious women and men in the capital. Francisca Josefa de la Concepción de Castillo (1671–1742), who lived in the convent of Saint Clare in Tunja (now Columbia), wrote her autobiography on her confessor's orders, as well as some poems and a collection of mystical pieces. Sor Paula de Jesú Nazareno (1687–1754) was a poet and writer from the Lima elite, who professed in Nuestra Segnora da las Mercedes; she composed her biography and some rhymes (both under her confessor's supervision). Sor Catalina de Jesús Herrera (1717–95), from Guayaquil (now Equador), lived in the Dominican house of Santa Catalina, where she held the office of abbess and mistress of the novices, and wrote about her spiritual experiences.[33]

Living in the newly created Catholic societies, these colonial '*apostolas*' reproduced in their narratives the main motifs of the Western European hagiographical tradition, but embellished it with images of the new religious, and ethnically mixed, American culture: 'as I passed the staircase I encountered the Devil, who was seated on the bottom step in human form, like a naked mulatto', wrote the Mexican Maria de San José (1656–1719) in her autobiography, remembering an episode of her early childhood:

> Just as I saw him, he raised a finger as if to threaten me, and he said to me: 'You are mine. You will not escape my clutches.' I saw this more with inward vision than with my bodily eyes. The words he said to me sounded in my ears; I heard them spoken. But, comforted and aided by Him who can do everything, who is God, I managed to enter the chamber where my mother was.[34]

In both the New and the Old worlds, nuns presented themselves to their audience of faithful as spokeswomen for God, religious leaders, and living proof of the successful exportation of the Catholic faith to transatlantic societies. In many different ways, mystical writing provided them with an opportunity to shape and define the contemplative dimension of their lives, and their spiritual role in the world in which they lived.

Writers of Lives and Historians

As well as their spiritual meanderings, nuns also recorded much more factual matters. They threw themselves into historical writing, describing past and present times. They mostly concentrated on the histories of their own convents, which they knew by direct experience, and about which they could write as authoritative insiders. They wrote biographies—or 'lives' as they were more appropriately called—and a variety of chronicles, annals, and foundation histories.[35] They worked individually and also collectively, efficiently maintaining continuous historical records. Unlike spiritual autobiographies and letters, historical writing was not a task required by the confessor, although some wrote about their past as part of their monastic duties. Most of these works remained unpublished, or else were published posthumously.

Mystic or saintly nuns, abbesses, and founders, and very learned or skilled nuns, were the key figures in this collective memory, and were portrayed as images of unblemished perfection in many biographies. These exceptional holy protagonists ennobled their convents, and served as role models and sources of inspiration for their present and future sisters, a guide and help against spiritual weakness and devilish tempta-tions. Illuminata Bembo (d. 1483), a Poor Clare from the Corpus Domini in Bologna, opens the *Life* of her mystic sister Caterina Vigri as follows:

> In the name of our eternal and glorious God, of our Seraphic Father Saint Francis...I have wished to write and note what I have seen with my own eyes in the years lived here and in her company, narrating with truth and certitude as briefly as I am able...I only intend this for my own contem-plation, so that when I tread the lake of tepidity or the tedium of doing things properly, seeing with my own eyes these things written down, may I see more easily...the great power of God...and ruminating on the excel-lent life of our great Mother, may I more joyfully fight off my enemies and temptors.[36]

Bembo celebrated Caterina's holiness by describing a number of episodes of her life: the saintly visions and miracles, her love for poverty and humble duties, her desire to found a new and reformed convent. Both nuns did indeed fulfil this latter aim when they moved together from Ferrara to Bologna—in a short though adventurous trip by carriage—to found a new Observant Franciscan house.

The holy and perfect women portrayed in the biographies could also be presented as ordinary nuns, who had shared important moments in the lives of the authors. Bound to Caterina by love and spiritual affinity, Bembo depicted her as a woman who was as 'feeble flesh like me'. A similar human portrait of holiness can be found in the biography of Catalina de San José written by Marcela de San Felix (1605–87), a Discalced Trinitarian nun from the convent of San Idelfonso in Madrid. Catalina's life had been a mixture of greatness and humility. She had been a privileged woman, and 'one of the most richly bejewelled and elegant women of Madrid,... who had not been raised in some little corner but rather among people of good taste and fine conversation'. She had left all this behind, 'the village of her birth and the house of her father',[37] in order to become a bride of Christ and a champion of holy perfection. Her virtues included humility, obedience, prudence, devotion to holy poverty, and industriousness, and she had a powerful positive influence on her sisters: 'all I could do', wrote

Marcela, 'was marvel, and often, I was simply baffled . . . And this was true with me: merely at the sight of her, I became calm both within and without'.[38] This holy nun, however, was also 'entirely and essentially a woman', her life being in many respects simply 'uneventful'. In these cases, writing grew out of the personal relationships and spiritual friendship which ran through the religious family.

Convent history was not reserved exclusively to holy nuns: unusually learned nuns, rich and aristocratic nuns with generous families, and exceptionally courageous nuns who endured painful deaths, all gained a special place in the collective memory of the community, and were portrayed in very detailed fashion. Fiammetta Frescobaldi (1518–86) was an aristocratic Florentine woman who died in the convent of San Jacopo di Ripoli in Florence. Afflicted by an illness lasting thirty-eight years, she was bedridden and consequently exonerated from administrative duties. But her physical ailments did not affect her mind: she was sharp, learned, and blessed with an extraordinary memory:

> Mother . . . Fiammetta Freschobaldi passed from this life to a better life as we believe on the sixth of July, Sunday, at 20 hours in 1586 and was 68 years old . . . she was a very spiritual nun . . . endowed by God with great intelligence and a sharp memory and could talk about anything and understood so well that it seemed that she had been in so many faraway places and countries and it was to the marvel and amazement of the people who had been in those places that she could describe all things as they were.[39]

Fiammetta spent her time reading and writing about a variety of things. Her creative drive produced an impressive opus: as well as a diary covering her life from 1575 until her death, Fiammetta wrote a range of historical works: a history of the Dominican order in Florence, a four-volume history of the East and West Indies, a history of the kings of Persia, a work on the patriarch of Venice, a compendium to Guicciardini's *Storia d'Italia*, and a five-volume history of the world focusing on extraordinary events and disasters. History had always interested her: 'because I have always enjoyed, as you know, reading and investigating the things of the past times that have been written by historians, a few years ago I had the whim of taking from these histories all the prodigious things, the calamity of the world, the malignity of men, the oppression of the just, and similar things like that'.[40] Fiammetta was also a restless translator and turned 118 saints' lives by Lippomano and Surio from Latin into the vernacular. Her genius was probably also fuelled by the desire to let her mind move with a freedom that was denied her body. She set an extraordinary example for the nuns, who could observe her achievement of perfection not simply by championing chastity, poverty, and obedience, but also by means of intellectual passion. Women like Fiammetta fitted the familiar spiritual feminine model which was extensively reproduced in the religious literature and in the lives of saints, but also uncovered a further dimension, associating nuns with virtuous and learned women.

In some cases, lives of nuns celebrating their individual merits, virtues, and actions, served the purpose of defending the community from external threats and criticism. One such text was written by Jacqueline de Saint Euphemie Pascal (1625–61), the sister of the philosopher Blaise Pascal and a nun in the Jansenist convent of Port-Royal, near Paris. A very productive author who wrote poetry, letters, and a *Rule* for the spiritual education of girl boarders, she recorded short memoirs of her mother superior, the controversial reformer Mère Marie Angélique, who had imposed on the convent a rigorous and ascetic discipline. One of Pascal's main aims was to report conversations she had with Mère Angélique in order to attest her orthodoxy, at a time in which anti-Jansenist forces had called it into question. Indeed, when Jacqueline entered Port Royal the community was in the midst of one of the most debated religious and political polemics of the time, and the nuns were overwhelmed by the attacks of the Jesuits and political authorities, who accused them of being in opposition to royal absolutism and sympathetic towards Calvinism.[41]

If nuns wrote many biographies of their sisters, they were also very keen to celebrate and preserve the collective memory of their community. They compiled chronicles and histories of their convents in which they recorded the names of all the sisters who entered their community, and the dates of their profession and death.[42] These works mainly addressed a convent audience, and some of them may well have been read out loud to all the nuns gathered together in the refectory, or in the chapter. While reading or listening to these rather monotonous narratives, the sisters would pray for the souls of their ancestors in purgatory, to win them entry to paradise.

They would also learn who their ancestors were, and what they had achieved. These texts allowed nuns to extend their sense of collective self through history, acquiring a permanent spiritual family inside their convent, to add to their biological families outside.

In this context, the chronicling of the origin and the foundation of convents played an important part in their narratives. For instance, narratives of foundation were produced by the Poor Clares who—sponsored by wealthy families—founded many religious houses—in the wake of the Franciscan Observant reform in fifteenth-century Italy. They celebrated the lives of their sisters and companions, such as that of the blessed Eustochia da Messina (1434–90).[43] Another Poor Clare nun, 'sister Caterina' was the anonymous author of the chronicle of the convent in Foligno, near Assisi. She described the arrival of the 'ancient' foundling mothers in the city, and their immediate success in recruiting many patrician women to religious life:

> [1425] As the...holy women lived a holy life according to observant principles, the fame of their sanctity spread throughout the country, and [patrician] women,... left the world and submitted to the yoke of the holy religion, so that in a short time they grew in number and quantity;... and many of them performed miracles during their life and talked to God.[44]

Caterina's task as a chronicler was continued by a long series of nuns for over three centuries, until 1733.

The Spanish Discalced Carmelites followed a similar path and the companions of Saint Teresa wrote of her as lifelong friends with great esteem and affection, narrating the foundation of the many convents headed by the saint, and her sisters, in Spain and in Europe.[45] In Mexico and Peru, Josefa de la Providencia and Mariana de la Incarnación took the pen to compile volumes containing triumphant descriptions of their foundations' adventurous histories.[46] Aimed at glorifying the community and instilling the sisters with courage and strength, these narratives celebrated their achievements, advertising convents as earthly paradises. At more or less the same time, Visitandines and Ursulines in France wrote biographies of their founders, collections of lives of their past and present sisters, and chronicles of their orders. They hoped to disseminate their spirituality, social influence, and success, in order to attract protectors and affluent sponsors.[47] Furthermore, by praising the founders of the convents these narratives enhanced their legitimacy while encouraging future sisters to perpetuate the spirit of their origins.

More rarely, nuns collected and translated ancient documents founded in their convent archive, in order to include them in their histories. Angelica Baitelli (1588–1650), from the northern Italian city of Brescia, included a long collection of imperial and papal documents in her *Annali Historici dell'edificatione Erettione et Dotatione del Serenissimo Monasterio di S. Salvatore, et S. Giulia* (published in 1657). These documents attested to the many privileges, exemptions, and freedoms enjoyed by her community. As she explained in the introduction of *Annali*, the translation from the Latin was her own work.[48] Compiled and published at a moment in which the centralizing plans of the Roman Church sought to place convents under the jurisdiction of their bishop, her annals were clearly aimed at supporting her convent's claim for autonomy from episcopal authority.

In spite of the emphasis on the individual community, nuns' historical works also evoked the external world, and their close involvement in events outside their cloister. New kings and emperors, the election of popes, and natural calamities such as plagues, earthquakes, floods, and wars filtered through the grilles of the parlour and found their place in the nuns' historical texts. Nuns were naturally aware of the most violent, cruel, and dangerous developments for society outside, and therefore of the limits of convents' isolation. And they dreaded war, more than anything else.[49] They described the arrival of soldiers, the horror of pillaging and destruction, forcing them to flee and abandon their cloisters. Nuns escaped death by becoming refugees, moving in with other nuns, or returning to their relatives' houses. Convent chronicles dedicate a good deal of attention to the tragic events during the sack of Rome in the sixteenth century, the Thirty Years War (1618–48) in Germany, or the Napoleonic invasion in late eighteenth-century Italy. Unfailingly the same litany is presented: pillage, theft, profanation of sacred objects and relics, fear of being raped or killed: 'We lost everything, lots of wheat, flour, oil, wood, and every good that was in our convent, . . . but because we did not lose our honour we could say that we lost nothing',[50] wrote the Roman Orsola Formicini (*c.*1548–1615) describing the Sack of Rome in 1527, and the arrival of German soldiers in the city. In Germany, the prioress Clara Staigher (1588–1656), in the convent of Marienstein near Eichstatt, described how Swedish soldiers attacked her convent in December 1633: 'In the morning...as the day broke we heard shots in the darkness and screaming in the alleyways. The enemy broke in through the doors...; the mother superior ran away immediately with a sister'; not all of the nuns were able to escape and those unfortunates that remained had to face the soldiers.[51] Other German nuns witnessed and described this war.[52] These historians wanted to record for posterity the troubles they had gone though, and their heroism in never betraying their duties as faithful and cloistered brides of Christ.

Nuns' historical works also addressed the political and religious changes of their times. The example of the advent of the Protestant Reformation in Germany is just one such event. It is not surprising that the nuns' writings reflected the powerful impact it had on their lives. Caritas Pirckheimer was the abbess of the Poor Clare convents in Nuremberg, who gave voice to the nuns' vehement resistance against the Protestants' attempt to close down the convent. She chronicled these events in great details and with strong emotional participation. Caritas reported the exact words of the nuns, describing a quite dramatic chain of events. The city authorities had allowed nuns to be released from their vows, and their parents to remove them from the convent. Three young nuns from Caritas convent, all in their early twenties, were taken away, against their will. She painted the picture of a battle between opposing forces: on one side the mothers and families arriving in their carriages to remove their children and on the other the children taken away screaming and crying. As abbess, Caritas found herself caught in the middle, like a powerless arbiter. She was determined to defend her nuns—her 'children'—but did not want to confront the families. Above all she wished to ensure that all this was not hidden from public view. She insisted that the parents who wanting to remove their girls were to use the front door of the chapel, where many people had gathered, packing the nearby streets and the churchyard. 'I did not want the matter dealt with secretly. I said that if they were in the right, then they should not be ashamed. I would not give the sisters back at any other spot than where I had taken them in, that was, the chapel door.'[53]

Having described the terrible morning in which all this happened, she added a laconic note on the difficulty of returning to ordinary life:

> What later happened to the children among the wild she-wolves [i.e. the mothers] we cannot know, for four days later we were told that Klara Nutzel had not yet eaten a bite in the world, and that others wept without ceasing. They had done everything they could, I give witness to this before God and men. Afterward they never spoke ill of the convent, rather, on the contrary, when given the occasion, they said the best of us, and bore within them a great yearning and desire to return to the cloister. God help us to be reunited in joy! Each of us parted with great pain in our hearts. We truly had a sorrowful eve on Corpus Christi; it was afternoon before the convent went in to the midday meal.[54]

Holy nuns, intrepid founding mothers, the echoes and implications of main events of public life, do not represent however the full range of topics which nuns contributed to historical memory, but only a part of them. Their biographies and chronicles are crammed with detailed descriptions of the day-to-day routine of life. So we read about their religious celebrations which took place in their cloister, such as the translation of precious relics of holy mothers,[55] the visits of important ecclesiastic or princesses who came to the convent, the distribution of monastic offices, and sometimes even of murder mystery stories involving the drunken lay servants who worked for them. Interestingly we also learn a great deal about economic and material aspects of life. Chronicles are full of notes regarding the restructuring of the convent building, the acquisition of works of art and breviaries, the donations and gifts received by the nuns from their patrons and protectors. Behind the everyday material concerns of the community we can discern not only financial difficulties but also the symbolic importance of material objects in forging the memory of the community.

Defenders of their Sex

If the past and present history of their communities drove nuns to write, those who felt the irrepressible urge to put their thoughts on paper could venture into another territory, that of the much-debated nature of the sexes, later known as the *Querelle des femmes*. A very small number of nuns authored tracts in defence of the female sex, praising women's strength, moral virtues, and intellectual skills, challenging the widespread belief that they were morally and physically inferior to men. Here nuns were not writing for the convent audience; instead they particularly addressed their writings to learned male scholars outside, often authors of polemical works against women. By doing this, they were participating in what is universally considered as the Western intellectual tradition leading to modern feminist thought.

Texts in defence of women usually took the form of biographical collections of illustrious women, describing the merits of female heroines taken from classical and Christian literature, often opposing them to the failings of men. The subjects of such works included mythological figures, saints, and other exceptional women celebrated for their courage, strength, or learning.[56] Nuns openly speculated on the position of women in the world: 'Lord,' wrote Teresa,

> you did not abhor women... when you were on earth, instead you favoured them with great piety and found in them such love and more faith than in men... Is it not enough, Lord, that the world keeps us enclosed and incapable of doing anything useful for You in public or daring to state truths that we weep in secret, for You to hear our rightful plea?... Yes, one day my King, we must all learn to know each other. I am not speaking of myself, since anyone knows my own unworthiness, and I am happy that it be public, but because I can see that in these times no virtuous and strong souls should be wasted, even if they are women.[57]

These lines from Teresa's *Way to Perfection* were actually censored and did not appear in the published version of the work. But less than a century later, another nun, the Venetian Arcangela Tarabotti, presented a similarly lucid analysis of women's lives and constraints. 'God', she wrote, 'loves all creatures, particularly the woman and then the man'.[58] A bright young woman who professed the sacred vows in 1620 at the age of 16, she spent her life in the Benedictine convent of Sant'Anna in the Castello neighbourhood of Venice. She dedicated herself—self-taught—to study, and kept books in her cell borrowed from friends outside. Well read, she was familiar with religious and profane literature, including major Italian authors such as Dante, Ariosto, and by her own admission 'most of my time...I use to read vain books'.⁵⁹ Although she may have always read many of the books she quoted, it is likely she also drew on published collections of quotations from various authors, which were widely used by scholars at that time. Lacking any interest in a monastic career, she never held the most important offices, and from her earliest times in the convent wanted only to write. She mostly wrote at night by candlelight, or when she was ill, keeping her rough notes in a box which was placed in her cell. From the beginning of her writing career Tarabotti was quite productive and managed to have some of her works published: *Monastic Paradise* in 1643, *Antisatire* in 1644, *Familiar Letters* in 1650, *Women Are No Less Rational than Men* in 1651, and *Simplicity Deceived* printed posthumously in 1654. Two other works—*Monastic Hell* and *Paternal Tyranny*—remained unpublished and circulated in manuscript form amongst her friends and acquaintances. Her literary success was complemented by her ability to develop social networks and maintain connections with powerful and learned cosmopolitan elites; her friends and protectors included Nicolò Bretel de Gremonville, the French ambassador in Venice from 1645 to 1649; Giovan Francesco Loredan, a politician and founder of the Academy of the Incogniti; and members of the ecclesiastical body, to whom she dedicated some of her works. Her intellectual originality resided in her skills as a polemicist as well as in her devotion to the early women's cause. In this she was almost certainly influenced by the Venetian literary tradition, and the proliferation of Venetian writers who wrote in defence of women, including such female names as Moderata Fonte and Lucrezia Marinelli.⁶⁰

As has been underlined, Tarabotti spoke in the name of womankind.⁶¹ Of course she was deeply concerned with spiritual matters, but these were addressed in the light of her insightful analysis of the female condition, which remained her main interest. Criticism of patriarchal society and the disadvantages faced by women, from their exclusion from education to their subjection to male guardianship, were central to her discourse. Patriarchy strictly constrained the opportunities open to women, forcing upon them a simple choice between marriage and the cloister. The economy of the marriage market, and in particular the ever-increasing value of marriage dowries, provided ruthless fathers with a good reason to shut up their daughters in convents: convent dowries were a cheaper alternative, and this was an effective strategy for safeguarding family financial interests, keeping their wealth intact for their male heir. Grounding her observations in her own times, Tarabotti aspired to a range of improvements for women, in particular equal shares of inheritances between male and female siblings, and the right for women to be partners in their husbands' businesses, and to act on their behalf. And following earlier polemicists—above all the just-mentioned Moderata Fonte, the author of *The Worth of Women*—she argued that unmarried women should also have the chance of a life of chaste spinsterhood in the paternal house, thus escaping the binary decision between the wall or the husband. Access to educational institutions, according to Tarabotti, was also crucial for women. The denial of education, she contended, was a major constraint 'in prejudice of women', deliberately engineered by men 'who keep them far from the world of study in order to make them unwilling or unable to defend themselves when the need arises'.[62] Without education women would be lost and incapable of responding to paternal control, whilst through learning, on the contrary, they might acquire self-awareness and even challenge paternal authority.

Tarabotti's articulate arguments went a step further. In *Monastic Hell*—written before 1643—she advocated women being able to act according to their own will. Placing particular emphasis on the issue of female monasticism, she argued that the convent was a desirable place only for those souls blessed by true vocation and genuine desire to become brides of Christ; for the unwilling, in contrast, convent life would be a life of immeasurable pain: 'It should be then known that just as enforced nuns experience in their life all the pains of hell, . . . voluntary nuns feel inside themselves all the sweetness of paradise'.[63] Indeed, if fathers were often guilty of forcing their daughters into the convent against their will, they were equally to blame in the opposite scenario, where they dissuaded their virgin daughters from taking the veil, sending them off instead to unwanted husbands. These were the truths that she was delivering to her readers, mostly men, through her sharp pen: 'The father must not and cannot marry off the daughter who wants to be a virgin; nor should she be obliged to respect his determination, and he cannot oblige her with violence to profess the vows against her own free will.'[64] As well as denouncing fathers, Tarabotti also laid bare the complicity of the state and ecclesiastical authorities, who tolerated this system of sacrificing daughters in the economic and political interests of the wealthy ruling classes and political elites. In her view, the duty of the prince was to care for the wellbeing of his subjects, including nuns, and for the salvation of their 'souls'. Too often they focused on the interests of their states, at the expense, amongst others, of women.[65]

Tarabotti's tract *Women Are No Less Rational than Men*, published in 1651, continued this line of argument. It was written as an answer to the writer Orazio Plata who had published, four years earlier, in 1647, a poisonous attack on women.[66] On the basis of the Holy Scriptures, Plata had argued that women—amongst their other defects—had no human soul, and were as lacking in rationality as animals. Tarabotti answered by considering each section of his treatise, refuting his statements one by one in order to demonstrate that the opposite was the case. She drew on the Holy Scriptures, but on her own interpretation of them, a rather unusual exercise for a nun. As she wrote in the short introduction to her work:

> a modern heretic—who believes himself very knowledgeable—wanted with the testimony of the Holy Scriptures . . . to make people believe that women are less rational than men and that consequently they do not save themselves and God has not died for them and humanised them. . . . I will do a brief survey of the thorny field of this impious composition only in order to cut off the malicious twigs of slander and heresy with the scythe of reason, knowing well that in questions of controversy words to words, reasons to reasons, concepts to concepts, must serve as answers.[67]

The polemical nature of Tarabotti's work meant that she was treading a delicate path between intellectual success and the dangers of censorship. Indeed she was subject to a good deal of criticism, her detractors dismissing her as a frivolous 'high society' nun, and having some of her works banned and listed in the *Index* of prohibited books. Of course, she was well aware of the potential scandal that her written words might cause. She declared of two of her unpublished works that if 'they were to see the light of day, I protest before God and my superiors that this would greatly mortify me, not because I know that they contain scandalous or less than pious claims, but because I believe that men care more for politics than for observing the divine teachings'.[68]

Like Tarabotti, the Mexican Sor Juana Inés de la Cruz (1648–95) penned rhymes to amuse her sisters, but also placed her intelligence at the service of the probably more complex and difficult task of defending women. 'Sor Juana' was born in San Miguel de Nepantha, two days' travel from Mexico City.[69] The illegitimate daughter of a low-ranked Spanish nobleman and a Mexican mother, Juana grew up on her maternal grandfather's large farm, in strict contact with the multi-ethnic cultural and linguistic environment of the countryside. Educated at home and in an *amiga* local school for girls, she benefited from the books collected in her grandfather' library, and was exposed, from her early years, to music, art, and magic, and to Spanish and Indian languages, as well as the rural, *ranchero*, dialects. Her stay in the country did not last long, and a major change in her life occurred when she was sent to live with relatives in Mexico City. She was introduced to the court of the viceroy, and became the lady-in-waiting of the vice-reine. In the following years she came into contact with the privileged and learned society of the capital and had the possibility to pursue further education. Apparently the young Juana soon became a prodigy. At the age of 14 she had already written her first poem, soon followed by a few sonnets and plays, and she had also begun learning Greek and Latin. Illegitimate daughters were not highly valued in the marriage market, and anyway Juana felt 'aversion' towards matrimony. Entering a convent was the obvious option. In 1669 she professed the vows in the Hieronymite convent of Mexico City, a rather large community which hosted forty-nine nuns, from *criolla* and *mestiza* families, and at least 150 servants and slaves. She had a cell of her own and benefited from servants and a mulatto slave given to her by her mother.[70] The Hieronymite house was not a particularly strict institution as far as religious discipline was concerned, and Juana managed to maintain many contacts outside the cloister, receiving visitors and corresponding with them. She remained here for the rest of her life. In the convent she was also able to satisfy her intellectual hunger, maybe more than her spiritual vocation, and found the time and means to express her multifaceted creative talents. She wrote and became well known, maintaining the protection of the viceroyals and developing many ties with secular and religious illustrious patrons, with whom she engaged in learned conversations.

Juana composed an astonishingly varied corpus of texts, amongst which we find sixty-five sonnets, sixty-two romances, a number of plays, and a treatise entitled the *Answer to Sor Filotea de la Cruz*, which she completed in 1691, though it was printed posthumously. Perhaps her best-known work, the *Answer* was written as a response to an attack by the bishop of Puebla. Juana, during a conversation with guests at her convent grilles, had dared to criticize one of the sermons of the very influential Portuguese Jesuit Padre Antonio Vieira, which had been published forty years earlier. Amongst the guests was the bishop of Puebla, Manuel Fernández de Santa Cruz, who was visiting Mexico City. Shocked and annoyed by her self-confidence in criticizing the theological work of a known author, the bishop decided to react. He invited her to put her criticism on paper. Juana accepted the invitation—her only written venture into the slippery domain of theology. It was a great mistake. Without her permission he published her theological critique, choosing the title *The Athenagoric Letter* (or *Letter Worthy of Athena*), and adding a preface in the form of a letter, which he wrote himself under the pseudonym of Sor Filotea de La Cruz. In this preface he declared that women should renounce all but divine knowledge, and that in particular they should renounce theology, because it produced disobedience and inclination towards presumptuousness. Juana was hurt, angry, and perhaps fearful. She quickly responded to his attack, and three months later completed the *Answer*. In this work, she contradicted his assertions point by point, and at the same time described how her immense love for learning had led her to embark on a life of study. Her work was autobiographical, but she spoke in the name of all women[71]— similarly to Tarabotti—claiming for them the possibility of learning and practising erudition, eloquence, and 'the queen of sciences' that was theology:

> I went on in this way, always directing each step of my studies, as I have said, toward the summit of Holy Theology; but it seemed to me necessary to ascend by the ladder of the humane arts and sciences in order to reach it; for who could fathom the style of the Queens of Sciences without knowing that

of her handmaidens? Without Logic, how should I know the general and specific methods by which Holy Scripture is written? Without Rhetoric, how should I understand its figures, tropes, and locutions?[72]

Juana saw no limits to the knowledge women could access, from physics and natural sciences, to music, arithmetic, geometry, architecture, history, and law. Far from subscribing to the Pauline silence, which in her opinion relied on an erroneous interpretation of the Scriptures, she redefined it. The Church never had forbidden women to write, she claimed. Indeed if it had done so, how could there have been so many nuns amongst women writers? She explained that Paul's famous passage 'Let women keep silence in the churches' must have been intended as a prohibition of public preaching but not writing:

> how is it that we see the Church has allowed . . . a Teresa, a Brigid, the nun of Agreda, and many other women to write? . . . And in our own time we see that the Church permits writing by women saints and those who are not saints alike; for the nun of Agreda and María de la Antigua are not canonised, yet their writings go from hand to hand. Nor when St. Teresa and the others were writing, had they yet been canonised. Therefore, St. Paul's prohibition applied only to public speech from the pulpit; for if the Apostle were to prohibit all writing, then the Church could not permit it. . . . If my crime lies in the 'Letter Worthy of Athena', was that anything more than a simple report of my opinion, with all the indulgences granted me by our Holy Mother Church? For if She, with her most holy authority, does not forbid my writing, why must others forbid it?[73]

The *Answer* defended the female intellect—which Juana shared with the whole of womankind—and connected her argument to the tradition of famous and illustrious heroines of the Western past:

> I confess . . . I had no need of exemplars, nevertheless the many books that I have read have not failed to help me, both in sacred as well as secular letters. For there I see a Deborah issuing laws, military as well as political, and governing the people among whom there were so many learned men. I see the exceedingly knowledgeable Queen of Sheba, so learned she dares to test the wisdom of the widest of all wise men with riddles, without being rebuked for it; indeed, on this very account she is to become judge of the unbelievers. I see so many and such significant women: some adorned with the gift of prophecy, like an Abigail; others, of persuasion, like Esther; others, of piety, like Rahab; others, of perseverance, like Anna [Hannah]

the mother of Samuel; and others, infinitely more, with other kinds of qualities and virtues.[74]

Because of the nurturing nature of women, Juana saw them as particularly appropriate for educating girls:

> For what impropriety can there be if an older woman, learned in letters and holy conversation and customs, should have in her charge the education of young maids? Better so than to let these young girls go to perdition, either for lack of any Christian teaching or because one tries to impart it through such dangerous means as male teachers. . . . Indeed, I do not see how the custom of men as teachers of women can be without its dangers, save only in the strict tribunal of the confessional, or the distant teachings of the pulpit, or the remote wisdom of books; but never in the repeated handling that occurs in such immediate and tarnishing contact.[75]

Juana's disquisition on the appropriateness of women's teachers had little to do with their intellectual capacities, which she took for granted, but instead focused on the moral and sexual risks of leaving girls in the hands of older male teachers.

The *Answer* is one of Juana's last works. Although it was circulated widely on both sides of the Atlantic, and increased her fame, gaining her the name of the Minerva of America,[76] it also brought her problems, and certainly did not make her life any easier. In Mexico, where the Jesuit she had criticized was highly respected, she was scolded and reproached for what she had done. In Spain, although the ex-vicereine in 1692 had some of Juana's works published in a volume containing writings in her defence, Juana's fame irreversibly tarnished. Decline was almost inevitable. The year after the *Answer* was published, Juana sold all her scientific and musical instruments and her library, and gave her money to charity. In 1694, as a sign of her abrupt change from a life of intellectual adventure to one of penance and self-sacrifice, she renewed her profession of faith. The year after that she died during an epidemic, while nursing her sisters. But why did she give up her instruments and tools of learning? Was it forced upon her or was it her own choice to give up the burden of being different? These are difficult questions to answer.[77] However, her experience stands as a reminder that even publicly recognized merit could not remove the restrictions on women making their way into the world of learning.

Thus, the works of Juana Inés de la Cruz—like those of Arcangela Tarabotti—departed from religious intellectual tradition by focusing on Christian virtues, spiritual perfection, and the celebration of monastic values, and merged with the more secular tradition of writing in defence of women that would later become part of modern culture. For this reason, Sor Juana in particular has been considered by scholars as the last great author of the Spanish Golden Age, and compared to poets such as Francisco Quevedo or John Donne. Labelled as the first feminist of the New World, she has won her place amongst learned women writers such as Christine de Pizan and Mary Wollstonecraft, for her contribution to the Western feminist tradition. And, as Nobel Prize winner Octavio Paz has shown, she has also been a fundamental figure in the creation of Mexican cultural identity. Today, a research institute built on the ruins of her convent, and one of the most important Mexican cultural festivals, organized by the Mexican Museum in Chicago, both bear her name.

FOUR

Theatre and Music

Performances

> [Antwerp] January 2 [1617/18] . . . : Here there has been much gaiety, for I had [the nuns] doing all sorts of nonsense; and they made sport of Monsior de Beruel and his associates, and Madame Acarie played Dionisia so that we were dying of laughter; and Angelito did Ymon, to the same effect. . . . Angelito played the Prioress on the feast of the Holy Innocents, and did it famously. . . . I tell you this to give you some recreation, and hope you are amused; and be sure that I love you well and fondly, my Daughter. May you be with God.[1]

When Ana de San Bartolomé wrote this letter to her friend Ana de la Ascensión, the two of them were both living in Antwerp, in the Spanish and English Carmelite convents respectively, Ana de la Ascensión being the prioress of the latter. Undoubtedly busy running their monastic foundations and organizing convent life, and perhaps slightly bored with the monotony of their days, both were eager to mix with their sisters not only at prayer and at work, but also to talk about humour and the theatre, and indulge in playful mockery of their superiors and of each other. Ana, on this occasion, wished to share with her friend—if only by means of a letter—some of these jovial moments of her life, and to apologize for not sending the rhymes that she had 'made up while [she] was in bed' in order to raise her spirits.

Recreation was an important feature of collective life. By reciting rhymes together and staging plays often embellished with music, nuns were able 'to laugh, cry, sing, dance, act, speak, and dress in costume', a form of collective relaxation which, far from contrasting with the discipline they had to observe, was in fact an integral part of it.[2] 'When [the nuns] are through with the meal', Saint Teresa contended, 'the Mother prioress may dispense from the silence so that all may converse together on whatever topic pleases them most as long as it is not one that is inappropriate for a good religious.'[3] Too harsh a regime would have been bad for the nuns' spiritual and physical health. It was therefore established that everyone should enjoy these moments of relaxation and pleasure, providing some relief from the burden of ordinary discipline, and acting as an antidote against boredom, the 'scourge' of cloistered life.

From the Middle Ages on, nuns wrote poetry and plays which they staged on holy festivities. The Saxon abbess and playwright Hrotswitha of Gandersheim and the visionary nun Hildegard of Bingen—a pioneer in many fields—are two well-known examples. Theatrical performances were also written by nuns in English and French convents.[4] Nuns threw themselves wholeheartedly into theatre as actresses, directors, and authors, as we learn from chronicles and documents from European and American nunneries. They wrote, copied, adapted, or commissioned plays, and sometimes developed complex mechanical and pictorial installations for the stage, all within the convert walls. They directed rather sophisticated performances, combining written words in prose and verse, song and dance. They were aware of the theatrical trends and novelties of their time, and often maintained close links with local circles of playwrights and literary society. Maria de San Alberto (1568–1640) and Cecilia del Nacimiento (1570–1646), two Spanish Carmelite sisters from Valladolid, scripted several religious plays—*fiestas* of *fiestecicas* as they were called. Both sisters were strongly influenced by the seventeenth-century Hispanic tradition. Like many of their contemporaries, they liked to use both words and music in their works, and their characters acted to background music provided by a guitar—a *vihuela*—and other instruments. Maria in particular has been seen by modern critics as one of the best Spanish examples of the impossibility of separating early modern theatre from music.[5]

The fame of theatrical nuns rarely came to the attention of the wider public. Sor Juana Inés de la Cruz, whose many theatrical works were known to her contemporaries, was one of few exceptions. Another was the Portuguese Violante Do Ceu (1601–93). An acclaimed poet, considered one of the great names of Baroque poetry in the Iberian peninsula, she was the author of plays, including one performed in honour of a visit by Philip II to Lisbon.[6] But an extraordinary number of lesser known nuns also wrote plays and developed local theatrical traditions. For example, a number of mystery plays, tragedies, and comedies authored by Italian nuns—nearly all of them from Tuscany—have only recently been rediscovered by Elissa Weaver.[7] The work of Antonia Pulci (1452–1501), the wife of the writer Bernardo Pulci, was circulated widely in Florentine convents, although most of it was written outside the convent before she entered religious life as a widow. Beatrice del Sera (1515–85)—a cousin of Michelangelo—wrote plays and poems, few of which have survived. Some succeeded in publishing their writings during their lifetimes, such as Cherubina Venturelli (c.1600–46). The abbess of the Benedictine house of Santa Caterina in Amelia, near Orvieto in central Italy, she composed a spiritual comedy in five acts, the *Rappresentazione di Santa Cecilia vergine e martire*, with great success: published for the first time in 1612, her comedy was reprinted at least six times in the following decades. Not surprisingly, the nuns who had the skill, motivation, and social connections to become published authors were members of the convent elite, and held the most prestigious offices. The Augustinian Raffaella de Sernigi (c.1473–1557) from the convent del Portico in Florence, published a mystery play entitled *La rappresentazione di Mosè* before 1557, while she held the office of abbess. Annalena Odoaldi (1572–1638), from the convent of Santa Chiara in Pistoia, wrote five farces between 1600 and 1604, while she was the mistress of novices (the likely audience for her farces).[8] Many more examples could be added to the list. Of course monastic theatre developed in male houses too, but monks and friars were more likely to attend outside theatrical venues than nuns, since the latter were bound by enclosure and had little or no access to cultural events beyond the convent walls, in particular after the Council of Trent.

When, where, and for whom did the nuns perform? Communal life, with its festivities and rites of passage, provided a variety of opportunities for creative expression.[9] Key moments, such as the entrance of women into religious life, the clothing of the novices, and the profession of nuns, were celebrated with readings of rhymes and theatrical events which took place in the convent. Nuns also wrote and performed at festivities such as Christmas, Carnival, birthdays and funerals, or for moments of communal recreation, as we learned from the example of Ana de San Bartolomé, quoted at the beginning of this chapter. The convent refectory—often mentioned as a place to accommodate the stage—provided a suitable space for a theatrical venue, as did the courtyard or the parlour. The latter in particular allowed nuns to perform their plays not only to the convent audience of novices, choir nuns, servant nuns, and boarders, but also to outsiders. Here nuns could perform in the internal part of the parlour, whilst their visitors watched from the external part. The public attending these theatrical venues were usually female relatives and patrons associated with the convent, including former boarders who had remained in close contact and would attend or even sponsor events. Invitations to convent plays were publicized and read to the nuns, or placed in visible corners in the common rooms: 'at 2 hours at night come to the room in which the curtained stage has been set up, and watch the generous exploits of the gracious Judith'[10] read one such notice in a Tuscan convent.

But what was the purpose of convent theatre? Here we can let the nuns themselves answer this question:

> we beg you, dear [reverend] mothers,
> to be pleased to listen in silence,
> and, if to these our young women
> some good fun of this sort is permitted,
> it is so they may improve themselves;
> but if they don't do well enough to please
> this worthy and excellent group,
> they ask, they beg forgiveness from all.
> Keep in mind that they are beginners,
> and, if someone is not so adept
> at delivering her lines, it is appropriate
> to be a student first, then a teacher.[11]

Theatre—as this anonymous *Commedia di San Raimondo* points out—was an important way of promoting both recreation and spiritual learning. The 'young women' players were nuns and novices and, in some convents, boarders. For them, reading their lines, and learning from the actions they performed, was an educational experience and in the process of self-improvement they could entertain and also instruct the 'reverend mothers' and the other nuns who made up the audience. In this respect, female convents resembled the male institutions of the time. Theatre featured prominently in the pedagogical activity of Jesuit colleges for the education of young nobles and the members of the European elite. Similarly, religious groups of young boys in Italy, known as *compagnie di fanciulli,* prepared theatrical performances as a way of educating boys to become better Christians, and learn proper decorum of bodily movement as well as speech.[12]

How exactly did this educational process work? Convent plays conveyed spiritual messages, drawing on narratives and teachings found in devotional literature, the same type of literature that nuns themselves contributed to as authors. Devotional literature, and hagiographical works such as lives of martyrs and saints, laid down moral examples and good Christian values. Women, religious and lay, were encouraged to emulate these values in order to make sense of their lives and strengthen their piety and religious commitment. The lessons of the devotional literature were embedded in convent theatre, which reproduced on stage the lives of biblical heroines and saints. But, unlike the written texts, plays were more accessible to women lacking the necessary literary skills to read them, as many nuns did. First, theatre possessed an intrinsic visual dimension that made the meaning of words and actions immediately understandable to the convent audience. Second, theatre provided opportunities for nuns to participate themselves, acting out the roles of the different characters and therefore identifying with them, if only fictionally and for the short duration of a play. The nuns and boarders who performed were able to act out the lives of the holy women and other characters they played, absorbing their moral values. Furthermore, by performing on stage they practised the art of rhetoric, proper pronunciation and delivery, and the control and decorum of their bodily movements. The audience, albeit passively, had a similar learning experience. Theatre was therefore an effective and entertaining educational tool for women, teaching them how to behave in the situations they may face in their lives as nuns or as wives.[13]

We can get a clearer idea of the full spiritual and educational meaning of these plays by looking at their content. The characters played were often allegorical and moral abstractions. The nativity play *Fiestecilla del Nacimiento*, composed by Maria de San Alberto in the late sixteenth century, presented the nuns with four female characters: four virgins embodying the four virtues of poverty, chastity, obedience, and patience to which the nuns bound themselves by solemn vows. By portraying her characters in adoration of the Child and offering him gifts, Maria emphasized their spiritual role and pointed at the meaning of the symbols and visual signs—a homespun, a lily, a yoke, a cross—which identified them, symbols that nuns would probably see in the many images decorating the walls of their cloisters and churches:

> The first of the Virgins is Poverty,
> known by the homespun she wears,
> and now, before the newborn Baby
> she offers up her gift, a mighty treasure.
>
> The second one is Chastity
> and she offers Him a lily,
> for it so closely imitates
> the King Himself in spotless sanctity.
>
> The third of these is Obedience,
> who has a yoke to offer,
> as full willingly she bends
> her head in meek submission to His power.
>
> And Patience gives the Child a cross,
> for He's eager to receive it,
> as He has taken human form
> that by His death we might all be saved by Jesus.[14]

The stories and characters nuns acted out on stage reproduced key features of female religious disciplinary models. Virginity—what else?—epitomized the nun's condition more than any other virtue. The lives of the saints Agnes, Catherine, Agatha, and Lucy, who died in chastity for their faith, provided dramatizations of this supreme purpose, stressing the superiority of virginity to married life and the need to remain chaste for the heavenly groom.[15] *Judith and Holofernes* was a very popular choice. It was recommended to religious women not least by Angela Merici the founder of the Ursulines, who in the first chapter of her rule invited her 'virgins' to follow the example of Judith, in order to reach the 'celestial homeland'. As the biblical story goes, Judith freed the city of Bethulia from the Assyrian army by deceiving the general in charge, making him drunk and cutting his head off, while managing to preserve her body inviolate. As has been suggested, the story of Judith—like all stories reproduced on stage—had multiple messages for the convent audience. On the one hand, Judith glorified chasteness: she was a woman and a faithful widow prepared to fight the enemies—in this case the enemies of Israel—but not to lose her purity. Her struggle evoked the nuns' own battle against temptation to preserve their superior virginal state, as well as their fight against the enemies of God. On the other hand, Judith embodied female courage, strength, and wisdom, and her image unmistakably conveyed a powerful message for the nuns to reflect on as an inspiring lesson for their own lives.[16]

Plays also touched on other related aspects of female life such as honour and marriage, the latter often represented by negative images of unfaithful husbands and terrible pain in childbirth. The *Rappresentazione di Santa Cecilia vergine e martire*, by Cherubina Venturelli (1612), included the story of Cecilia's dowry, in material and financial detail: the trip to the countryside by the father of the bride, Signor Gabbinio, and the future groom in order to assess Cecilia's dowry, a property on the outskirts of Rome; the words and promises exchanged by the two men; the couple's satisfaction at receiving such a generous dowry; and the final act of counting the money at the bank. In the passage below, two of the characters, Ascanio and Cassandra, describe the entire sequence of events:

> ASCANIO: They went to that country property with the beautiful palace a half mile outside of Rome.
> CASSANDRA: Do you think he wants to give such a beautiful thing to Cecilia as her dowry?
> ASCANIO: I think so, because he told him 'all this is yours,' and he turned over everything to him, even those beds with the beautiful canopies.
> CASSANDRA: What did they say? Were they satisfied?

ASCANIO: You bet. They were both very satisfied, and I just left the three
of them at the bank where signor Gabbinio (father of the bride) was
having the bridegroom count out a large amount of money.[17]

Allegorical characters were also very popular, as we can see in some
of the works of Marcela de San Felix.[18] The illegitimate daughter of
the well-known playwright Lope de Vega, Marcela was in touch
with theatre from her very earliest days. After a childhood spent in Toledo
with her siblings and her mother—the talented though illiterate actress
Micaela de Lujan—she moved to Madrid with her father. Here she came
into direct contact with Lope's circle of friends from the world of the
theatre, before taking her vows in the Trinitarian community of San
Idelfonso—where the nuns were fervent followers of Saint Teresa.[19] This
monastic house had close connections with the city's literary elite, and
many of the forty nuns living there came from theatrical families. It was
also a privileged burial site for Madrid's literary personalities, including
the writer Miguel de Cervantes, which of course gave the nuns visibility in
the city and its literary world. Deeply influenced by her intellectual
background, Marcela was a most productive author, stealing time from
her duties as teacher of novices, cellaress, and later mother superior, in
order to write. The result was impressive: she completed six one-act
allegorical religious plays, more than twenty romances, biographies of
nuns, and apparently burned—in the best female mystic tradition—
parts of her own *Life*, which her confessor had requested her to write.[20]
Her plays presented characters such as the Soul, Mortification, Negligence,
Faith, Prayer, and Fervour, symbolizing monastic discipline and the
lessons nuns had to learn in order to live a life of spiritual perfection, material
abnegation, and detachment from earthly matters and pleasures. References
to food—its acquisition, preparation, consumption, and donation—
were frequent in some of her works. On the one hand, food symbolized the
broad range of desires and sensual pleasures. On the other, it reflected nuns'
charitable practices, such as offering food to the poor outside the convent, as
well as the difficulties of living within the discipline of privation. In her *Death
of Desire* Marcela used food to satirize monastic life, mocking its spiritual
meaning and highlighting the very real conditions of communal need
and poverty which often afflicted convents. The characters in this play

interpreted—and ridiculed—conflicts amongst the sisters, the harsh
material deprivation and discipline, and the peculiarities of living enclosed,
not least the pathological tightfistedness of the cellaress whom she derides
because 'Although all her store may rot, she worries not a bit'.[21]

> DESIRE: I suddenly have quite a longing
>   to eat two sweet cheese pastries.
>   When will you make meatballs?
> SOUL: Hush now, you've gone mad.
>
> ...
>
> DESIRE: Till now I have requested little;
>   I'll require much more, in time.
> SOUL: Well, I shall not give it
>   if you keep on pestering me.
> DESIRE: You want me to go without food
>   when I'm nearly faint with hunger?
>
> ...
>
> Slice me a bit of that ham,
> for it was dispatched to you
> by my mother, Greed.[22]

Comic motives fitted neatly into the religious plots of convent performances, as we see in this play which reveals Marcela's comic vein.[23] This not
only confirmed the importance of humour and recreation amongst nuns,
but also left room for less conventional messages that could include mild
criticism of monastic life.

Tragic or comic, the lives of martyrs and virgins, the episodes from the
Holy Scriptures, or the allegorical characters embodying main virtues,
brought many other aspects of female life onto the convent stage. Audiences were invited to reflect about women's subjection to men, their desire
for education and preference for study over marriage, and perhaps the
most dramatic obligation for religious women, that of enclosure.[24] In
some of this theatrical work, attention shifted from the spiritual dimension of the nuns' lives to a more material, even political, dimension. This,
at least, is what is suggested by the words of two Florentine playwrights.

At the end of the sixteenth century in Florence, whilst the archbishop
Alessandro de' Medici was closing doors, building grilles, and reinforcing

walls in line with the Tridentine order to segregate nuns, the convent walls
became a recurrent image in nuns' plays, a symbol of imprisonment and
exclusion from the world. 'I know of no world but the closed quarters
within these four walls where I enclosed myself when I was nine years
old',—wrote Maria Clemente Ruoti (*c*.1609–90) in her *Jacob the Patriarch*;
'I have no experience with theatrical machines, nor ability to operate
them, for which reason I have thought it better to adapt my poetry to
my own means rather than the purse of others to my inventions as poets
do'.[25] In spite of her complaints, Maria Clemente did pursue her art, and
was very successful in expressing her aspirations within the narrow cloistered world of her San Giorgio convent, where she lived with her sister. She
wrote six comedies and won entry into one of the very distinguished
academies of Florence, becoming the first woman, and only nun, to have
the privilege of joining the Accademia degli Apatisti. Hers was only an
honorary nomination, usually reserved for foreigners, and she was not
allowed to attend meetings (which she would not have been able to attend
anyway, due to enclosure).[26]

The walls assumed a different connotation for one of her contemporaries, Beatrice del Sera, though rather indirectly. As this nun admitted in
her only surviving play—*Amor di virtù*—people marvelled at her because
they could not understand how 'a woman who has always been enclosed,
who hasn't studied or seen the places and the ways of the world, can
produce such things as they see coming from me'.[27] A self-taught woman,
aware of her skills, she portrayed the walls as rocks, towers, or prisons, and
suggested ways of coping with physical barriers. For her isolation could
also be an opportunity for evasion, and the creation of a space in which to
express her creativity and talent. *Amor di virtù*[28]—a dramatic adaptation
of Boccaccio's *Filocolo*—contains numerous references to walls, though
not necessarily convent walls. In a passage of this play two women—the
protagonist and a servant—are enclosed in a prison and engage in a
conversation which touches on the unhappiness of female existence.
Here the theme of the walls appears to be slightly revisited: these are not
convent walls but the more immaterial barriers that constrained women's
lives. While the servant explains that women are born to be trapped by
their subjection to males—a state symbolically represented by the prison

in which they find themselves—the protagonist confesses how, in her imprisoned condition, she finds consolation for her soul through dreams and the life of the mind:

> I feed and live on thoughts alone.
> And all that I enjoy is in my dreams.
> I believe the gods gave dreams
> to our souls for consolation,
> just as sleep comforts the body;
> and I am happy for a while, but often
> even as I sleep I recognize my plight.[29]

Theatre exposed nuns not only to spiritual teaching, but also to discourses about gender constraints, and their impact on the lives of both religious and lay women. Nuns did want their peers to learn about and reflect upon the perfections and imperfections of a life of monastic duty.

Bloody Heads, False Noses, and Male Dresses

Organizing performances in enclosed convents was a complex matter, due to physical restrictions, scarcity of resources, and the dearth of well-trained actors. Nuns faced difficulties in getting hold of voluntary performers, so the actresses often played several parts in the same play, and the objects, fabrics, and materials necessary for props and costumes and staging were usually lacking. We should also assume that nuns had only limited access to a public audience, making acting a less appealing prospect. In the face of these difficulties, they planned their performances, writing precise directions on every detail: the accompanying music, the decorations and objects for the stage, the costumes, the actresses' position and movements on stage, and their facial expressions and physical gestures. The stage directions given by Maria de San Alberto, for one of her two nativity plays, carefully explained what each actor should do on stage; for the character of Chastity offering a lily to the Child, she envisaged that the actor 'reaches the place and does the same [makes her offering]. If there is no lily, make it in paper'.[30] As far as objects, clothing, shoes, and wigs were concerned, details were crucially important. The stage directions for a sixteenth-century performance of *Judith and Holofernes* stated that Judith should be dressed

> [with a black frock ... She should have her hair beautifully done with curls and plaits, and she should wear beautiful sandals. She should be beautiful ... because all the point of this story consists in the beauty of Judith. When it is time for her to come out adorned, she should walk [onto the stage] with a solemn, modest, and honest air, ... and as she has to throw herself on the floor in front of the prince the ornaments on her head in particular should be firm so that they do not fall].[31]

Other stage directions from the convent of La Crocetta in Florence—known also for its active music tradition—give specific instructions for the Devil's disguise in the play *The Spiritual Struggle between the Angels and the Devil*: 'Devil, in a robe that hits him at mid-leg, with hair that covers his entire face, and in his hand a straw club covered in cloth. When he appears in the form of a merchant he should have a man's hat, his face uncovered, and over his Devil's clothes a big coat'.[32] Elaborate costumes, false noses and beards, fake blood and worldly clothes borrowed from outside relatives and friends were also widely used, allowing nuns to follow the example of fashionable secular theatre, which emphasized the visual, as well as the spoken and textual, aspects of performance.

The suggestive picture created by stage directions illustrates the nuns' enterprising nature, but it also reveals a theatrical problem typical of convents. Since nuns were obliged to do everything themselves, they had to play lay characters, both female and male, which implied wearing worldly and male clothes. Such behaviour risked provoking their superiors' suspicions: 'Profane, loving, and secular gestures corrupt the will of the virgins', advised a decree of the Council of Cologne in 1549, prohibiting convent theatre and lay clothing.[33] Male disguises and cross-dressing were strictly forbidden for both women and men: 'The woman shall not wear that which pertaineth unto a man' spelled out Deuteronomy, 'neither shall a man put on a woman's garment: for all that do so are abomination unto the Lord thy God'.[34] Avoiding transvestism was imperative, and sexual boundaries should not be crossed. Cross-dressing suggested a blurring of gender distinctions, leading to social disorder and sexual as well as moral perversion, even if only in the fictional space of the theatrical stage. Dressing up in male clothing might induce nuns to secular practices and trigger sexual desire. At the beginning of the seventeenth century, the Roman congregation in charge of governing nuns—the Sacred Congregation of Bishops and Regulars—recommended nuns 'not to take off their habits, nor should they put on men's hose, . . . and those who play female roles are not to grow back their hair since nuns who have taken the veil must keep their hair cut off'.[35] As we might imagine, nuns obviously disregarded these prohibitions. In Venice, at the convent of Miracoli they used to 'sing profane songs, and they play the guitar and the lute, and they dress up as men in order to put on plays'.[36]

But what terrified the Church authorities the most was the notion of nuns using theatre to make contact with outsiders, whether they be professional performers or male and female members of the audience. Indeed, this kind of contact was not entirely unknown. In Spanish convents, as well as in the New World, nuns would invite drama companies—made of actors of both sexes—to perform and play music in their churches and convents.[37] In 1660, the nuns of the Misericordia convent in the northern Italian city of Reggio Emilia performed in front of secular women and men; they allowed them to gather in the external courtyard facing the carriage gate so that they could watch from outside. The nuns were later reported to the Sacred Congregation for this public exhibition.[38] Many nuns were enthusiastic participants in the performing arts, and were understandably keen to play before city audiences. Public performances were a just reward for their efforts which gave meaning to their art. Invitations to convent plays went out to circles of acquaintances outside the walls, and patrons, relatives, and ex-boarders watched the nuns perform, mainly from the parlour and the external part of the grille. In Florence one evening in November 1623, several members of the Medici family left the Pitti palace to go and see a play performed at La Crocetta. This family group included Maria Maddalena of Austria, Prince Leopoldo, the princesses, and other members of the court. The arrival of such a group, the grand dukes, and their attendance, surely must have made a big impression on the nuns:

> On the 22nd of the month, the feast of Saint Cecilia...the Serenissima
> [Maria Maddalena of Austria], after dinner got in a carriage with Prince
> Leopoldo and the two young princesses and with her court and went to the
> convent of the Crocetta to see a performance of a play called the *Dialogo
> de l'anima e del corpo* and also in attendance was Madama Serenissima
> [Cristina di Lorena] with the widowed Princess of Urbino [Claudia de'
> Medici]. And their Highnesses had a good time and then returned to Pitti.[39]

Naturally, theatre ran the risk of exposing religious women to the values of
the secular world, and to the kind of urban social life enjoyed by the
various secular women and men associated with the convent. And if
female and male outsiders could see the nuns perform, the reverse was
also true: from the inside of their grilles, nuns could enjoy recreation
activities taking place outside or in the parlour, including shows and
theatrical performances. Some eighteenth-century visual sources confirm
this. Paintings like Guardi's *The Parlour* (fig. 15) previously mentioned—
which show nuns gathered in their parlour, entertaining their visitors
while watching puppet shows performed in the external part open to the
public, clearly suggest a parallel between the parlour and the eighteenth-
century salon.[40] It is hard to judge how accurate the painter's version of
the female monastic space was, but he did grasp the significance of these
theatrical performances.[41] For the nuns, theatre brought together learning, recreation, and contact with outside society, affording them a glimpse
of the world beyond their community.

Angelic Voices

On Christmas Day 1615, a Habsburg princess, the Infanta Anne of Austria,
married Louis XIII and became queen of France. Before leaving Madrid
she gave a public farewell to the city and acknowledged her devotion and
personal ties to some of the most prestigious female monastic houses.
Educated to piety and charity, this daughter of Margaret of Austria and
Philip III of Spain made an official visit to the convent of Las Descalzas
Reales, the home of several Habsburg nuns, then visited other houses:
first 'Santa Clara, and then without waiting any longer she went to

Costantinopla where there was sophisticated music'. The nuns of Costantinopla were famous amongst the *madrilenos* for their excellent singing and playing. It was their privilege and honour to bless the future queen with their sacred music, offering her a farewell tribute and spiritual protection into the future.[42]

Ever since the Middle Ages, music had been a powerful devotional tool. Cathedrals, courts, chapters, confraternities, and monasteries, both male and female, performed music for religious and political ceremonial occasions, such as for example Anne of Austria's departure for France. Medieval traditions included liturgical chants of nuns and monks with sacred dancing at particular feasts, such as Christmas lullabies.[43] In early modern convents, sacred music permeated all aspects of the nuns' daily lives, and contributed to their presence and visibility in the city.[44] Singing in the choir was an act of prayer. Musical skills and beautiful singing voices were so valuable that convents could even offer discounts on the dowries of gifted nuns, and decorous religious houses accepted girls from modest backgrounds. Certain feast days and liturgical services required music and singing. Nuns sang the divine office at Christmas, Purification, Ascension, Assumption, Maundy Thursday, and Good Friday. They organized public processions and singing to celebrate their collective devotion towards the saints and protectors of the convent. They made music and organized choirs, in order to celebrate their primary monastic rites and key rites of passage: clothing and profession ceremonies, and burial services.[45] These ceremonies combined music and choreography, bringing together religious practice, music, and theatrical performance.

Convent architecture and visual setting enhanced the impact of the music, and the fact that nuns' voices were heard while their bodies usually remained unseen emphasized their symbolic resemblance to angelic creatures.[46] Federigo Borromeo, the archbishop of Milan, took a rather mystical view on the issue. For him cloisters were earthly paradises and the music their inhabitants performed akin to celestial music. This idea was shared by many of his contemporaries. In Spain, Dona Alfonsa Gonzales de Salazar, from the nunnery of Costantinopla of Madrid, inspired her admirer the poet Miguel Toledano to just such a comparison: 'You converted the Earth into Heaven, with the celestial voice, the beauty, which make you resemble a divine Angel.' In one edition of his works, Alfonsa was portrayed playing the harp, her mystical and intercessory powers reflected in the caption: 'Before the angels I will sing for you.'[47]

But the spirit of Trent and the Counter-Reformation raised a set of questions concerning music and its compatibility or incompatibility with enclosure. Saint Teresa had already observed that music was a sensitive area and should be subject to the discipline and control of the father superior:

> He must listen to the choir offices, both sung and said, and find out if . . . all singing . . . is edifying and this in keeping with our profession. For to sing on a high tone has two disadvantages: first, it sounds ill, as we do not sing in harmony; secondly, it conflicts with the modesty and spirituality of our way of life. [. . .] Let the voices be those of persons who practice mortification and not convey the impression that they are anxious to be well thought of by those who hear them.[48]

Teresa was not the only one to worry that music could corrupt a nun's body and spirit. Particularly after Trent and the imposition of strict enclosure, music became a more and more contested matter. Music, with its intrinsic and impalpable power to break barriers and create links between individuals across different spaces, was a potential challenge to nuns' material and symbolic separation from the rest of the world. While singing, playing instruments, and organizing public musical performances, nuns could see, and be seen by, the public gathered in the external church or outside the parlour. Even when hidden in their choir or behind the curtains of their parlour, singing nuns might be heard by outsiders, triggering fantasies about their forbidden bodies. Worse still, through music lessons nuns might meet male teachers, although they were only to be allowed in the parlours. Music could become a source of corruption, and although some conceded that nuns were entitled to 'honest and virtuous recreations', music was suspected to be spiritually disruptive and therefore unacceptable.

The Tridentine Church's response to the nuns' musical enthusiasm was consistent: control, restrictions, and prohibition. Several laws discouraged musical learning and banned nuns from playing instruments, in particular wind instruments, and singing for outsiders.[49]

[1606] Sister Felicita Stellini, Sister Anna, and Sister Armellina Uberti...all considerably versed in music, and desirous to study how to sing some spiritual motets *alla Romana*, humbly request that you permit Canon Manzini to come...to the public parlatorios to explain and teach the above-mentioned nuns the way they are sung...in the presence of the Abbess and the appointed chaperones.[50]

'Nihil' was Rome's inflexible response to these three Italian singing nuns from the convent of San Biagio of Cesena in northern Italy. Nuns were ordered to limit their musical activities to the internal grounds of the convent, and receive instruction from their sisters only. Only sacred music, related to religious subjects and episodes from the lives of saints, was permitted. Musical misdemeanours were severely punished. Nuns found in possession of madrigals and amorous sonnets were condemned to saying penance in the refectory for three months. Others who disobeyed the rules faced penances such as being deprived of the veil for three months, being relieved of their duties as organists, or a three-year ban on singing the office. Punishment extended to their musical instruments too. Harpsichords or other instruments kept in cells for private and individual use without the explicit consent of the mother superior would be confiscated, and the guilty nuns could be denied the right to sing polyphonic chants for several years.[51] Outsiders who sought to use music as a means to break strict cloister rules were also punished. As always, these regulations addressed the very real threats to convent order: musicians and singers did indeed often transgress codes of behaviour when they came in contact with the female monastic world. In June 1658, a band of male musicians performed at the church of Santa Marta in Venice, with grave consequences for the nuns:

In the music at Santa Marta directed by Giovanni [da Pesaro], some of the musicians...went into a corner of the music platform, and there between the organs and the wall, they lowered their trousers and displayed their shameful parts, touching each other's asses, and displaying their pricks, taking them in their hands in front of the nuns, who were standing nearby to hear the music; they did all this just so they would be seen by the nuns...The music master admonished these singers, and knows all about this, and he would know how to bring them to justice, if you want to avenge an offended church and scandalised nuns.[52]

It is hard to say whether the nuns were impressed, amused, or horrified by their musicians' lewd performance and demonstrations of masculinity. They wisely decided to let the matter drop. Maestro Giovanni and the other musicians denied everything and the case was closed.

Much to the horror of advocates of strict discipline and public order, a flexible approach to convent music often prevailed. Indeed, nuns' opportunities to express their musical creativity depended entirely on ecclesiastical authorities' interpretation of enclosure, and the extent to which these men were attracted by the religious charm of music.

Whether hindered or encouraged, nuns of every religious order and in every country made music with varying degrees of ability. Many of them sang, though not all of them read music, and some had to learn the music by heart. They played instruments, promoted musical performances, received musical compositions dedicated to them, composed their own music, and collected a wide variety of musical manuscripts in their convents. What seems evident is that nuns in Europe and the New World, shared a common musical culture. Striking similarities has been observed between music composed in different houses, such as for instance the resemblance between the miscellaneous choirbook from the fourteenth century found in the nunnery of La Concepción in Palma de Mallorca and contemporary Italian manuscripts.[53]

By looking at specific cases we get a vivid picture of convent musical production. In Italy—where convent music has been extensively researched—between 1593 and 1607, the Dominican nuns at la Crocetta of Florence regularly paid for polyphonic music and music for liturgical services and masses. This involved choirs formed by up to fourteen singers, a maestro, and musicians playing a variety of instruments such as the organ, violin, viola, horn, trombone, flute, and guitar. They regularly paid musicians to play at the Holy Cross feast, on 16 September.[54] In early seventeenth-century Siena, nine out of twenty-one female religious houses had musical ensembles, a practice particularly common in the oldest Augustinian foundations. Lay musicians taught singing and playing: the nuns of San Paolo, for instance, were taught by a range of organists, violinists, maestri, sopranos, and bass singers in the last two decades of the seventeenth century.[55] In Milan 'nearly all monasteries of nuns cultivated music as a profession'. In the convent of Santa Redegonda, which housed more than a hundred nuns, it was reported that 'music is cultivated as a profession, and there are fifty nuns counting singers and instrumentalists of utter perfection, divided in two ensembles, with two madri di cappella, who seek daily to make themselves more skilled, competing with each other'.[56] When the Grand Duke of Tuscany Cosimo III de' Medici arrived in Milan and visited the convent in 1664, these two *maestre* gave their best performance: Signora Clerici sang solo, while Signora Ceva sang a motet for a full choir. In the cloisters of Bologna, nuns owned music books and instruments. In Santa Cristina, they kept 'organ rooms'. Accessible only through the internal parts of the convent, these rooms had grated windows overlooking the public church, from which they could hear and see the singers and musicians who had come to perform.[57] In Santa Margherita they owned a spinet, a guitar, a lute, clavichords, violins, and several trombones; one of them had her own 'books to sing and play' as well as musical instruments. They probably inherited such expensive instruments from relatives or friends, like the nuns of San Guglielmo who inherited a trunk full of vocal music from one of the convent's benefactresses.

In Spain, too, convents were active in making music, and invested money in the maintenance of organs, in bringing in outside organists to play, and to buy musical instruments, as in the case of the nuns of Santa Isabel in Toledo who bought a consort of dulcians in order to save on the cost of minstrels.[58] Since music was expensive and finances were often strained, nuns preferred to learn how to play themselves—investing in their musical education instead of relying on external musicians.

What were the names of these 'convent divas' whose musical compositions were widely heard, and sometimes even published? The early modern period spawned several examples of talented musical religious women. The Bolognese Lucrezia Orsina Vizana (1590–1663), whose *Componimenti musicali* were printed in 1623, published her music for a wider and public audience. Born into an aristocratic family, Lucrezia entered the Camaldolese convent of Santa Cristina della Fondazza—today the home of Italy's main women's research library—as a

10-year-old, along with her sister. Here the two girls came under the secure protection of their maternal ancestors in the persons of three aunts, all very dynamic women: two served as abbesses and one died in odour of sanctity. Santa Cristina had quite a musical tradition, and Lucrezia probably sought artistic inspiration from other nuns, some of whom were well known outside the convent. One of her relatives, Camilla Bombacci, was the 'first organist, three time mistress of the novices and subsequently abbess' of the convent.[59] The nuns were also exposed to the external influence of the city's lively musical scene. Bologna was an important musical centre and a pole of attraction for musicians and composers, including Claudio Monteverdi who regularly visited the city in the years in which Vizana wrote her *Componimenti*.

Milan was also a centre of monastic music in this period: the Umiliata Claudia Rusca (1593–1676) composed sacred concertos, Chiara Margarita Cozzolani (1602–76) from Santa Redegonda wrote motets, and the Ursuline Isabella Leonarda (1620–1704) from Novara left nearly 200 religious compositions of vocal and instrumental music, published between 1640 and 1700. Trained by the composer Gaspare Casati, Isabella was mistress of music and taught her sisters. She was an expert in plainchant and polyphonic music, and wrote non-liturgical music, achieving international recognition: in the late seventeenth century the French music collector Sebastien Brossard, who had some of her music in his library, described it as 'so beautiful, so gracious, so brilliant' that he regretted not possessing more of her work.[60]

Singing, playing, and composing music brought fame to the nuns and their houses. Travellers marvelled at their musical gifts and performances, and contemporary authors dedicated verses to them: 'To the Most Reverend Mother Donna Claudia Sessa Excellent in Singing and Music' wrote the Italian writer and actress Isabella Andreini, dedicating one of her sonnets to this musical Milanese nun.[61] The Camaldolese Adriano Banchieri dedicated his *Messa solenne* to the Bolognese Emilia Grassi, writing that 'I desire no other reward, only that on occasions when you perform [these concertos] you and your dear sisters would remember to pray God for me in your devout and holy prayers'.[62] Emilia was quite an all-rounder and 'in addition to [her] most honourable qualities [she was] highly skilled both in singing and playing'.[63] Finally, by making music nuns could even make their names known in faraway lands. The English Dominican friar Thomas Gage, who travelled in Central America between 1625 and 1637, reported in his writings of Juana de Maldonado y Paz from La Concepción in Guatemala City: 'In her closet she had her small organ, and many sorts of musical instruments, whereupon she played sometimes by herself, sometimes with her best friends of the nuns; and here especially she entertained with music her Bishop.'[64]

Education and Public Devotion

Nuns' interest in music was not only about their devotion or creative drive; they also valued the educational opportunities it provided. Convents—in particular those strongly committed to female education—offered music lessons as part of their curriculum, and respectable musical training for young women was welcomed, especially for those from wealthy backgrounds. The Ursulines and Visitandines, for instance, taught vocal and instrumental music, and had their own chants. Saint François de Sales, one of the founders of the Visitandines (1610), wrote the 'Chant des trois notes' for his nuns, and prescribed chants for reciting the offices in his *Coustumier et directoire pour les sœurs de la Visitation de Sainte Marie.*[65] In the seventeenth century, the Ursulines of Graz counted amongst their number two choirmistresses who were also composers, Maria Therezia von Gall (1665–1741) and Viktoria Maria Wohl (1676/7 –1755). These two sisters sang, played a variety of instruments, and ran a school teaching music and dance to girls from the city, who came daily to take lessons. According to the records Maria Therezia was a brilliant orator, blessed with a wonderful memory, and committed to sacred convent life and teaching. Hailing from a local aristocratic family, she marked her entry into the Ursuline order with a striking public statement: she donated her wedding dress to be turned into sacred ornaments for the church.[66]

Convents in the new world also saw music as an educational tool. The Ursulines of Quebec owned copies of French musical manuscripts and liturgical chants, some of which were translated into Indian languages. In the time of Louis XIV, in particular, music was played at all the religious ceremonies of this transplanted European society: in the governor's chateau, in the intendant's palace, in the cathedrals, and in the nunneries.[67] These nuns who settled across the Atlantic therefore contributed to creating musical culture in the New World. They organized musical activities and concerts jointly with male missionaries, and sometimes performed in the local idiom, seeking to educate and convert the Indians (see fig. 13).

Convent patrons took musical education very seriously as an important expression of religious discipline. The French 'royal house' of Saint-Cyr, near Versailles, is perhaps one of the best-known examples of this. A convent school for impoverished aristocratic girls, Saint-Cyr was founded in 1686 by an Ursuline nun, and quickly won the patronage of Louis XIV's wife, Madame de Maintenon. Because of Maintenon's influence in the French court, her close involvement in Saint-Cyr helped turn it into a kind of 'annex' of Versailles, which continued to operate under royal patronage until its closure after the Revolution. The girls who studied at Saint-Cyr followed a systematic educational programme. A group of twenty-four nuns—living under the Augustinian rule—acted as teachers and assisted by lay servants. Girls were admitted between the ages of 7 and 12, and were divided into four classes by age group, each class wearing a different coloured ribbon. They left at 20, after having completed their education, and received 3,000 *livres* as a dowry. This money served either to enter a convent or to marry, hopefully maintaining aristocratic status for these girls fallen on hard times. The curriculum followed by the girls included history, geography, calculation, literature, and music—the only art they studied. Musical education served a double purpose: it not only shaped the morality of the girls for a future in the convent, but also prepared them for married life, acquainting them with the aristocratic world of the salons and the court. For these future wives of—possibly—aristocratic men, learning music made them more competitive in the marriage market. This is probably the reason why the music taught in Saint-Cyr was not merely devotional, but also in touch with worldly cultural life. The nuns at Saint-Cyr were careful to hire musicians of note who were active within the king's entourage. The first two organists who taught at Saint-Cyr were both well-known composers. The first, Guillaume-Gabriel Nivers (c.1632–1714) was one of the king's four organists as well as being a music theorist. The second, Louis-Nicolas Clerambault (1676–1749), was a highly regarded musician and composer of French secular cantatas. Both men wrote chants, motets, and *petit motes* to be used by the girls at Saint-Cyr. It appears they were not sufficiently devoted to sacred religious music for a convent environment, and their performances did not quite match the patron's plans and recommendations. Indeed, Madame de Maintenon was particularly keen on music, and recommended it as a way of strengthening piety and simplicity. She thought that Nivers was too interested in music for its own sake: 'All I can tell you', she confessed to one of the nuns in a letter written in 1686,

> is that the king wants nothing more than simplicity and modesty in our house; . . . I am not satisfied with Nivers. He deviates from the unison chant I have requested . . . I will be much obliged to you to rectify this and instruct [Nivers] to come only on Saturdays and the eves of feasts as it is not necessary to excite the girls just to have something to sing. On that pretext, they would do nothing but go to and from the parlour.[68]

We do not know what happened next. Probably neither the nuns nor Nivers took Maintenon's worries about her girls' behaviour, and her concern with satisfying her king's expectations, very seriously. In any case, Nivers remained in place at Saint-Cyr well after this episode. His music continued to influence convent education in France, as well as in New France where his *Antiphonarium romanum* also circulated in Indian translation.

Alongside education, one of the primary functions of music was to contribute to public devotion. Convents were poles of civic religion, deeply rooted in the sociability of the city, and took part in a variety of public celebrations, giving nuns the opportunity to perform their music for the city. The civic demand for sacred music encouraged the nuns' involvement in musical events. They performed for relatives, acquaintances, and patrons who enjoyed hearing the nuns singing for their own entertainment, particularly on days when 'nothing was going on in the Piazza' as some Italian records reported.[69] Music was also performed on special occasions, such as visits of illustrious people or propitiatory processions, in which nuns participated from their cloisters. In 1649, the nuns of Santa Maria degli Angeli in Siena, one of the largest communities in the city, honoured the Low Sunday procession by lending a precious relic to the lay confraternities organizing the event. The relic was the head of San Galgano, a saint to whom the whole city paid great devotion. It was displayed in the external church of the convent for an entire week, with great affluence of visitors. The nuns, as official owners of the relic, did not disappoint public expectations: they had adorned the walls of the church with decorative brocades, and organized prayers almost daily, singing as loud as possible so that their voices could be heard outside. This was their way of celebrating the event. On the day of the public procession, the Medici prince and his court visited the convent church, and the relic was exhibited through the city. Afterwards, the relic was returned to the nuns who took it inside their cloister and organized an internal procession though their garden. While the nuns honoured their relics within enclosure, the confraternities and other citizens followed the event and sang along from outside. Nuns from nearby convents did their best to participate in the procession too. The nuns of S. Monaca—the convent adjacent to S. Maria degli Angeli—proved to be quite inventive in making their voices heard outside; they

> stood atop a cloister wall . . . They were well aligned and had lighted candles in their hands, [a sight] that brought both devotion and delight. And when the procession passed by that wall and arrived under a window of the refectory, one could hear those virtuous women sing, to the accompaniment of the organ, a most beautiful and lovely motet in honour of S. Galgano.[70]

Music, a powerful devotional tool, strengthened the link between the city and the nuns, affording them a central, though hidden, role in public devotion, if just for one day.

The Sienese show was not an isolated musical performance. Indeed, it paled into insignificance compared with the musical celebrations which took place in Rome for holy years. From the beginning of the sixteenth century and with the advance of Protestant reform, holy years increasingly became associated with religious propaganda. In this context, architectural grandeur, beautiful art, and religious ceremonies were marked by ever greater magnificence and splendour, focused on celebrating the power of Rome as the capital of the entire Catholic world. Nuns were at the forefront of these holy celebrations, for which the usual musical restrictions were temporarily lifted. For the 1675 Holy Year, the nuns of several Roman converts very cleverly manipulated religious and political authorities in order to win exceptional licence for a series of lavish celebrations of their saints' days and the profession of new members of their community. They laid on shows with no sparing of decorations such as fine tapestry, curtains, ribbons, silk, and offered the people who attended their ceremonies flowers and refreshing water.[71] Given women's traditional association with the preparation of food, and nuns' expertise in making sweet and savoury delicacies for sale outside, they also distributed food. To the public eye, the nuns symbolically nourished the city with their music, and their patrons, families, and friends with pastries, fruits, and chilled wine after the musical shows.[72]

Thus, it appears that the Church authorities were right to suspect that music and the sacred celebrations which went along with it could create palpable and impalpable links with the outside world. For the nuns these celebrations were a way of enhancing their symbolic presence in society. The outside world, for its part, also valued their presence, as the nuns themselves confirmed from all corners of the globe. On 2 June 1778, the nuns of one of the convents of Lima organized a grand traditional ceremony known as the Paseo de Alcaldes, an institutional colonial procession symbolizing the foundation of the city. This event took place entirely within the walls, the nuns turning their cloister into something similar to one of the city squares. The citizens knew about the event, and gathered outside the walls, then entering inside. As they entered they marvelled at the scene: nuns offered fruits, pastries, biscuits 'as if they were on the public square of this city'. Twenty-three nuns and servant nuns, some on horseback and dressed in male clothing, representing the viceroy and the other authorities:

There were also two nuns dressed in clerical habits, one wearing a tassled hood, another as a captain of halbardiers, and another as a captain on horseback. The latter carried a taffeta flag. The accompaniment, who were laypersons, dressed as maids or as halbardiers in their respective uniforms. All the leading roles recited a eulogy in verse to the mother abbess and threw silver coins into the air.[73]

The public spectacle carried on until half past nine at night. Then all the nuns retired to the abbess's rooms, played minuets, and danced.

FIGURE 1 **Detail from Hans Memling,** *The Moreel Family Triptych* **(1484)** Women who entered the convent and became nuns instead of marrying, often remained in contact with their world of origin. Despite their cloistered position, relatives still regarded them as part of the family, and included them in pictorial representations of their family life. On the internal wings of this triptych, destined for the church of Saint Jacob in Bruges, Memling painted the two donors, with their five sons and eleven daughters, one of whom is portrayed in the garb of a nun, behind her mother.

FIGURE 2 **Hans Holbein,** *Portrait of Veronica Welser* **(1504)** Nuns often commissioned works of art to be exhibited in their convent public church, as well as in the internal space of their cloister. These commissions could be on behalf of a whole convent, or of individual nuns. Veronica Welser, a nun in the Dominican convent of Saint Catherine in Augsburg, commissioned this painting representing the Basilica San Paolo in Rome, which included an almost full-size portrait of Veronica herself. The painting was to be displayed in the convent's new chapter hall. A member of a prominent local family, Veronica was serving as abbess of her community at the time of this commission.

FIGURE 3 **Jean Bellegambe,** *Jeanne de Boubois* **(before 1534)** Abbess Jeanne de Boubois, from the convent of Flines in Belgium, commissioned this work for the convent's Cistercian superiors. Her portrait in adoration of the host before an open book of prayers—with her heraldic device above—matches the figures of the two nuns reading by a window reproduced in the right-hand corner of the painting. The whole image offers an insight into convent interiors, while suggesting the nuns' devotion and pious reading practices.

FIGURE 5 *The Miracle of Ana de Jesús* (1621) Nuns were active founders of new convents. The Spanish Discalced Carmelite Ana de Jesús was a tireless supporter of the reform of her religious order initiated by Saint Teresa of Avila in the mid-sixteenth century. One of Teresa's most faithful companions, she travelled—with a small group of nuns—from Spain to France and Flanders, where she founded a number of Discalced convents. She died in Antwerp in 1621, in odour of sanctity, assisted and revered by her sisters, as shown in this print which celebrates her fame as a holy woman.

FIGURE 4 *(opposite)* **Giulio Morina, *The Miracle of the Bread* (*c.*1594)** Holy nuns and their miracles were publicized by paintings and prints. The life, death, and miracles of the fifteenth-century, Italian mystic Caterina Vigri, from the Corpus Domini convent of Bologna, were illustrated in a series of twenty-one small paintings by Giulio Morina. These paintings were to be displayed in a chapel where her preserved body was located and visible to the public through a small window. In the miracle represented here Caterina, charged with baking bread for the community, left to listen to a preacher visiting the convent. When she came back with her sisters four hours later the bread, which should have been burnt, was perfectly cooked.

FIGURE 6 **Andres de Islas, *Sor Juana Inés de la Cruz* (*c.*1772)** This is one of the several portraits of the acclaimed Mexican prolific poet and writer Sor Juana Inés de la Cruz. Following a fashion used in previous portraits, she is here presented in the act of writing at her desk, while she stares at the viewer. In the back are books lined up on a shelf, the symbols as well as the tools of her work, which she kept in her cells together with a number of scientific instruments. 'Sor Juana' was praised by her contemporaries for her amazing knowledge which extended to different disciplines.

BONVM EST PRESTOLARI CVM SILENTIO SALVTARE DEI·

FIGURE 7 Velázquez, *Portrait of Madre Jerónima de la Fuente* (1620) Nuns participated in the missions in America and Asia and contributed to the making of colonial society. In Seville in 1620, Velázquez painted the Poor Clare nun Jerónima de la Fuente from Toledo, as she waited to sail to the Philippines to become the first abbess of the new convent of Santa Clara de la Concepción, in Manila. She left Spain at the age of 66, in the company of three other nuns. As the writing on the lower middle part of the painting underlines, this painting celebrated Jeronima and her three sisters as missionaries, and 'very important women' suited for 'such a high calling'.

FIGURE 8 **Philippe de Champaigne,** *Jacqueline Marie (Angélique Arnauld)*
(1653) The portrait of the well-known seventeenth-century religious reformer Angélique Arnauld, from the French convent of Port-Royal. She poses armed with her
rosary and book, and behind her we see the window-framed image of the convent of
Port-Royal-des-Champs, outside Paris, where she was shortly to move. Placed upon
the door of the chapter room, her portrait would make her a permanent and visible
presence in the community.

FIGURE 9 *Reformed Prostitute wearing the Habit* (**eighteenth century**) Convents opened their doors to women from all walks of life, including widows, abandoned wives, battered women, and prostitutes willing to reform. For all these women the convent might represent a refuge, which could end the difficulties of their lives. They were, however, required to embrace monastic discipline.

FIGURE 10 **Plautilla Nelli,** *The Last Supper* (1550s) Nuns were active in the visual arts as painters, sculptors, and illuminators, and in the making of art objects and textiles of various types. The Dominican Plautilla Nelli lived and worked in Florence in the sixteenth century. She completed a number of works for her convent, as well as others for outside patrons. This large painting, intended to adorn the refectory of her convent, is signed 'Sister Plautilla. Pray for the painter.'

FIGURE 11 **Lucrina Fetti,** *Portrait of Eleonora Gonzaga* (1622) Lucrina Fetti—
the sister of the painter Domenico—lived and worked in the convent of Saint'Orsola
founded in Mantua by Margherita Gonzaga, a member of the ducal ruling family. She
established herself as a painter and portraitist of the Gonzaga women.

FIGURE 12 **Brooch showing the Virgin of the Apocalypse (eighteenth century)**
Small devotional objects served the nuns in their daily prayers, or were used to decorate their monastic habits. In Spanish American convents, nuns wore brooches like this one clipped on their breast. Commissioned or sometimes painted by the nuns themselves, these brooches often displayed variations on the theme of the Virgin and Child. They extended divine protection to the wearer, and at the same time reminded her—and whoever was viewing them—to pray.

FIGURE 13 'Asperges', *The Micmac Messenger* (1866) Singing was an important devotional practice which nuns taught to novices as well as boarding girls who received education in the convent. This practice was reproduced in the convents founded in the New World. In Canada, where nuns taught Amerindian pupils in the hope of converting them, books of prayer and chants were sometimes translated into American languages.

FIGURE 14 **Antonio Allegri, called Correggio, Detail from Convent of San Paolo, Diana painted on the fireplace** (*c.*1518–19) Convent interiors included communal areas for the various functions and rituals of collective life, as well as cells and personal apartments. These personal areas featured different rooms, kitchens with fireplaces, latrines, and were fully furnished and decorated with tapestries, and sometimes personalized with the nuns' family coats of arms. The fireplace of the particularly lavish apartment of abbess Giovanna da Piacenza, in the convent of San Paolo in Parma—for which she contracted Correggio—reflects one of the many similarities between the convent and domestic interiors.

FIGURE 15 *(opposite)* **Giovanni Antonio Guardi (?),** *The Parlour* (*c.*1740–50) Convent parlours allowed nuns almost direct contacts with visitors such as relatives and acquaintances of various ages. This eighteenth-century version of a parlour suggests a strong link between the convent and other social spaces: conversation, smart outfits, and fun. Particularly noticeable is the range of convent visitors: men and women of different ages and even children, such as those playing close to a puppet show. Visitors also accessed the convent in order to trade products, like the woman holding a basket, pictured in the background on the right of the painting.

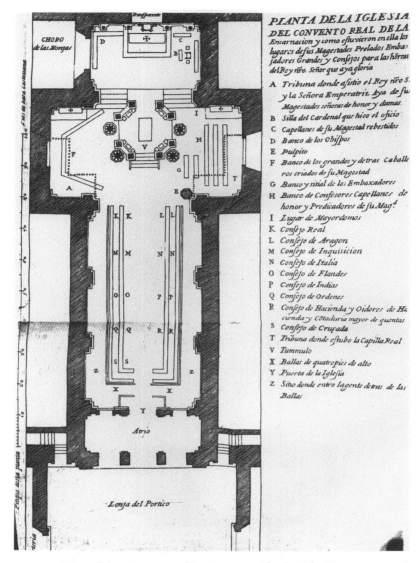

FIGURE 16 **Plan of the Convent of La Encarnación** (1665) Convents turned, on occasion, into burial sites making the nuns hidden participants in public life. The funeral of King Philip IV of Spain was held in the church of the royal convent of La Encarnación, in Madrid, in 1665. The plan of the church shows the position of the various participants, ecclesiastical and lay, at the event. The choir of the nuns—which connected the convent to the church—was positioned just on the left hand side of the main altar. From here they were present at the ceremony without coming into contact with the public.

FIGURE 17 **Pedro de Villafranca y Malagón, Catafalque Inside the Church of La Encarnación, erected for Philip IV (1665)** Particular of the catafalque for Philip IV.

FIGURE 18 **Denis van Alsloot,** *The Religious Orders and the Clergymen Process* (1616). While convent churches hosted public celebrations, no female religious presence was allowed in public processions to women who were members of religious orders, as they were subjected to enclosure. Nuns therefore were excluded from direct participation in public life. Noticeably, in van Alsloot representation nuns are absent from the scene.

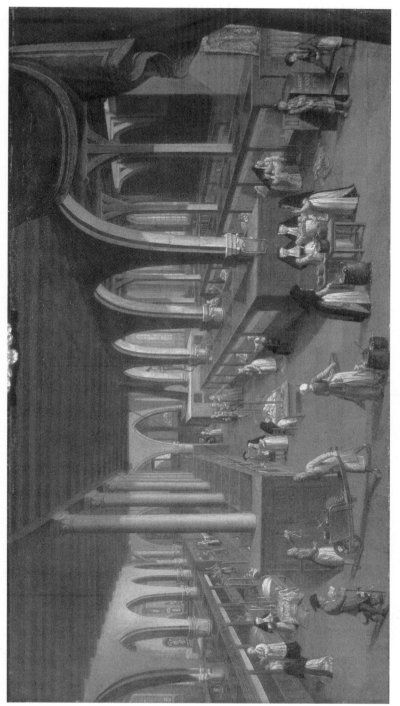

FIGURE 19 Jan Beerblock, *View of the Ancient Sick Wards* (c.1778) The seventeenth century saw a proliferation of new socially oriented religious formations. Women who joined these groups engaged in social services such as caring for the poor and the sick, and working in hospitals, orphanages, and prisons—all activities that brought them in direct contact with the community. As this hospital image suggests, by the eighteenth century religious women, as well as laywomen, had become more and more a frequent feature of such caring places.

144

FIGURE 21 **Begiinhof in Leuwen** Female religious institutions are still part of the urban landscape, like this house for beguines in Leuwen. Frequently turned into museums, houses of beguines preserve collections of objects and images attesting of the life and work of many generations of religious women.

FIGURE 20 *(opposite)* **Michael Wening, (Munich)** *The Institute of the English Ladies* **(eighteenth century)** The Institute of the English Ladies was founded by the British-born Mary Ward at the beginning of the seventeenth century, and it was devoted to the education of Catholic women. Ward's initiative had an almost immediate success and the English Ladies spread in many countries such as France, Italy, and Germany, also thanks to the support of many rulers. The shape of the Munich Institute reproduced here shows how such institutions, without being enclosed, often resembled convents and retained a rather closed architectonic structure.

FIVE

The Visual Arts

Anyone visiting the old Franciscan church and convent of the Corpus Domini in Bologna, located in a narrow street at the heart of the old city centre, will be able to see the body of its founder, the famous visionary saint Caterina Vigri, whom we have already encountered in this book. A rather slight female figure, whose complexion has been darkened by the centuries, Caterina's body is enclosed in a small chapel next to the main church of this large architectural complex. She sits on a throne, surrounded by relics and pictorial images which furnish the chapel. The nuns jealously preserve her crucifix, her violin, her breviary, and twenty-one small panels illustrating her life, death, and miracles, painted by Giulio Morina around 1594, more than a century after her death. Venerated as a living saint, Caterina's existence was a prolific series of ecstasies, prophecies, and miracles. In Morina's panels, these extraordinary episodes become vivid images of the nuns in their habits, veils, and clogs, busy with their daily duties while witnessing her exceptional life. These episodes include her vision of the Virgin handing the baby Jesus to her one Christmas night; the miracle of the bread that did not burn when she left it for four hours in the wood-oven while she heard a sermon by a venerable father (see Fig. 4); and the healing of a nun afflicted by dropsy. Manifestations of her holiness continued well after her death. Eighteen days after her death, in 1463, on a Saturday, the nuns exhumed her body—induced by the sweet odour emanating from her grave—and found no sign of its decomposition, her flesh and skin still fresh, her nails untouched.

Joyfully they moved her from the grave to the convent church, placing her body in a coffin. As the fame of the holy woman spread, the nuns displayed her body to faithful outsiders, who could admire it though the communion window connecting the public church to the convent's internal choir. Twelve years later they witnessed yet another miracle when the saint's body sat up at the order of the abbess, remaining in the same position ever since. Later the nuns placed her on a throne and displayed her in the chapel, protected by curtains which could be drawn when necessary.

The Chapel of the Saint, and everything it contains, represented a joint effort by nuns and citizens to make the convent an artistic as well as a devotional site. In the case of these Bolognese Poor Clares, this effort continued long afterwards, reaching a peak in the eighteenth century when the civic Academy of Fine Arts—the Accademia Clementina—proclaimed Caterina patroness of the arts, although there is little certainty that the pictorial works attributed to her were indeed her work.[1]

Like many other shrines, convents—in particular rich and aristocratic ones like the Corpus Domini—owned relics, sacred objects, and the most remarkable variety of images. These images came in pictorial and plastic forms, were engraved or embroidered on textiles, and could be made of precious or poor materials: there were paintings of various sizes, statues made of clay or wood and dressed with fabrics, altarcloths, furniture, canopies decorated with golden threads, and clerical vestments. Images were everywhere: hung or painted on the walls, in small niches, in the external church, and in the internal areas. Nuns produced images them-selves and also commissioned them from artists and artisans outside the cloister. Images were also received as gifts, legacies, and donations from their relatives, acquaintances, and patrons, sometimes the same ones who built the convent and its church, or endowed it with land. Female monastic interiors speak therefore of the nuns' spirituality and perception of sacred objects, as well as of their taste, and the way they wished to be seen. They also speak of the lay community's expectations of them. Indeed convent art and architecture was also the result of a joint effort, made up of a variety of contributions from religious and lay people, insiders and outsiders, the nuns on the one hand, and male and female patrons on the other.

Making Convents

Supporters of convent art and architecture were devout men and women of means. They expressed their devotion in the form of material investments in convent churches and chapels, and in return expected the nuns to pray for them and fulfil their primary intercessory role between worldly society and heaven. These investments were also motivated by the patrons' family interests and financial strategies. As we have seen, they often expected convents to open their doors to their daughters and female relatives and wanted the building to be appropriate to their rank. Furthermore, through their financial and material efforts to enhance the convents' physical appearance—endowing them with works of art, precious relics, and sacred objects—patrons expected to leave a visible mark on the city, a sign of their status and power, benefiting from the prestige traditionally associated with ecclesiastical institutions.

Convent patrons commissioned building works, hired architects and builders, contacted artists, and paid for expensive decorations and artistic devices, even providing all kinds of furniture. Sometimes they gave the nuns the very roof over their heads, and contributed houses to be converted into suitable monastic buildings. The Dominican nuns of Santa Caterina da Siena in Florence, for instance, started their convent in 1496 in the wake of Gerolamo Savonarola's call for spiritual reform. They went to live in houses donated by a patrician relative of one of them, not too far from Savonarola's monastery in San Marco. More than one century later, in Rome, the grand constable Filippo Colonna generously contributed to financing the construction of a brand new Discalced Carmelite convent in Rome, so worried was he by the appalling physical conditions of the old one, the convent of San Egidio in Trastevere where his daughter intended to take the veil. Here his personal concern for his daughter combined neatly with the benefit to his family's social prestige of sponsoring sacred architecture, a very public demonstration of Colonna's magnanimity.[2] In France, Queen Anne of Austria had a much more important and quasi-political reason to sponsor a convent. Indeed, she attributed her conception of the future king, Louis XIV, to the propitiatory intercession and prayers of the mystic Marguerite du Saint

Sacrement, a Carmelite nun. She therefore enthusiastically rewarded her and her convent with a bronze sculpture of Louis as a child, which she commissioned in 1638 soon after his birth.[3]

Women played an active part in convent patronage, confirming the long tradition of female support of charitable institutions such as hospitals, churches, and monastic houses.[4] These female patrons shared certain characteristics, the most obvious being that they came from exclusive and wealthy circles. Their generous and benevolent patronage drew on both their husbands' finances and their own resources, namely their dowry, jewels, and other valuable goods. Most of the time, they were wealthy widows, enjoying the economic and financial freedom that was often associated with the state. Widows, for instance, were numerous amongst the sponsors of the early Jesuits.

The lives of prominent patrician women from Rome show how female convent patronage might work.[5] Francesca Baglioni Orsini (1543–1626) was an aristocratic woman whose family was well connected with the papal court, her mother being Catherine de' Medici, the niece of Pope Clement VII.[6] According to her biography Francesca, who married at 14, was very devout and had a strong inclination towards spiritual life. Benefiting from a personal allowance from her husband, she dedicated herself to pious actions. She visited hospitals, took care of the sick and the dying, and sheltered women in need of protection, including a woman rescued from the Turks, taken in at the request of Pope Gregory XIII. When her husband moved to Florence, she followed him and took up yet another caring (though less charitable) task, by becoming the governess of the Medici children and the mentor of Christine of Lorraine. A few years later, her husband died and she returned to Rome. Free from her marriage duties, she began a more ambitious activity in support of convents, involving very generous financial outlays. In 1600 she bought a site near her house at the Quirinal hill in order to found the convent of Santa Maria dell'Umiltà, specifically dedicated to accommodating poor noblewomen, the construction of which began the following year. On top of endowing the convent with the large sum of 63,000 *scudi*, she ran down her dowry, sold her jewels, carriage, personal possessions, and clothing (to the point of causing her servants' embarrassment at her untidy appearance), and spent a fortune arranging the convent's internal spaces.[7] She also supplied it with valuable silver furnishings and two large and elaborately worked silver vases, which she had inherited from her father. Finally she hired the Milanese painter Francesco Nappi to decorate the church with painted images of the Virgin, and Saint Michael the Archangel.[8] But this was not enough for her, and she extended her charity network still further, founding chapels in other churches, amongst them the chapel of the Nativity in San Silvestro al Quirinale, which was frescoed by well-known artists. Having used up a substantial portion of her wealth in support of female religious buildings, Francesca crowned her religious aspiration: she abandoned worldly life and entered her convent, without taking the three solemn vows. Only at the very end of her life did she explicitly claim glory for her pious actions, having her name and coat of arms placed on the altar of the convent church. After her death, the nuns added the final touch, placing celebratory inscriptions on the walls of the cells she had occupied.

In the same period another noblewoman followed Francesca Baglioni Orsini's example and chose convent architecture and art as the main focus for her charitable activity.[9] Seventeenth-century Rome was an ideal place for this. The centre of the Catholic world and at that time one of Europe's capitals of the visual arts, Rome was a city of state dignitaries and prominent members of the Church. It needed magnitude and splendour to celebrate its power and that of its most worthy citizens, and had a great supply of painters, sculptors, and architects ready to produce the finest and most beautiful architectural and artistic works. Princess Anna Colonna Barberini (1601–58) grew up in a wealthy privileged family, and cultivated a strong attraction for religious life, which she put to one side to marry Don Taddeo Barberini, the nephew of Pope Urban VIII.[10] Her marriage reinforced her social position and she came to be regarded as one of the most influential aristocratic women in the city. Devoted to Saint Teresa of Avila and the Discalced order—to which two of her sisters belonged—she founded the Discalced convent of Santa Maria of Regina Coeli in 1654, not without the help of her paternal family and of the pope who donated 4,000 *scudi*. To put her plans into practice she used her husband's allowances and his networks, hiring artists and architects well

known to her family, such as Francesco Contini. Like Francesca Baglioni
Orsini, she also drew on her own resources, selling her jewels in order to
complete two chapels and three altarpieces in the convent church, and
paying for furniture, utensils, religious books and breviaries, clocks,
liturgical furnishings, and the crucifix for the chapter room. Her enthusiastic involvement in this enterprise included close attention to aesthetic
decorations, as well as comfort. Her will states that her convent had fresh
water, a large enclosed garden, and a great collection of paintings. She also
chose the subjects of the three altarpieces for the convent church: the
Presentation of the Virgin in the Temple by Giovan Francesco Romanelli, a
scene directed particularly at women entering religious life; the *Death of
Saint Anne*, centred on the saint traditionally invoked for a good death;
and the *Ecstasy of Saint Teresa*, presenting a model of piety and female
leadership for the Discalced nuns, and in particular for those of Santa
Maria who were fortunate enough to have Teresa's index finger, 'with
which the Saint wrote her admirable works' amongst the convent relics.[11]
By embarking on this project Anna showed her charity and altruism
and above all her desire for personal prestige.[12] She ensured some
money was set aside for her own celebratory monument, a sumptuous
though severe tomb placed in the convent church, at the right of the high
altar. Made of black marble and decorated with putti and columns and
her coat of arms, the tomb displayed her bronze figure dressed in a
widow's garb, kneeling on a prie-dieu as if in perpetual adoration of the
sacrament of the Eucharist. An inscription praised her charitable works,
her virtues of prudence, modesty, and chastity, and her important family
connections, adding further prestige to her memory.

　　Convent patronage had different meanings for women and men. By
building and decorating convents, men and women fulfilled their duties as
good Catholics working for the honour of their family and society in
the name of God. However, convent-focused patronage had additional
implications for women. By commissioning self-celebratory inscriptions,
statues, or busts, women not only contributed to shaping urban architecture, they also developed their own public image in a world that usually
associated them, no matter how rich and noble, with a private and
rather enclosed domestic domain. More important still, funding convents,

furnishing and embellishing them with paintings, sculptures, and precious objects, and possibly joining them as lay or religious members, satisfied their desire for spiritual and community life. By using the money from their dowries, jewels, and clothes, or the wealth of their deceased husbands, they cancelled out the signs of their previous existence as wives, and turned their attention outside the family, toward the making of communities which were an alternative to it.

Sacred Images

> It was decided to order a panel or large icon for the main altar of the external church...decorated with the Assumption of the Virgin Mary, as befits this church.... [the abbess] found the best master, recommended by many citizens and also by our venerable fathers who had seen his works; his name was master Raphael of Urbino, and a contract was signed with him,...and our steward *ser* Bernardino da Chanaia paid in his hand... 30 golden ducats, which was the price this master Raphael charged.[13]

In 1505, the nuns of the aristocratic Perugian convent of Monteluce, headed by the newly elected abbess Battista Alfani, commissioned Raphael to produce a painting for the main altar of their church. As they openly expressed in this brief note, they wanted Raphael's painting to resemble Ghirlandaio's *Assumption*, which was located in a male Franciscan church in the nearby city of Narni. It is unlikely any of them had ever seen Ghirlandaio's work, which they probably only knew through their intermediaries. Nevertheless they requested preparatory drawings from Raphael, so as to have an idea of the final product, and his project won their approval. Unfortunately for them, Raphael died leaving the work unfinished, and two other artists, Giulio Romano and Gian Francesco Penni, completed it five years later in 1525.[14]

Abbess Battista was determined to boost the prestige of her convent, as well as the nuns' self-understanding. A few years earlier, she had established a convent chronicle to celebrate the glories of its founders and 'ancient mothers', and preserve their memory within the community so that her sisters, present and future, would know what a great and worthy community they belonged to. Now, she was pursuing a project of refurbishment and redecoration of the convent, which included building new rooms, extensions to the main building, and a new wall between the vegetable garden and the hen house. She also commissioned—in keeping with the artistic trends of her times—a wide range of sacred furnishings for the external church—as well as contracting Raphael for the Assumption: crimson velvet clerical vests, brocade, and silk cloths embroidered with golden threads for the altar and sacristy, and for the infirmary where ill and dying nuns received their communion. Her artistic plans were helped by generous support from her family, including her mother who a few years earlier had donated money to acquire a marble tabernacle to be placed on the church altar.[15] Battista Alfani was by no means exceptional in her artistic aspirations and aesthetic concerns. Other nunneries' acquisitions included various pieces of interior decorations and religious gadgets, brass candlesticks, crucifixes, marble sculptures from Florence and Venice.[16]

Nuns involved in commissioning artworks acted more or less as lay patrons would do. Like the Monteluce sisters, they hired artists, signed contracts, approved preparatory sketches, and demanded information about paintings and buildings which they had not seen. Although they often used intermediaries, they dealt directly with the painters and artists they wanted. In Florence, for instance, the nuns of San Francesco de' Macci instructed Andrea del Sarto, though the grilles of their convent, to paint a Madonna and Child and two crowning angels and saints for 40 golden florins, a work he eventually finished in 1517.[17] Similarly, in 1554 the nuns of San Maurizio in Milan hired the famous organ maker Gian Giacomo Antegnati to build their organ, and negotiated their business with the painters and workers who decorated it, signing the contract under the supervision of their superiors and witnesses.[18] Sometimes nuns introduced new artists into their superiors' circles. Around 1510, the Benedictine abbess of San Paolo, in Parma, hired Correggio to paint her quarters. The result was the beautifully frescoed Camera di San Paolo, a masterpiece of Renaissance art whose images and motives were associated with mythology, pagan religions, and profane love (see fig. 14). Correggio made a great impression on the nuns' superiors, the monks of San Giovanni

Evangelista, who later on commissioned frescos for their own church from him. The monks also borrowed a series of decorative motifs and images from the nuns for the decoration of their church, thus indirectly acknowledging the women's influence over their own iconographic choices.[19]

Since these works were collectively financed by the convent, or commissioned by individual nuns and sometimes paid for with their own personal allowances, it is not surprising that every stage of the process was carefully supervised.[20] When the Benedictines of San Zaccaria in Venice ordered their new choir, they stipulated in the contract that in the event they were unsatisfied with the finished work, they would refuse to pay, and the costs would be covered by the craftsmen.[21] The Poor Clares of Murano, one of the islands facing Venice, turned out to be rather choosy about their new choir stalls. They asked to try out the sample stalls, and after sitting on them they gave their verdict: they would have to be modified. They wanted simpler carving, the hoods half a foot further back, and the arm rests longer and lower. As the sole users of these stalls, they wished—understandably—to ensure that the appearance, functionality, and dimensions of the stools met their tastes and fitted the shape of their bodies.[22]

What type of images furnished the convent and surrounded nuns? Theoretically, nuns were not to look at profane images that could distract them from their devotional duties. In particular their eyes should not fall on 'lascivious paintings, above all portraits of people whom they... loved'.[23] Naturally, their visual imagination at times deviated from religious topics—as the just-mentioned pagan themes in Correggio's frescos for San Paolo suggest. Nevertheless, scholars have illustrated the variety of sacred images and edifying scenes that were most frequently found in convents. The Virgin Mary, Jesus Christ, and male and female saints were very popular. So were the saints associated with the convents' name or religious order: Catherine of Siena in Dominican convents, Clare of Assisi for the Poor Clares, Teresa of Avila for the Discalced Carmelites. Nuns prayed before these images, found spiritual comfort in them, and viewed the models of divine perfection that they were recommended to imitate. Specific themes, such as mystic marriage—representing the union

between a female saint and Christ—stood as a metaphor of the monastic
condition, and were displayed in order to facilitate identification with the
nuns' role as 'brides of Christ'. Specific images were displayed in particular parts of the convent. For instance, scenes from the Last Supper
accompanied the nuns as they ate in the refectory (see Fig. 10). Images
of the Archangel Gabriel watched over conversations with visitors and
meetings with messengers in the parlour. Saint Jerome removing thorns
from the lion's paw was to be found in infirmaries, where nuns were taken
if they fell ill or were about to die. This scene offered comfort to nuns in
need of relief, evoking the defeat of disease and curing of pain.[24]

Amongst the devotional objects circulating within convents Christ-
child dolls also figured.[25] The presence of such holy dolls, representing
Jesus as a child, has been attested to in Italy, particularly in the fourteenth
and fifteenth centuries, and similar dolls were in circulation in
German convents too.[26] Sometimes owned by individual nuns, devotional
dolls were part of the monastic trousseau they had carried with them on
entering religious life. Although sacred dolls were possessed by married
women, and often donated to them when they married, they acquired
particular meaning within the female monastic context where they were
used by the nuns in rituals of symbolic care. Nuns would take care of
these dolls, make clothes to dress their naked bodies, and on certain feast
days of the year hold and cuddle them, thus symbolically acting as the
Virgin Mary. Through the rituals associated with these dolls nuns,
although dedicated to virginity for life, could ever experience a kind of
symbolic motherhood.

Nuns also owned other types of sacred images of the Virgin and
Child, which they kept attached to their bodies and clothes. Saint Teresa
recommended prominent display of effigies of Jesus in convents and
encouraged her sisters to 'display him on their breasts' and 'to frequently
talk to him'.[27] In practice nuns did carry painted icons portraying Christ,
the Virgin, and saints, on their breasts and wore them as religious jewellery
on their monastic habits (see Fig. 12). These icons extended their protection to the bearer and reminded her to pray. They seem to have been
very popular in Latin America, in particular amongst Conceptionist and
Hieronymite nuns, until the eighteenth and early nineteenth centuries,

although they were also in use in Italian convents, as shown by seventeenth-century portraits of nuns wearing brooches with the Virgin and Child.[28] In his chronicle of his Peruvian travels, Fray Antonio Vazquez de Espinoza reported that the Conceptionists '[wore] white habits, and blue mantles with the insigna, and an image of Our Lady on the breast and another on the mantle at the shoulder'.[29] Framed in gold or silver, mother-of-pearl, and tortoiseshell, or else embroidered, these circular or oval discs were the size of small paintings which were fastened to the nuns' habit with clips or cords, like brooches—or *escudos*. Nuns sometimes possessed more than one of them. The three portraits of the famous Mexican poet and writer Sor Juana Inés de la Cruz show her wearing three different brooches all of them representing the Annunciation (see Fig. 6). She was eventually buried with a fourth oval tortoiseshell brooch, with painted effigies.[30] Commissioned to artists or painted by the nuns themselves, each brooch was a distinctive sign on the body that made the nun who bore it different from the others. Sacred images were both sources of protection and markers of individuality.

Like all sacred art, convent art often evoked supernatural events. Nuns used images and objects to interact with the divine and invoke the protection of the saints for a variety of purposes. In times of war, holy crucifixes would be carried around the church and common rooms by barefoot nuns imploring protection before the imminent arrival of the enemy armies. Icons and statues of the Virgin were displayed in processions organized within the convent walls in order to invoke rain in times of drought, or food in times of scarcity. These objects carried around or kept privately within the walls could be called upon to intervene in moments of crisis. The nuns of the Castilian convent of La Concepción, in Valladolid, owned a miraculous image of the Virgin and Child which they used on various occasions. As the sources report, the image served its owners well in at least one case. One morning in August 1629, the image spoke to one of the nuns, telling her that she would become the abbess: 'You must take this post-the Virgin had apparently said.' A couple of days later the nun won the election for abbess, and obediently accepted.[31] The nuns attributed the happy outcome to divine intervention. A few days before that fatal morning, the Conceptionists—aware of the very delicate nature of the voting, and fearing conflicts—had appealed to the Virgin's icon. They had placed it on the empty chair reserved for the abbess, praying the election would go smoothly, which ultimately it did. Now they could say that the Virgin did not disappoint them. In other convents, nuns were reported to use *agnus dei* to request flour to make bread in time of famine. For example, one day in 1630, when the plague and crisis was afflicting them, the sisters of San Clement, in Prato near Florence, went to the room where the flour was kept, knelt down, and prayed. Then they took an *agnus dei*, drew a cross in the flour, and left it there. Over the course of a few days more flour appeared and the nuns were able to bake bread, which 'they felt multiply in their hands'. To capture this memorable event for eternity, the nuns commissioned two ex-voto paintings narrating the miracle.[32]

In investing in artistic works, using images for their private and collective devotion, and appealing to the multiple sacred icons that were available in their cloister, nuns were not only concerned with the spiritual wellbeing of their sisters, or the everyday material needs of their community. Abbesses and nuns were also eager to address specific political issues. Two examples—from Belgium and from Germany—serve to illustrate this point.

Around 1509, abbess Jeanne de Boubais, from the Belgian convent of Flines, near Douai, commissioned the painter Jean Bellegambe to produce two large pieces of artwork. These works were meant for the clerics of their Cistercian order and superiors of the nuns. One was a triptych, later known as the *Cellier Altarpiece*, which portrayed *The Family of Saint Bernard in Adoration of the Virgin and the Child*, and the *Miracle of Lactation*. The other was a diptych representing *A Cistercian Cleric, St. Bernard, and the Virgin and Child*, and *Jeanne de Boubais in Adoration of the Host*.[33] In offering two paintings to their superiors, the nuns were undoubtedly well aware of the impact such a gift would make within their religious order. But they also had a more precise goal: to win their superiors' benevolence and declare their subordination. In the previous years, the nuns of Flines had gone through a difficult moment of great change that had put their community under strain. The monastic reform promoted within the Cistercian order obliged all female houses to accept strict cloister rules, and greater submission to the male hierarchy of the order. These were the principles pursued by other reform movements in those same years, such as the Franciscans for instance. In the case of Belgian Cistercian nunneries, the implementation of the new rules had been particularly tortuous, with nuns putting up such resistance that some communities had subsequently been dismantled and expelled from the order. On pain of dissolution, other nunneries had accepted the new restrictions, and Flines was amongst them. Jeanne became abbess one year after the new rules had been introduced in her convent. She was expressly chosen for that role by the convent confessor, on condition that she would comply with the rigorous application of the reform and of enclosure. But this was not an easy task judging from the accusations of indiscipline and rule violation directed at the nuns.[34] It was in these troubled circumstances that Jeanne commissioned—at the convent's expense—the two Bellegambe paintings for the clerics who had brought the reform to her house.

The iconography of the two paintings is revealing of the message that Jeanne and her sisters wanted to convey to their superiors. Set in context, the paintings conveyed a precise message of the obedience and acceptance of the reform, while celebrating Jeanne's leading role in its implementation. Jeanne is portrayed in both of them, and so are the heraldic devices which identify her as the patron. In the exterior wing of the diptych (see Fig. 3) she is positioned in a closed space, kneeling in adoration of the host, her eyes fixed on an open manuscript. Behind her, in a separate window in the upper right-hand corner, two nuns are reading in their cell furnished with bed, fireplace, and clock. These scenes emphasized the nuns' cloistered position, their devotion to the sacrament, and their willingness to learn from written texts how to access spiritual perfection and salvation.[35] In the triptych, a series of images also speak of the nuns' respect for monastic discipline. The *Miracle of the Lactation*, depicted on one of its exterior wings, recalls the Marian devotion so crucial to the Cistercian tradition, and more generally to the Christian ideal of femininity. In addition to this in *The Family of Saint Bernard in Adoration of the Virgin and Child*, depicted on the interior wing of the triptych, Jeanne is portrayed as Saint Bernard's sister Humbeline, a Cistercian nun, while the father superior of Flines is portrayed as Bernard. These images clearly identified the nuns of Flines and their superiors with Bernard's family and more generally with recognized members of the Cistercian order.[36] The paintings therefore declared to the superiors that the good nuns of Flines, having fulfilled their duty under the direction of the abbess, Jeanne, regarded themselves as perfectly entitled to remain an integral part of the order. We do not know whether this message reflected the nuns' genuine desire to accept the reform, and convent art did not necessarily reflect the sentiment of the whole monastic community. But whatever the nuns' views, they certainly saw art as a medium for communicating with the Church hierarchy, and negotiating their position and authority in the ecclesiastical establishment.

As we see here, convent art articulated discourses about power, discipline, and obedience, addressed to an external audience made up of their father superiors and the wider order. At roughly the same time these Belgian sisters of Flines went through their transition to strict cloister, the German nuns of the Dominican convent of Saint Katherine in Augsburg were facing a similar experience.[37] Saint Katherine's was one of the wealthiest religious houses in town, packed with names of local patrician and mercantile families.[38] The nuns enjoyed privileges, papal and royal protection, and a degree of political and economic autonomy. They were exempted from the control of the bishop, ran a textile business, and were allowed to appoint their own administrators to run the convent estate. Traditionally, Saint Katherine's community had not been subjected to strict enclosure and the nuns had always maintained their uncloistered state. In the late fifteenth century they successfully resisted two attempts at reform by religious and state authorities. It is reported that when the city council sent workers to fit new grilles and build walls, the nuns spat at them, causing the workers to give up the job. In the years that followed, between 1499 and 1504, the nuns commissioned six panel paintings from Hans Burckmair and Hans Holbein. Commissions were made, individually, by five wealthy nuns, one of whom—the abbess Veronica Welser—paid for two panels, one of which included her portrait (see Fig 2). The six paintings—known as the *Basilica Cycles*—represented the seven basilicas of Rome, with images of the Virgin Mary, Christ, pilgrims, and a number of Christian saints and early Roman martyrs, some of whom were related to the Dominican order. Placed in the new chapter hall, where the nuns gathered for prayer and for discussing important decisions, the six panels were intended to be used as 'goals' of their symbolic spiritual pilgrimage to Rome.[39] For this devotional act they would be granted papal indulgences just like the pilgrims physically travelling to Rome. But the panels also acquired another meaning for the nuns, linked to their recent experience. Indeed, the panels portrayed the Virgin and many of the female saints and courageous women who had fought for their faith, some of whom also had temporal power such as Helena, empress of Rome; Ursula, princess; Dorothy, daughter of a Capedocian senator. All of these women embodied total dedication to God, purity of faith, as well as strength and power. The *Basilica Cycle*—and its heroines—presented a full range of powerful women from the past, which the nuns could seek to emulate in their own present in order to resist external pressures and the imposition of unwanted rules. Commissioned after a rather turbulent period of struggle against the externally imposed restrictions, the paintings reminded the entire community united in the chapter of their righteous choices, and legitimized within the community the uncloistered state that the nuns sought to maintain. As in the outside world, convent art and patronage served multiple purposes, both private and public, and served the nuns' political agenda as well as their spiritual aims, the two proving remarkably closely intertwined.

Nuns as Artists

She labored diligently...and used her skill for painting, drawing, embroidering, and other painstaking work, to fashion the corporal cloths, and made lovely flowers; she cut the fabric and made altar cloths for this purpose also, using things given to us as alms,...And when she finished they were so fine and so perfect, they did not seem to be the work of human hands.[40]

This gifted nun was the Carmelite Maria de San Alberto from Valladolid. An artist, as well as an acclaimed poet and writer, Maria restored ruined paintings and painted herself. One day the nuns of her convent lent a table portraying the Veronica to one of their dowers, the Marquis de Poza. The table was returned in such a poor condition that even the finest painter in town did not dare to touch it. Luckily Maria could take on the job: she chose all 'the oil colors that she deemed necessary, [and] repaired it so that it was perfect as it had been before, as though it had never been touched by human hands'.[41] Maria's activity as a restorer—and an almost celestial worker—was hardly unique. Painter nuns were often charged with repairing the pictorial and monumental images in their convents, both to save the community money, and in order to avoid direct contact with male workers coming from outside. For example, in 1488 three nuns from Wienhausen in Saxony—amazingly all of them called Gertrude—restored the mural paintings of their choir.[42]

Following the monastic dictum 'pray and work', nuns were encouraged to collectively engage in 'writing, sewing, embroidery, tapestry, weaving, spinning, crocheting, combing and carding the wool, hooking and weaving cloth'.[43] Naturally, some of them became quite skilled. They painted, sculpted, worked as miniaturists or engravers, and were involved in all kinds of art and craft works, bookmaking and decorating, needle and textile works, which provided income for their houses. The Cistercian sisters of Bijloke, in Ghent, specialized in liturgical embroidery that they sold to the town's churches. In some convents, such as fifteenth-century German Dominican houses, the nuns wove devotional tapestries with sacred scenes and images of themselves sitting at the loom, which suggest deep awareness of the spiritual and economic significance of their work, and of their own creative identities.[44]

The separation from the outside world inherent in the cloistered condition created obvious practical difficulties for nuns interested in actively exploring the visual arts. Although many nuns received an artistic education from their families before entering the convent, and some even came from artistic families and could emulate the skills of parents, siblings, and relatives, access to visual education and artistic training was very limited under conditions of monastic reclusion. Nuns' links with the extramural art market were mainly indirect, and they had little exposure to contemporary artistic trends. Nevertheless, nuns did paint. They helped decorate their convent spaces and produced paintings for outside patrons, learning from their more experienced sisters, and engaging with them in collaborative work. From inside their convents, they even managed to attract an outside audience for their art. Nuns could transformed their convent space into something similar to their own art studio.

In his work on female monastic art in late medieval Germany, Jeffrey Hamburger has offered the most thoughtful insights on how to interpret the nuns' creativity. Images created by nuns for the convent audience were devotional tools, primarily used for inculcating the sisters with the basic principles of spiritual experience in an accessible manner.[45] Impossible to detach from its devotional function, the nuns' art was less concerned with reproducing aesthetic forms and concepts than with providing visual examples of how to pray and participate in collective devotional practices.[46] The series of devotional drawings by an anonymous nun from the Bavarian convent of St Walburg, near Eichstatt, dated around 1500, represent images of the Virgin and Child, saints, narrative episodes from the Gospel, and key moments of the nuns' cloistered life. They focus on themes, like for instance the Consecration of Virgins, which hinted at the nuns' entrance into religious life. Similarly, devotional tapestries produced in this convent narrate acts of devotion to Saint Walburga. The *Newer Walburga Tapestry* portrays four nuns in their choir, and on their right two pilgrims entering the crypt where Walburga's bones were preserved. From these images nuns learned about the meaning of their collective and devotional life, and about the importance of performing everyday liturgical acts other than attending the mass and divine office. In these cases they learned about the importance of their consecration to God, and would be reminded of their duty to venerate the saint who gave his or her name to their convent.[47]

The evidence suggests that this devotional, rather than purely aesthetic, understanding of art was well entrenched in the early modern mind. Examples of this can be found in the writings of nuns, and in their references to the artistic and visual culture of the convent. In one of her writings, Maria de San Alberto—the extraordinarily gifted and already mentioned Carmelite from Valladolid who restored the Veronica painting—describes an image of the Virgin owned by her convent.

She specifies that it was made of rather poor material but that it nonetheless mattered a lot to the nuns, because 'although [it was] not beautiful, it inspired devotion'.[48] A series of examples from hagiographical texts reporting the lives of early modern nuns suggest a connection between artistic creativity and devotion, or even ecstasies. The mystic Caterina Vigri decorated her breviary with small images of Jesus, the protagonist of many of her visions; after her death the nuns of her convent kept this illustrated devotional text as one of many relics of the saint.[49] Maria Maddalena de Pazzi, the Florentine visionary saint, produced images while she was in ecstasy: 'enraptured by God, with her eyes fixed to the sky, she ... painted devout images on paper'.[50]

The deeply devotional nature of female monastic art can be seen in the work of artist nuns such as—once again—Maria de San Alberto and her sister, Cecilia del Nacimiento. The two were born in Valladolid of Antonio Sobrino, secretary of the city's University, and Cecilia Morillas, who was admired by her contemporaries for her learning and for being an artist and illuminator. All the children became painters, musicians, and writers. Both sisters received a scholarly education of letters, Latin, music, drawing, and embroidering, and they learned to write, paint, play the guitar, and sing, apparently very beautifully.[51] Both of them embraced religious life in 1588, in the Carmelite community of La Concepción, and penned autobiographical writings on the request of religious men in their circle. After Maria's death, Cecilia composed her *Life* in which she praised her sister's extraordinary virtues and merits. Surely influenced by their family background, they both painted, although they could count only on the convent's limited resources to work with, and mainly used rough canvases made of second-hand materials.[52] Together, and perhaps with the assistance of other nuns, they completed a total of five paintings: a *Man of Sorrows with Roundels of His Suffering*, a *Christ at the Column*, a *Christ as the Word*, and two *Ecce Homos*. These images, displayed inside the convent, would assist the nuns in their daily prayers. According to the Teresian tradition, very strong in seventeenth-century Spain and in particular in Carmelite convents, nuns were encouraged to contemplate images of Christ in order to see their own imperfections, and subsequently engage in spiritual exercises to begin the long journey towards final purification and union with God. They were also encouraged to follow a precise liturgical format, which included meditating on the passion of Christ, and focusing on specific moments of his suffering, one episode at a time.[53] As an aid to following this pattern, the nuns could transfix the passion scenes—such as those represented in the roundels surrounding Christ in the *Man of Sorrow* by Cecilia and Maria—and complete their inner pilgrimage to God. Interestingly, in the case of the Sobrino sisters, they adapted their aesthetic creativity to the female audience they addressed. As has been pointed out, in the images created for the convent, the two artists visibly emphasized the feminine traits of the body of Christ. Their Christ has narrow shoulders, a soft belly, and very small hands. In proposing this feminization of the body of Christ they actually deviated from the established iconography. This interpretation of the divine minimized the gender difference between the female viewers and the image of Christ.[54] In doing this they did not mean to challenge the most traditional images of the literary and artistic traditions but instead aimed to stimulate the nuns—the only audience for their art—to identify with Christ.[55] On a more practical level, this feminized version of Christ was probably also a consequence of their greater familiarity with the forms of the female bodies they would use as models for their work.

The visual discourses elaborated within the convent delivered important messages to the community about the deep meaning of religious life. This is revealed, for example, by the work of the Italian Maria Eufrasia della Croce (1597–1676), a Discalced Carmelite nun from the convent of San Giuseppe a Capo in Rome.[56] Maria Eufrasia came from a patrician family, and was the sister of the art collector and amateur architect Abbot Elpidio Benedetti. Some time after 1627, when she entered religious life, she completed an altarpiece, *The Nativity of Christ*, for her convent church, and she was charged with painting a series of large murals on the walls of the refectory and other collective rooms. She also painted the nuns' choir, including the partitioning wall between the choir and the public church. This was the wall of the *comunichino*, the little window through which the nuns took their communion while mass was performed in the church. Here, on the left side of the communion window was featured a *Christ and the Samaritan Woman*. On the right side of this window stands the figure of Mary Magdalene. In between these images there is an *Annunciation* and above it *God the Father*.[57] These scenes evoked rejection of sin and worldly life embodied by Mary Magdalene—the repentant prostitute that God had redeemed—and the Samaritan woman elegantly clothed and adorned with jewels. They also evoked the universal model of purity represented by the Virgin. All these were crucial values that the nuns were to follow and that they would have been familiar with since the first day they set foot into the cloister. Such a visual portrayal of the meaning of monastic life covered a wall that, by dividing the nuns from the outside church while allowing them to take communion, materialized the powerful tension between religious confinement, on the one hand, and the ability to reach God, on the other. Maria Eufrasia here deployed her art and visual language—which she assumed her sisters were able to understand—to encourage them to reflect on their existence and to make sense of it.

The role of art and artworks conceived within closed communities raises an important question. Did nuns create their work exclusively for the convent audience, or were they also addressing society outside? Although we still know very little about nuns as artists it is clear that some of them did reach an external audience. Nuns were not the only viewers of these works, some of which were sent out of the cloister to be exhibited in public.

Plautilla Nelli (1523–88) is an example of an artist whose works reached external destinations.[58] A nun in the Dominican convent of Santa Caterina da Siena, in Florence, Plautilla spent the years of the Council of Trent in a community where nuns were fiercely opposed to the new rules, and in particular to strict enclosure. As enclosure was implemented only slowly in her convent, her life was not too heavily affected by it.[59] In the convent she lived with her sister Petronilla, the probable author of a copied manuscript version of the *Life* of the Florentine Dominican reformer Gerolamo Savonarola. This convent was one of a group of artistically active communities. In the sixteenth and seventeenth centuries several Tuscan Dominican nunneries were known for the production of sacred images and small terracotta figures that were profitably sold outside.[60] In Plautilla's convent nuns were engaged in similar kinds of work, as well as pursuing painting activities to decorate the internal spaces of their building.[61] They almost certainly benefited from the influence of their artistically active superiors, the fathers of San Marco. In this favourable environment Plautilla conceived her many works. They included a *Lamentation with the Saints*, originally installed in the outer church of the convent; a *Christ, the Madonna, and Three Dominican Martyrs*, and a *Last Supper* respectively for the infirmary and the refectory of her convent; a *Descent of the Holy Spirit* for the church of San Domenico in Perugia; a *God the Father with Angels, Saint Dominic, and Saint Catherine of Siena* (now lost) that she painted with her sisters for the chapel of the dormitory of her convent, and that was largely financed by the nuns' families.[62] For these and others of her works Plautilla gained reputation as a painter amongst her contemporaries. She was one of the few women—and the only nun—whom Vasari allowed to appear in his collection of great artists' *Lives*. He thoroughly praised her, although he thought that her lack of artistic training weakened her work and that 'she would have done marvelous things if, like men, she had been able to study and to devote herself to drawing and copying natural living things'. According to Vasari, Plautilla completed works for churches and convents in Florence and outside, as well as for Florentine patricians, and he mentions two *Annunciations* which he saw in the 'homes of the gentlemen of Florence'.[63] Certainly, Plautilla conceived her art for her sisters as well as for a public of outsiders which probably included—as Vasari claimed—the wealthy patricians of Florentine high society.[64] Furthermore, as has recently been argued, her activity was profitable. She received money from commissioned works, and had close contact with external patrons through her own networks of acquaintances. This allowed her to move beyond the convent to a wider audience, making steps into the 'world of the professional'.[65]

Like Plautilla, other nuns also exhibited their work in public. The Spanish Teresa del Niño Jesús (1662–1742) for instance 'employed all the very great ability that the Lord gave to her in the service of the cult' and produced artworks for her Bridgittine convent in Valladolid, including a much-praised life-sized Virgin for the public church.[66] Lucrina Fetti (*c.*1595–*c.*1637), for her part, established herself as a portraitist in the Gonzaga court in Mantua.[67] The Mantuan court, with its refined cultural and artistic activities and its ruling family eager to celebrate its power, stoked demand for the visual arts, providing opportunities for artists to find commissions and work. Lucrina found an audience for her works in both the closed space of the cloister and the more public world of the court. She arrived in Mantua from Rome with her father and her brother Domenico who was a painter and probably her art teacher. The same year, she entered the convent of Sant'Orsola, a community founded by Duchess Margherita Gonzaga. Here many women of the ducal family spent part of their lives in education. Duke Ferdinando—a keen patron of artists—provided for the Fetti family, paying for Lucrina's monastic dowry. In Sant'Orsola she started to paint.[68] On the whole her production comprises a series of more than ten paintings—including those she painted maybe with the help of her brother—representing religious themes which were exhibited in the convent's public church. Lucrina also completed four life-size portraits of Gonzaga women: Eleonora I Gonzaga (see Fig. 4), Eleonora II, Duchess Margherita Gonzaga (the founder) depicted in a widow's garb, and Caterina de' Medici Gonzaga, second wife of Duke Ferdinando. Displayed in the Duchess' apartment—where she lived attended by her ladies-in-waiting, and surrounded by works of art—these images would be seen primarily by the nuns and by the selected group of visitors officially allowed to come inside the cloister to visit her. The images of the four noblewomen would act as visual reminders of the prestigious ties that linked the convent to the ducal family, and to some of the most distinguished ruling dynasties of Europe, with whom the Gonzaga were related through carefully chosen marriages. Set in the semi-open convent space of the Duchess' rooms, Lucrina's art acquired a political dimension. Her portraits celebrated the patrons of her convent, and reminded the nuns, as well as their distinguished visitors, of the importance of dynastic alliances, and of the crucial role women played in them.[69]

In addressing an audience outside the convent, nuns devoted their attention towards non religious subjects. One example of this is Orsola Maddalena Caccia (1596–1676), the daughter of the painter Guglielmo Caccia, who inherited her artistic vocation from him in more ways than one. Not only did he bequeath to her—and to her sister Francesca, who may also have been a painter—the usufruct of 'all his drawings and paintings, small or medium size', and his colours and brushes. In his last will, he also specifically ordered his daughter Orsola to finish one of his uncompleted works for the altar of the Franciscan church of Montalvo, in the hope that she would follow on from his own artistic career.[70] Orsola certainly lived up to her father's expectations and, in the years following his death, she completed his work, and began to paint a number of panels for local churches. Her skills won her important engagements and in 1643 she received a double commission for a *Nativity* and a *Saint John the Baptist* from Christina of France. Orsola however also painted a number of still-life pictures which she filled with flowers, fruits, berries, and birds. For her pictorial creativity she acquired posthumous public recognition. In the eighteenth century, she and her sister were praised and equated with their well-known lay predecessors Artemisia Gentileschi and Lavinia Fontana. They were defined as 'the Gentilesche and Fontana of Monferrato'.[71]

A few decades later, Isabella Piccini (1646–1734) made a name for herself as an engraver. The daughter of an engraver, Isabella began her successful artistic career in the convent of Santa Croce, in Venice, which she entered at the age of 22. Here she maintained contacts with authors, typographers, and the most important Venetian publishers. Her work focused on religious narratives, and mystic subjects and events, like the image of Saint Teresa of Avila writing in the solitude of her cell, which was published in a 1694 re-edition of Teresa's works, or the anatomic dissection of a holy nun from Nocera—a rare representation of the frequent ecclesiastical investigations aimed at assessing the presence of miraculous signs on the human female body.[72] But the objects of her many works were also official portraits, including those of exemplary learned and illustrious laywomen. Her engravings were published in many of the books, breviaries, and rituals printed in Venice in the late seventeenth and early eighteenth centuries.

Portraits of Nuns

Before leaving the subject of convent visual art we need to look at one final genre associated with nuns: the portrait. Portraits were painted of many nuns, including mystics such as Caterina Vigri, Teresa de Avila,

Maria de San Alberto, and others. Nuns were portrayed in various states: their eyes turned to God in ecstasy, praying in front of the sacrament, holding their crucifix or instruments of self-inflicted bodily mortification, reading their breviary, or surrounded by their books. Great abbesses and founders of religious houses in the Old and New Worlds also had their portraits painted. Images of particularly pious and holy nuns were painted after their death, their heads crowned with flower girdles. Anonymous images of nuns found their way into paintings representing holy scenes, or into prints classifying monastic orders and their habits, and were used to illustrate nuns' work of preparing food and herbal potions, making silk flowers, cutting liturgical clothes, and caring for orphans. Nuns were portrayed in the sacred space of their convent monastic cell, or on their deathbed, or more rarely in the communal spaces of the convent, or in an imaginary, sometimes quite empty, eternal space. These images tell us a great deal about nuns and the place assigned to them in the world.

Convent spaces were decorated with portraits commissioned by the nuns or their families. One of the best-known examples is that of the royal convents of Madrid, where many full-length paintings of Habsburg nuns—founders, abbesses, and novices—hung in chapter rooms, in parlours, and in nuns' cells.[73] These images celebrated the women who had ennobled the community by professing and living their lives there, while fixing in the minds of nuns and visitors the idea of inextricable connections between the crown and the convent, as in the case of the portraits by Lucrina Fetti which we have just mentioned. Convents also had portraits of nuns who had become famous or acquired particular merits. One of the three portraits of the writer Sor Juana Inés de la Cruz was painted after her death and is attributed to Juan de Miranda. The panel, painted before 1713, immortalized her in a room that was probably her cell, fully dressed with her garb, veil, and brooch on her breast. She is at her desk, pen in hand, looking at the viewer. Behind her a number of volumes are lined up on a bookshelf and on the side of her desk an inscription praises her virtues. We do not know exactly where the painting was positioned, nor if it was accessible from outside. However, it served the purpose of celebrating the intellectual gifts of this renowned nun, and—by extension—her community.[74] A very similar image of Sor Juana is also presented in later portraits (see Fig. 6).

Convents also owned portraits of missionary nuns who had since left. The first public painting made by the young Velázquez was a portrait of Madre Jerónima de la Fuente, completed in 1620 shortly before the departure of this Poor Clare from Toledo for Manila in the Philippines, where she was going to found a convent with three other sisters. The nuns of her convent who commissioned this portrait probably knew Velázquez through his teacher, the pious Francisco Pacheco, a well-known Sevillian portraitist and author of a tract on the arts, who had connections with the Franciscan order. Fearing that they might never see the 66-year-old again the nuns had decided to eternalize her presence. Jerónima posed for the artist in Seville, while waiting to sail. A rather austere and solemn full female figure standing in an empty space, Jerónima is dressed with the Clarissan habit and the veil, branding a large crucifix with one hand, and a prayer book in the other—the two spiritual weapons for winning souls and confronting the unpredictable challenges of the New World (see Fig. 7). This portrait conveyed an important message to the present and future sisters of the Toledo convent: through Jerónima, a member of their community who answered such a high calling, they could claim their own indirect association with the missions in the Philippines.[75] By commissioning this nun's portrait for display in the convent, the nuns were honouring her with leave to remain in the community as an immortal presence, reflecting the community's achievements. At the same time they were reinforcing awareness of their community's contribution to cultural life or to colonial expansion.

Other portraits celebrated the religious community by hinting at more local forms of expansion. The portrait of Mère Angélique Arnauld, the founder of the Jansenist convent of Port-Royale in Paris, was completed in 1653, as she was about to leave the city for Port-Royale-des-Champs, another Jansenist foundation. Made by the pious artist Philippe de Champaigne, and intended as a gift for Angélique's sister, her close collaborator, it was hung above the door leading to the chapter room for all the nuns to see (see Fig. 8). Mère Angélique sits on a chair holding a book, wearing a white habit with a red cross on the chest, and a black veil. In the background through a window we see the image of the convent she is about to join, surrounded by countryside.[76] The portrait transformed the departing Angélique into an eternal part of the Parisian convent, whilst at the same time perhaps suggesting the future expansion of Jansenist religious houses. This was a powerful and strengthening message for the nuns of this order, who had been subjected to fierce religious persecution in those years. In 1662, Champaigne completed another portrait for this house. It was the portrait of his daughter Catherine de Sainte Susanne. Champaigne wanted this portrait to be an ex-voto.[77] After a paralysis of the leg lasting fourteen months, Catherine—helped by the constant prayers of the nuns—had recovered completely: one day, while in the solitude of her cell, she heard the echo of the mass from the convent church, got up, and began to walk. To thank God for his benevolence, she renewed her solemn vows, while her father celebrated the miracle by painting her portrait. The portrait depicts Catherine lying on a chair and footrest, her legs covered by her long habit, beside a kneeling Mère Agnès. Both nuns have their hands clasped together in prayer, one facing a long crucifix hanging on the wall above her head, the other facing away from it. Hung in the chapter room where it could be viewed by all the nuns, this double portrait conveyed a visual revelation of the divine, reminding the sisters—including the artist's daughter—of the importance of their vows and dedication to God. In the light of the persecution suffered by the sisters in this period, this portrait also offered them a reassuring image of the divine majesty of God who protected and bestowed gifts on them, as his beloved daughters.

Finally, we should also add that portraits of young women who became nuns were sometimes included in pictorial representations of the family. As Diane Owen Hughes argued—focusing on a numbers of examples from early modern Italy—these celebrative representations might serve to reinforce the bonds between family members, such as those between parents and children, or between brothers and sisters. Portraying the female unmarried members of the family—including those who entered the convent—these images aimed to confirm their link with the family, and claim them as part of the lineage, even after they had left.[78] Examples from Spain and from eighteenth-century Mexico, show that families commissioned many portraits of their relative nuns, on the occasion of their profession, or after their death.[79] In these portraits nuns are dressed with their garb, or the lay clothing which they were about to abandon. The image of Doña Juana de Cortés Chimalpopoca, an Indian princess who took the veil in the Corpus Christ convent of Mexico City, presents her just before she entered religion, wearing the lavish clothes she wore for her parade though the city, held just before taking the veil.[80] This image catches the Indian woman in the crucial transitional moment of her life, though still locating her in the world. Some of these portraits of nuns-to-be clearly identify their subjects within their family by reporting inscriptions which specify the names of their father and mother.[81] Portraits of nuns, then, celebrated the holy brides of Christ, and more specifically the holiness acquired by families through their association with these women. We might also speculate that by immortalizing the women who were about to give themselves to God, these portraits openly claimed them still as members of this world. Indeed, they confirmed the nuns' intermediate position between heaven and earth, though firmly asserting their roots in their family and the terrestrial community.

SIX

Expansion:
Nuns across the Globe

The powerful image of women living in sacred cloistered spaces, dressed in their religious garb and veils, active in their spiritual and domestic duties, creative in all the arts, and sometimes endowed with mystical gifts, is now firmly established in our mind. There is, however, another equally powerful image which captures the nature of female monastic life: that of the founding nun. There are numerous examples of very determined nuns leaving their convents and moving to other cities, and even other countries, in order to found new communities. Their destinations ranged from Europe to the colonies of the New World, and included faraway places in Asia, America, and, in modern times, Africa. Wherever in the world they ended up, these nuns might enter into close contact with the society around them. They also maintained long-distance relations with the other members of their orders back home, receiving advice and instructions that they did not always obey.

Expansion was an implicit aim of monasticism from its very origin. By joining a monastic community, men and women could satisfy their need for a total spiritual experience following the examples of Christ and the Apostles, by preaching and instructing other people in the principles of Christian faith and setting an example of a Christian life. In the late medieval and early modern periods, waves of expansion brought the foundation of new orders and monastic houses, often as a result of dissidence, movements of spiritual renewal and religious reform, or the conquest of new worlds. In the fifteenth century, for example, the emergence of reform movements within the Franciscan and Dominican orders led to a number of new foundations of male and female 'Observant' monastic houses. In the sixteenth century, the renewed impulse for Catholic reform in response to the Protestant advance also brought about the creation of new monastic institutions and religious orders. In the same period, Europe's colonial expansion created a demand for monasteries and convents outside Europe. But if participating in new foundations and moving outside the walls of the religious house might be an ordinary feature of the male monastic experience, it had very different implications for nuns, whose integrity was inevitably associated with the protection of the walls, and the close guardianship of their male superiors. Perhaps because of this, the narratives celebrating the lives of founding mothers sometimes assume heroic tones, describing the importance of their spiritual mission, as well as its difficulties. They report the complications associated with the transfer of holy women from one convent to another, the hardship of beginning a new life, and even warding off physical threats to, and attacks on, their communities.[1] This sense of mission for the sake of God finds expression in some of the visual celebrations of these nuns' achievements, which provide us with images of veiled women when they are about to leave for their new destinations, or as they travel in rows of carriages hidden behind protective curtains, safely escorted by armed men on horseback, or when they finally arrive in their new place.

We can trace the movements of these nuns, and explore the meaning of their actions, by looking at three different examples of female monastic expansion: the new Carmelite foundations in France, Flanders, and Europe, the establishment of teaching monastic communities in New France, and the growth of convents in Spanish America. These three examples show, once more, how the history of nuns was always closely intertwined with the main political and religious developments of their times.

Teresa and her Sisters

From their very origins the Discalced Carmelites were deeply devoted to the missionary spirit. Indeed their creation owed everything to the determination of the strong-minded Teresa of Avila who, after twenty years of monastic life, first founded a reformed and distinct branch of her Carmelite order emphasizing strict discipline, spiritual renewal, and deeply introspective oration. Teresa then dedicated her efforts to extending and consolidating her monastic model by establishing a number of new convents. A letter to her brother talks of her early project of founding a reformed community 'of no more than fifteen nuns,... in such strict enclosure as to be prevented from even going out or being seen by anyone without a veil on their face, firmly rooted in prayer and mortification'.[2] Teresa's reform and apostolic ideal developed out of her deep concern for the Catholic faith. Well aware of the danger posed by the forces of the Protestant Reformation and by the many divisions within the Roman Church, Teresa-as we have seen-was determined to fight to defend her Church, firmly believing that women—including cloistered women— could play an important role in this fight, with the right guidance. By embodying a life of penitence and total communion with God, and above all by engaging in constant prayer for the benefit of the worldly community, the Discalced aimed to provide a model of perfection for other devout women and men to follow. Teresa even hoped they could win back souls lost to the Catholic cause.

The history of the early Discalced order shows how systematically Teresa and her sisters undertook their apostolic task. In December 1562, after two years of careful planning and many difficulties, Teresa founded the first Discalced Carmelites community: the convent of San José in Avila. The following year she became its first prioress. Initially small in numbers, the Discalced order grew rapidly and their convents flourished. In 1567, a first group of nuns left Avila for Medina del Campo. This foundation, which coincided with the beginning of the reform of the male branch of the Carmelite order, was followed by those of Malagón and Valladolid in 1568, Toledo and Pastrana in 1569, Salamanca in 1570, Alba de Tormes in 1571, Segovia in 1574, Beas and Seville in 1575, and Caravaca in 1576. In the last three years of her life, and after an interruption due mainly to conflicts within the reformed and unreformed parts of the order, Teresa continued her tireless activity and founded convents in Villanueva and Palencia in 1580, Soria in 1581, and Granada and Burgos in 1582. Negotiations were begun for the foundation of the Madrid house, which opened in 1586, just four years after her death. The impetus for the progressive institutionalization of the Discalced order was maintained after Teresa's death, and in 1593—at the time of the definitive separation of the Discalced from the Carmelites—there were thirty-one convents, located in Spain, Portugal, Italy, France, Flanders, Germany, Austria, and Poland.³ The geographical range of this expansion clearly reveals the participation of the Discalced in a campaign of spiritual conquest of Europe, which reached many corners of the Continent, including those riven by religious conflicts.⁴ It was a campaign orchestrated by the Spanish monarchy with the active participation of the Church and the Catholic elites outside Spain. It was also an operation punctuated with moments of failure and genuine despair, as emerges from the letters and spiritual works of the first generations of the Discalced, who wrote almost on a daily basis.⁵

Some of the early followers of Saint Teresa stand out from the crowd, such as Teresa's two earliest and most faithful companions, María de San José and Ana de Jesús (1545–1621). Devoted both to the saint and to the Discalced cause, they played a crucial role in leading the reform and supporting it against all odds.

María de San José—probably the daughter of converted Jews like Teresa—grew up in Toledo, as the lady-in-waiting of the aristocrat Luisa de la Cerda. The encounter with mother Teresa had a great impact on this young and well-educated woman, who—a few years after their first meeting, in Toledo—joined the Discalced convent of Malagón. This was the beginning of her peregrinations, which took her first to found a house in Seville, where she became abbess, and then, in 1582, to direct the foundation of the Discalced convent of Lisbon. Sponsored by Cardinal Prince Albert of Portugal, this foundation was the first Teresian house to be established outside Spain, marking the beginning of the Discalced presence in Europe.⁶

María was highly regarded and influential, but also a much-contested and persecuted figure. Attacked and accused by other nuns of heretical behaviour while she was still living in the Seville convent, she later became embroiled in the heated dissensions within her religious order over the leadership of the reform, and ended her eighteen years in Lisbon with

confinement in a monastic cell of her convent. It was there that on Good
Friday 1593 she wrote her *Letter written by a poor Discalced Carmelite
prisoner, for her own consolation and that of her Sisters and Daughters,
who seeing her thus imprisoned, were sore grieved.* Conceived in solitude
and conviction, her words reveal her sense of grief and pain, but at the
same time restate the importance of the Discalced collective mission, as
well as infusing in her sisters the courage and strength to pursue their
mission:

> We have embarked with Christ in the little boat; the storm must rise; and
> though the Lord sleeps and it seems that we are foundering, his Majesty will
> remember us in time and will save us. Do not be dismayed, dearest
> Sisters...Nor should you think that this is an evil particular to all we
> have worked for these many years, in service to the Order, exiled in so
> many lands, enclosed in the greatest poverty, suffering the intolerable
> hardship that are undergone in founding and sustaining the convents....
> I humbly beg you all...that we all agree in this: to love those who afflict us,
> not as enemies but as true friends and benefactors, and for the sake of our
> great friend Christ.[7]

If María de San José saw the missionary task as one of her primary
duties, Ana de Jesús, who took the reform into the heart of Europe, was
just as committed. Born into a Castilian family of the lower nobility, she
first entered the Discalced convent in Avila and then moved to Salamanca
where she became a close collaborator of Teresa. After more than twenty
years spent moving within Spain, where she founded two convents, she
went back to Salamanca in 1594, soon to leave again in the direction of
Paris.[8] The story of Ana de Jesús and her companions, who embarked on a
founding adventure in the first half of the seventeenth century, is an
intriguing one in a number of ways, not least for their leading and
pioneering role within their order.

It was common for religious orders to establish houses in regions where
they had little presence, but where the renewed Catholic spirituality they
advocated could attract support. The originality of the Discalced project
lies in the fact that it began under the impetus of the female branch of
their order, and under the influence of Teresa, and won the almost
immediate support of at least a part of its male component. Particularly

noteworthy was Jerónimo Gracian, Teresa's confessor and a very influential man, whose involvement was invaluable to the completion of the reform and the subsequent expansion of the order. Nearly always the nuns cleared a path for their male counterparts who would establish themselves later.[9]

Probably, Ana de Jesús's departure from Spain was motivated by her spiritual ambitions, as well as own personal circumstances, and her direct involvement in conflicts inside the order. These were mainly conflicts about the guardianship of nuns, as well as disagreements over the government of the order itself. Although Ana never openly admitted to having left Spain because of these difficulties, it is possible that her decision reflected a desire to distance herself from her opponents, whilst strengthening her reputation by association with the Catholic mission. She perhaps thought that by leaving Spain she would have won greater independence and autonomy in developing her own understanding of the Discalced form of collective life. Two years before her departure she had manifested her desire to take part in the prospective journey to France.[10] As she wrote to father Diego de Guevara in 1602, 'I pleaded with our General Father to request nuns to be founders in France, and that if he did, that I should be one of them '... and that this should all be agreed in Paris, and [I pleaded with] the great Lord with his pieties, who does everything to make use of them and find ways of showing his love'.[11] Her plea was received positively. She and her companions left Salamanca for Paris in 1604. Apparently they left incognito, in the middle of the night. As we gather from the journal of the voyage penned by one of the male participants who escorted the nuns,

> we had to leave the monastery in Salamanca one hour after midnight, otherwise the people would never have allowed us to be taken...and in order to do this more secretly, I left our hostel for the convent of the Discalced Fathers and accompanied them to the monastery of the mothers, who came out on our arrival.[12]

The six-week trip was disrupted by encounters with overly curious travellers keen to catch a glimpse of a group of nuns outside their cloister walls, and other difficult and even dangerous situations, but divine intervention ensured their safe arrival at their destination in Paris, in mid-October of that year.

The establishing of Carmelite foundations in France cannot be understood without considering the specific context in which the nuns operated. In those years, France—just emerging from religious and civil conflicts which had devastated the country—was the centre of great religious and spiritual Catholic revival. Many men and women from the Parisian elites were drawn to join small circles of devotees and immerse themselves in a life of deep piety and charity.[13] They actively sponsored new orders and welcomed new foundations. In Paris, between 1604—when the Discalced arrived in the city—and 1650, forty-eight new female religious houses were opened.[14] To the eyes of these devotees the austere Discalced nuns arriving from Spain, and taking with them the true spirit of Teresa's spiritual reform, embodied a series of values—extreme devotion, piety, and spiritual introspection—and the triumph of Catholicism over religious conflict. They might therefore be a weapon to restore peace in their country. It was in this framework that the Spanish nuns found the means to fulfil their plans.[15]

If we look at the networks surrounding the nuns we get an idea of the extent to which the foundation of the first Carmelite convent relied on the support of the French Catholic elite and owed its achievement particularly to the careful work of devout women, helped by powerful members of the Church. These female patrons offered strategic help, using—as women often did—the informal networks of power to which they had access, in order to guarantee their success. The Paris convent, the first foundation in France, was completed in 1604, with the invaluable help of three patrons in particular: Cardinal Pierre de Berullé; his cousin Barbe Acarie; and Catherine d'Orléans, princesse de Longueville. While Berullé had travelled to Spain, personally making sure of the nuns' transfer to Paris, Barbe and the princesse de Longueville worked at local level. Barbe was, for sure, an ideal benefactor. Very pious, she was particularly inclined towards monastic commitment, to the point that she ended her days in the Parisian Discalced convent having professed the vows after her husband's death. She was a main reference figure within the circle of distinguished and devout men and women who met in her Parisian house.[16] On top of her spiritual fervour, Barbe was extremely well connected to the key points of political power. She was able to ensure, amongst other things, favourable conditions for the establishing of the Discalced, and to act as a *trait-d'union* between the nuns and the court of King Henry IV. Furthermore, for her the Discalced mission was associated with divine will. A few years earlier, Saint Teresa had appeared to her in a vision, telling her to bring the Discalced nuns to France.[17] Together with Barbe, the princesse de Longueville, a cousin of the king, had a crucial part in the Discalced foundation from the start, assuring their safe arrival in Paris. 'I would like to say that I should be permitted to have your daughters here', she wrote to the general superiors of the Discalced:

> I have obtained from His Most Christian Majesty permission to have them here and to remove all obstacles to this journey. I believe that when your Fathers consider the progress of this enterprise, and see that other seminaries like this monastery will be founded all around, . . . they will see fit to make good use of this work and give responsibility for this house to the most experienced souls in the order.[18]

If the princess's support was vital for getting permission from the Discalced fathers, it was even more important in providing the endowment for the Discalced convent and finding the financial means to put plans into practice: 'I have chosen a place in a good location, with fresh air and open space', she wrote again to the Discalced fathers; 'I have provided eighteen hundred thousand escudos in rent for the monastery. In the name of this house I have hurried along the construction work with such diligence that it will all be finished and habitable within three months'.[19]

Just two years after the establishment of the convent in Paris, in Faubourg Saint-Jacques, the Discalced had set their sights on another destination: Brussels. Here the regent archdukes—Albert of Austria and the Infanta Isabel Clara Eugenia, daughter of Philip II of Spain—had officially requested the presence of the Discalced: 'For many days I have wished you to be here and to see in these states the daughters of Mother Teresa', declared the Archduchess Isabel Clara Eugenia to Ana de Jesús:

'Our Lord has not seen fit to fulfil this desire of mine up to now, and I hope you will not refuse my wish that you found a monastery here, . . . and I hope that . . . it will be possible to overcome all the difficulties that may arise, whatever it takes to do so'.[20]

As had happened in Paris, patrons in Brussels provided for the many material needs of the nuns. The infanta revealed to Ana her plans for the immediate arrangements of the convent building which would be located in close proximity to the archducal palace: 'the place I have for the monastery is next to our house, which is what I always wished, so that we too can take some of the goodness that is in your house'.[21] The archdukes endowed the Discalced with rents, money, and a range of precious gifts, such as 3,600 florins in cash, a set of silver chalices, and also an extraordinary collection of devotional images and paintings of different sizes, including portraits of the archdukes themselves which celebrate their roles as patrons. They maintained close contact with the nuns and were assiduous visitors of the convent that they treated as their own creation, and as a part of their palace:

on the eve their Highnesses came with their whole court and many ladies and they entered the chapel [. . .] and on leaving the chapel the Most Serene Archduke took the pallium with the most noble gentlemen of the court . . . the nuns came out with their white habits and passed through the chapel were the Infanta was waiting, and the Infanta took the hand of our Venerable Mother Ana de Jesús.[22]

The many precious gifts from the founders, the convent's proximity to the palace, and the lavish decoration of the building with no expense spared, were hardly consistent with the Discalced's ideals of frugality and essentiality, and caused some concern amongst the holy mothers. Nevertheless, they accepted their patrons' generosity. On the other hand, for the archdukes, the gifts and donations destined to the nuns were a means to strengthen their link with them, and even to appropriate their spiritual goals for political reasons. Indeed their association with the nuns reinforced the Catholic identity of the court and ruling elite, thus consolidating their power.

Following Brussels, further houses were opened in Mons, Louvain, Antwerp—which became the headquarters of Ana de Jesús—Tournai,

Bruges, Liège, and finally Ghent. As she approached old age, Ana desired to return to Spain. Hers was the desire of a woman who had spent much of her life far from her country, which she presented—not surprisingly—as the proper conclusion of a life entirely dedicated to missionary work. As she admitted, 'it is right to go to die amongst Catholics'.[23] Her wish was not to come true. She died in Antwerp in 1621, at the age of 76.

The proliferation of Discalced foundations must be considered in the light of the close links between religion and politics in Counter-Reformation Europe. Helped by the protection of Spanish monarchs and supported by the Catholic rulers and aristocracy, the expansion of Saint Teresa's followers had an obvious political dimension. In France they were instrumental to the Catholics' spiritual agenda and the clergy's attempt to reaffirm its power, with the help of that part of the aristocracy which was deeply supportive of the Catholic cause. In Flanders, they provided a symbol of religious orthodoxy. Their growing presence might have acted therefore as a catalyst for a spirituality which spread beyond the cloister walls, amongst the Catholic elites of post-Tridentine Europe.

It is hard to assess precisely how much influence the Discalced were able to exert over the political and religious events of their times. They were however keen to present themselves as women who made an impact on their world, so profoundly marked by religious and political divisions. They wanted to be seen as peacemakers, and as agents of spiritual conversion, thus reclaiming their role in political life: 'Everyone says it is a miracle and with us came peace', claimed Ana de Jesús in a letter written from Brussels in 1609 and addressed to father Diego de Guevara in Salamanca. She reiterated: 'since we arrived there was peace'.[24]

The Making of New France: Marie de l'Incarnation

If in Catholic Europe the founding of female religious houses was a means to strengthen Catholicism, so it was outside Europe too. Women were needed in order to recreate European society in the colonies: not only unmarried women who would become the wives and mothers of the early colonizers, but also nuns who could work to educate their female offspring, preparing them for marriage or for religious life. Nuns were part of the making of the colonial world, and convents were amongst the first institutions to be transplanted to the colonies. This happened almost everywhere. In Goa, the Portuguese crown set up convents and a religious house for repentant prostitutes;[25] in the Philippines, the Spanish Franciscans supported the opening of convents by moving their nuns there; in the Spanish and Portuguese American colonies convents were opened in order to host the 'daughters of the conquerors'. In French America the Ursulines taught Indian girls.

The life of the Ursuline Marie de l'Incarnation (1599–1672) provides an example of the crucial role played by mystic nuns in the religious conquest of the New World, and of the spirit of the early phases of colonization.[26] The first French woman to join the missions in Canada, and the first to found a convent there, Marie arrived in August 1639 at the age of 40. What had brought her across the Atlantic was her desire to take her strong and long-standing commitment to the service of God to new heights. The daughter of a merchant baker from Tours, with an early inclination toward monastic life, she was instead married at the age of 17 to a silk maker, Claude Martin. A rapid succession of events changed her life. One year after her marriage she gave birth to a son. The following year her husband died, leaving her a widow. She soon moved into the busy house of her sister and brother-in-law, who ran a transport business. The loss of her husband left her free from marital engagement and—since she had no wish to marry again—she was free to pursue her irresistible attraction toward a religious existence. Mystic experiences, frequent mental oration, and the subsequent acquisition of a spiritual director added a new impetus to her life. Following the example of other mystic and devout women, she engaged in penitence and practised extreme forms of bodily discipline including the hairshirt and chains, and privately took the three vows of chastity, obedience, and poverty, thus embracing a monastic lifestyle while still living in the outside world. She also engaged in charitable works, attending to the poor, sick, and dying in hospitals, visiting and caring for prisoners, and imparting her teachings about the Ten Commandments of God to the various workers who visited her brother-in-law's house.

Through her spiritual director—to whom she had begun to describe her inner life—she was introduced to the classics of devotional literature of her times, in particular François de Sales's *Introduction* to devotional life, and Saint Teresa's *Life*. This determined spiritual engagement finally found its full expression when she was accepted at the Ursuline convent in Tours, where she professed the solemn vows.[27] Marie's move into monastic retreat was particularly radical, as it implied separation from her 11-year-old son, Claude. Still, years later, she would justify her choice as a difficult but correct one because, as she wrote, 'I had to give way to the power of divine will.'[28]

After the arrival of the Jesuits in Tours, the year after Marie's entry into religious life, she adopted a new Jesuit spiritual director and sought to contact religious men already involved in missionary activity. The Jesuits were already very active in the colonization in Asia and America, but now they were also recruiting women to teach the Amerindians in their missions. Jesuits' writings and reports of their work in the New World, which were published at that time, probably impressed Marie, who became very interested in the matter. She was also influenced by Saint Teresa's work, and Teresa's *Way to Perfection* was amongst her favourite readings. Indeed, since Teresa was the founder of the Discalced order and of many new convents, she was almost certainly an important reference point for Marie. After all, the Discalced nuns were renowned for their missionary work in Europe and beyond, and this probably contributed to reinforcing Marie's growing interest in missionary activity, about which she even fantasized—seeing herself spiritually involved in it: 'My body was in our monastery, but my spirit was tied to that of Jesus and could not be enclosed . . . I walked in spirit in those great vastitudes, accompanying those working for the Gospel.'[29] Of course she was fully aware of how challenging the departure for the missions might be for a cloistered nun, but at the same time she was determined to go: 'I visualize the travail, both on the sea and in the country; I visualize what it is to live with Barbarians, the danger of dying there of hunger or cold, the many occasions when one might be seized . . . and I find no change at all in the disposition of my spirit.'[30] Canada, as she claimed, was a call and an act of obedience to the divine will. It was God who told her about her imminent future as a missionary there: 'You must go there and make a house for Jesus and Mary.'[31] In her writings she recalls a vision she had before leaving Tours, when she saw a 'very difficult place', and could discern a small hospice building, above which was the Virgin Mary holding the Child in her arms:

> this so afflicted place that I saw was New France. I felt a very interior attraction to found there a House for Jesus and Mary. I was then so strongly taken by this thought that I gave my consent to the Lord and promised Him to obey Him if He would give me the means.... And really, the vision and the strong faith that I feel will condemn me on the Day of Judgment if I do not act according to what the divine Majesty asks of me.[32]

Marie's vision became reality. She finally obtained permission to set sail from Dieppe in the company of a small group of women. One was the sponsor and patroness of the mission, Madame Madeleine de la Peltrie, a young, noble, pious, and wealthy widow who had planned, with the help of the Jesuits, to go to Canada with the Ursulines and engage in the Christian education of young Indian girls. The other three women were the personal attendant of Madame de la Peltrie, Charlotte Berré, and two Ursuline nuns, Marie de Saint Joseph and Cécile de Sainte Croix.[33]

When they arrived in Quebec, the heart of the Jesuits' mission, after a three-month journey at sea, the hard work of their new life began. Quebec was a centre of a few hundred people. The four women quickly got themselves organized for their new task. Just one year later their convent was one of the largest buildings in the whole of New France. It was located on the promontory of Quebec, slightly isolated from the rest of the community, and consisted of a main building—mainly made of cedarwood—and an extended green area boarded by a fence. By 1650, eleven years after their arrival, the Ursulines' numbers had grown from four to fourteen, all of them living in enclosure. By 1669 they numbered twenty-two.[34]

The Ursulines set up a school in their convent, where they taught Indian girls from different nations—Algonquins, Montagnais, Hurons, and Iroquis—as well as French girls and the daughters of colonizers. This amounted to a quite significant body of pupils—twenty to fifty—boarding within the convent. In order to address such a heterogeneous and multilingual audience Marie and her companions learned the Indian languages, rather than simply relying on French. Marie de Saint Joseph learned Huron, while Marie de l'Incarnation could speak Algonquin, Montagnais, and Iroquian. Most remarkably, Marie began to write in the native languages—following the Jesuit example—and completed a number of prayers, catechisms, and dictionaries in Algonquin and Iroquis. Equipped with all linguistic skills, the nuns were ready to take up the challenge of teaching the extraordinary variety of people with different languages in their convent.[35]

The nuns adopted a partially flexible attitude in dealing with their pupils, allowing them to retain elements of their own culture. On the one hand they aimed at 'Gallicizing' the 'savage girls', 'cutting their hair in French style', making 'long dresses' for them, and educating them according to European standards. They imparted the basics of Catholic religion and Christian beliefs, and instructed them in prayer. They taught them how to speak, read, and write in French, as well as teaching them embroidery and painting in the French and European style. The nuns also made their pupils cover their bodies with clothing that they provided. Indian girls entering their convent as boarders performed a kind of ritual act that marked their inclusion within the French community of the nuns, and possibly the first step towards their religious conversion. This ritual act consisted of dressing them in undergarments and a tunic, after they had been properly washed and cleaned, literally 'de-greased':

> When they are given to us, they are as naked as a worm, and one must wash them from head to foot because of the grease that their parents have smeared all over their bodies. And no matter how diligently one does it or how often one changes their clothes, it takes a long time before one can get rid of the vermin caused by the abundance of their grease. One sister spends part of each day at this. It is an office each of us seeks with eagerness. Whoever wins it esteems herself rich with a happy fate; whoever is denied it considers herself unworthy and remains in a state of humility.[36]

On the other hand the Ursulines had to come to terms with the difficulties and limits of their mission. By delivering their lessons and teaching songs and hymns in both the French and Indian languages, and both of which the girls would also be taught to write, the Ursulines allowed their pupils to develop knowledge of their own culture. In effect, they delivered a mixed form of education which was both French and American Indian.

This flexible educational approach reveals the determination with which the nuns prioritized their ultimate missionary purpose. For them, the primary aim of education was to convert their girls and inculcate the principles of Christian religion so that they abandoned all their own religious practices, shamanism, and rituals, in the hope that the girls would pass on what they had learnt to their own people. This would be the nuns' contribution to the evangelization of America.[37]

Through their teaching activity the Ursulines were at the heart of the mission's religious life. They acted as godmothers at their pupils' christenings and socialized with the numerous women and men who visited the convent, sometimes just to enjoy meals from the nuns' kitchen. Marie de Saint Joseph, for instance, entertained groups of visitors in the parlour, and Marie de l'Incarnation 'was delighted to hear her and see around her forty or fifty Hurons, as many men as women and girls, listening to her with unbelievable eagerness'.[38] Additionally, the Ursulines taught their pupils important and productive skills—above all spinning—which could enhance their economic position within the colonies.[39] A good indicator of the visible role of the Ursulines in the life of colonial Quebec was that public ceremonies and processions—in which both Europeans and Indians took part—never failed to include their convent as one of their stations, just as in Catholic Europe.[40] Of course, this did not mean that their relationships with the Indians were always amiable. They did become entangled in the conflicts that sometimes exploded in the colony. In one occasion, when the Iroquis became particularly aggressive, the nuns and their pupils had to temporarily abandon their convent for a safer location, while Marie remained, alone, to watch the convent. Marie spent a sleepless night fearing the worst, 'my ears were pricked all night for fear of an alarm and in order to be always ready to give our soldiers the munitions required in the event of an attack'.[41] The nuns were an integral part of the colony, with all the advantages and disadvantages this implied.

Besides, Marie kept her patrons and correspondents in France informed about life in the mission, thus publicizing the Ursulines' activity in Canada. She was a prolific letter writer, she wrote her spiritual autobiography on the request of her son, who arranged for its publication. She also completed a *Sacred History*, and she became well known in France for her missionary work, and for the knowledge she acquired in her American years. She was invited to contribute to the annual Jesuit *Relations* from the New World, and was asked by the Jesuit François De Creux in Paris to provide material for his *Historia Canadensis*.[42]

Although there is no questioning the Ursulines' dynamism, we do need to ask how much of an impact they had on their pupils, and to what extent they successfully accomplished their mission of evangelization. Indeed, there are clear indications that things did not always work out as hoped. Although they did manage to convert some of their pupils, who then went on to marry French colonizers, not one Indian girl took the vows to become an Ursuline nun.[43] The nuns probably understood that one of the reasons for this failure was the very cloistered nature of the Ursuline life, which could be counterproductive, discouraging vocations and diminishing the impact of the nuns' preaching and missionary work. Marie was the first to recognize that their cloistered condition could be an obstacle to their mission, undermining the process of assimilation of Indian women. As she recalled, on one occasion 'Several of them arrived from a far away nation and on seeing us they were distressed by our way of life. They asked me why we covered our heads and why we could only be seen through holes, as they called our grill.'[44] Enclosure probably reduced the attractiveness for Indian girls of remaining in the cloister as nuns, and may even have pushed them into leaving, as some did, with the help of their parents: 'as soon as they become sad their parents take them away lest they should die. . . . Others leave on a whim or when the fancy takes them; they climb our fence which is as high as a wall like squirrels and go off to roam in the woods.'[45] As Marie claimed, she had known 'savage girls' who could not 'survive claustration', becoming melancholic once they were no longer able to roam freely wherever they wanted. On the whole, she was rather pessimistic about the possibility of things changing:

> I do not know how all this will end, for, to be totally frank, it seems impossible to me. In all the years which we have been in this country, we have only civilized seven or eight, who were Gallicized; All the others have returned to their families, albeit as good Christians. The savage life holds such charm for them on account of its freedom, that it is miraculous if one can interest them in French ways which they see as beneath their dignity.[46]

Enclosure only allowed the Ursulines to interact with the Amerindians within the confines of their convent, but not outside it. When their girls left the convent and went back to their parents, the nuns were not able to go out and look for other women to convert as a male missionary would have done.

Marie was not alone in wondering about the drawbacks of enclosure. Some of her contemporaries shared similar concerns. The Saint Sulpice missionaries—the founders of Montreal—specifically requested secular women to be sent over, since they would have greater logistic freedom in dealing with the Indians, thus overcoming the limitations of missions run by cloistered nuns. In 1653, Marguerite Bourgeoys (1620–1700) began to found a female community of lay missionaries, the Notre-Dame teaching congregation in Montreal. This congregation, which provided education and care for Indian girls and young French female immigrants, was made up of religious women bound to simple vows of poverty, chastity, and obedience, but not to enclosure.[47] So must we conclude that Marie and her contemporaries were openly confronting the shortcomings of the centuries-old model of female cloistered life? Whether or not they thought about matters in quite this way, they were certainly aware of how thorny this issue was, and how deeply it conflicted with Roman Church directives regarding the discipline of nuns. Surely, Marie was torn between the desire to go out and perform her religious task outside the cloister, and her sense of obedience to the disciplinary requirements of her monastic condition: 'I am well aware that I shall never go out, but I have a consuming interest in the gaining of souls for God, while waiting for matters to reach the desired conclusion.'[48] In the event she stayed until the end and died in Canada at the age of 73.

Marie's words reveal the achievements and contradictions of the nuns' missionary adventure. Enclosure, the most distinctive feature of their public presence, appeared to be an impediment to the civilizing purpose of the mission. Indeed enclosure could be almost a 'metaphor' for the difficulty, even the impossibility, of bridging the gap between Christianity, on one hand, and the New World, on the other.[49] Monastic women found it impossible fully to accomplish their missionary task. It is no coincidence that the later female groups of missionaries arriving from France consisted of secular sisters.

Apostles in New Spain

By the time the French Ursulines and other lay teaching congregations were settling in North America, Spanish nunneries had been flourishing in Central and South America for over a century. Preceded by the male religious orders, communities of nuns began to develop from the very beginning of the Spanish conquest of American territories. Populated by the daughters and female relatives of the early colonizers, these communities mirrored the new society, in all its similarities with old Europe, as well as in its differences, including those of class and ethnicity.[50] They participated therefore in the social and cultural transformations on which Spanish-America was built.[51]

Few women made the journey from Spain to settle in the colonies in the early years. The first waves of the conquests were mainly made up of men, many of whom relied on the companionship and services of Indian women, inevitably contributing to the birth of a growing number of illegitimate children. Pressed by the need to maintain an ordered society, the Spanish authorities laid down strict criteria for unmarried men who wished to move to American territories alone.[52] But if there were very few women suitable for marriage it also meant that there were very few of them suitable for religious life and for setting up new monastic foundations. Requests were therefore made for nuns to be shipped over from Spain, such as in 1536 when the first bishop of New Spain, Juan de Zumárraga, demanded religious women be sent there to forge the emerging Christian civilization within the Indian territories. The inhabitants of the first convents were the few Spanish-born nuns sent over from their homeland, or widows of early colonizers who had entered religious life after their married existence had come to an end.

The first female religious settlements were established towards the middle of the sixteenth century, and lasted until the end of the colonial period, at the end of the eighteenth century, when they started to decline and many were turned into secular institutions.[53] Some of these convents were built on the basis of less formal female religious communities, such as previously existing *recogimientos*. A kind of asylum for women lacking family protection and support, *recogimientos* hosted a variety of women such as single women and single mothers, abandoned wives, or women vulnerable to being drawn into prostitution. For instance, the convent of La Concepción founded in 1550 in Mexico City, and the convent of La Encarnación in Lima founded in 1561, both developed from *recogimientos*. Convents were also created on the basis of already established *beaterios*, communities of pious laywomen who had embraced a monastic lifestyle without taking the solemn vows, and engaged in devotional and charitable activities.[54]

The growth of the female monastic population from the later decades of the sixteenth century onward attests to the social success of convents. Communities like La Concepción in Santiago grew from just ten nuns in 1578 to 150 in 1619. In La Concepción in Lima, nuns tripled in number in the space of just one century, jumping from eighty to 247 between the early 1600s and 1700. The success of convents also attests to their capacity to absorb an extremely heterogeneous group of people. If we look inside female monastic houses of Mexico and Peru, we discover that they were packed with nuns and girl boarders placed there to be educated. However, they also hosted an astonishingly high proportion of servants, slaves, and sometimes even abandoned babies who would grow up there, spending all or part of the childhood within the walls. Nuns were no more than a portion of the monastic community, sometimes a large minority. In 1700, the above-mentioned convent of La Concepción in Lima housed over one thousand individuals, of whom only three hundred were professed nuns, novices, or servant nuns.[55]

The reasons for this expansion of convents in the major cities of Spanish America were mostly similar to the reasons for their growth in the old world. The impact of the Catholic reformation in Spain, and in particular of the monastic reform inspired by Teresa of Avila, and the presence of the Discalced in continental Europe, had an echo in the American territories. This may have been enhanced by the canonization of Teresa in 1622, matched in the same year by that of Ignacio de Loyola, the founder of the Jesuits, an order that had been present in America since the 1560s. The female Discalced—following the example of their male peers—organized their first colonial foundations, beginning in 1604, when a group of four nuns opened the convent of Puebla de Los Angeles, in Mexico. In the following decades, female houses belonging to different religious orders emerged all over Spanish America.[56]

The growth of female monastic foundations was also a response to the economic interests of elite families. In the colonies, just as in the home-land, convents mainly recruited on the basis of wealth. Wealthy families did not always find it easy to place all their daughters in economically advantageous marriages, and some were inevitably pushed into the cheaper option of monastic retreat, often together with illegitimate siblings. At the same time, the rise of property-owning and merchant groups provided abundant financial support for the establishment of convents. One of the peculiarities of convents in the New World is precisely that they never recruited principally amongst the aristocracy, which remained quite a small portion of society until the mid-seventeenth century. Instead convents largely took the daughters of emerging wealthy groups of landowners, merchants, bureaucrats, and members of the military elite.[57] Additionally, the crown did not always welcome the foundation of female monastic houses, on the ground that they drained funds which might have been invested more profitably elsewhere. To make things worse, nuns were occasionally put under pressure and obliged to set aside a fixed number of places and scholarships for women from impoverished elite families—to the disappointment of the entire commu-nity.[58] When Madre Josefa de la Providencia, a Nazarene nun from Lima, entered into discussion with the viceroy about the foundation of a new convent which was being developed from an old *beaterio* with the support of a wealthy local woman, she was told she had to provide four scholarships for the daughters of respectable families who had fallen into misfortune. Her reply was firm:

> I said that I could not, because the convent was so poor: he said . . . that he didn't want them for himself, but for the daughters of poor judges: I said that the *beaterio* did not owe so much as one single grain of wheat to any judge, count, or marquis, and so I could not give him what he asked.[59]

Association with wealthy families did not prevent convents from reproducing the discriminatory attitudes embedded in colonial society. First of all, there was the distinction between Spanish-born inhabitants of the colonies and American-born inhabitants of Spanish origin. The Spanish-born claimed their superiority on the ground of their European blood. The American-born suffered a sense of insecurity because of allegations of part Indian or part African ancestry. Within the convent, this was reflected in the distinction between Spanish-born nuns, known as *gachupinas*, and the American-born *criollas*. The histories and chronicles of the nuns' foundations reveal clear traces of such discrimination. In her history of the foundation of her Conceptionist convent in Mexico City, the abbess Ana de San Miguel—herself a *criolla*, and a member of the largest group in the community—focuses on an episode that created great disruption in her community: the attempt on the part of some nuns to abandon the convent and found a new Carmelite house. She interprets this breakaway as a purely political, rather than religious, move clearly aimed at allowing these nuns, all *gachupinas*, to recreate their own privileged environment of Spanish-born nuns, separated from the others, all this with the support and benevolence of the archbishop, a *gachupín*. As she comments, 'it seems that things are working out for the foundation of the Carmelite convent. These Spanish people have their lucky star in the Indies. Ynes de la Cruz is *gachupina* and will get her foundation. There's nothing for us to do but retreat and leave it to her and those who follow her.'[60]

Contemporaries commented on the regrettable distinction between women of different 'nations', thus indirectly confirming that Ana de San Miguel's bitter insight into her Spanish-born fellow nuns was widely shared. Such a distinction was in stark contrast to the spirit and unity of the religious community, and therefore had to be banned, both inside the convent and outside it. As Juan Bautista Méndez argued, in his history of the foundation of the Discalced in Mexico,

> I would like to see the insults and discord between those of one nation and the other banished from [the realm of the] Religious Order where no notice should be taken if one is *criollo* or *gachupín*.... Arguing about the Indies and Spain, setting one country above the other, is to fulfill to the letter what the mystical doctor of the church St Teresa says: that it's like arguing over whether one land or another is better for building with bricks or with tiles. Let's try and forget countries—I speak to every monk and nun [...]. Let's

stop deceiving ourselves and acknowledge that the best thing is to seek to walk in perfection towards our true nation which is heaven.[61]

But in spite of the friars' determination to invoke equal treatment for all, in the name of God and of building a 'true nation', social discriminations were deeply rooted. *Criollas* were dismissed as lazy and 'spoilt chocolate-guzzlers'. They were the living proof of the belief that the climate had a negative influence on the inhabitants of the Indies, who were over-inclined towards pleasures. These pleasures included chocolate-drinking, a popular habit amongst the female elite, as well as smoking tobacco, which some nuns took up enthusiastically. The nuns of N. Señora de las Nieves, for instance, used to smoke tobacco, only giving up during days of fasting. One eighteenth-century chronicle describes one of these nun's weaknesses as follows: 'in all the bread and water fasts and others she kept she abstained from taking tobacco, keeping the box of powder in the cell from the night before the fast until the day after, at which point she would send for it while drinking her chocolate.'[62]

A second form of racial discrimination concerned the other groups who lived within the monastic community: mixed-race women or *mestizas* (women of Spanish and Indian origins), the Indians, the blacks, the mulattos (women of Spanish and African origins). Within the convent *mestizas* were often only accepted as servant nuns, a role they were condemned to for life. The convent rules established a clear division of roles and functions between choir nuns and servant nuns. Irremediably these rules bound the latter to the heaviest manual work, which the more fortunate choir sisters were not expected to perform. As servant nuns, *mestizas* could not hold high offices or take part in the government of the community, were not able to vote in convent elections, and were often required to tend and nurse their ill sisters, without such care being provided for them on an equal basis. Indian women, on the other hand, were usually not allowed to take the black veil of choir nuns and also entered as servant nuns; blacks and mulattos were found in great numbers amongst the convent slaves.[63]

In the heterogeneous society of the colonies the relations amongst different ethnic groups were difficult to manage, in particular within the circumscribed world of the convent. Some convents were created to host specific groups. Such was the case of Santa Clara in Lima, founded in 1558, which only accepted *mestizas*, with the purpose of preserving their honour and instructing them in the principles of the Christian faith.[64] Similarly, the Corpus Domini convent in Mexico City became the first institution to call noble Indian women to be officially part of the Catholic Church. Sponsored by the viceroy Marques de Valero, Corpus Domini was created in 1724, and remained reserved for Indian 'princesses'. The inclusive logic underpinning this new convent, providing Indian women with some opportunities for social integration, could not mask the fundamentally elitist nature of the convent.[65]

From within their convents, nuns played their part in the development of the new society, with its religious and cultural practices, hierarchical relationships, and ethnic differences. Not surprisingly, they came to embody the ultimate purpose of the Spanish providential mission in America.[66] As symbols of virginal purity nuns epitomized the pride and grandeur of the colonial enterprise, and their presence was welcomed with great celebrations. In *Parayso Occidental*, an apologetic chronicle of the Catholic missions in America, and the religious orders' contribution to it, the author argued that the city of Mexico deserved to be honoured and compared to heaven, because of the devotion of its citizens as well as the celestial purity of his nuns:

[Mexico] has become the head and metropolis of America not so much because of the wonderful pleasantness of her location or for the incomparable beauty of her spacious streets, or the opulence and courage of her ancient Kings, ... or the gifts which heaven has benignly distributed to her sons but thanks to this and innumerable other Temples with which her expansive area is adorned and could thus easily be mistaken for the empyrean heaven, both because of the sacrifice and tribute owing to God which are sent continually to Him ... and because they [the temples] are inhabited by those who live in celestial purity [the nuns].[67]

Conclusion: Missions and the Cloister

Around the year 1620, the Spanish mystic María de Jesús de Agreda began to experience the most extraordinary godly gifts. She claimed to have miraculously travelled across the Atlantic into colonial America in order to preach the Gospel to the Indians, with the intention of making good Christians out of them. Her travels had happened through bilocation, allowing her to visit America without ever leaving her Spanish convent. Furthermore, she was less than modest in her claim to have made not one but a number of visits to various tribes in New Mexico. All this conformed to the will of God. Even for a mystic, María's American adventures appeared particularly daring. Nuns from her convent, however, attested that she was subjected to many supernatural experiences, and that they had seen her, for instance, levitating in the air while praying. Moreover, friars from her order confirmed her words. Indeed, María's story was not entirely the product of her mystic creativity. The Franciscan Alonso de Benavides, a missionary in Mexico, actively contributed to it. In 1629, he heard of some Indian tribes who had seen an apparition of a lady in a blue cloak. Having previously come across the news of this Spanish nun from Agreda, and her mystic trips to America, Benavides identified her as the lady in blue the Indians had seen—blue being the colour of the religious habit of María.[68] He did not attribute the Indians' vision to the more likely possibility that what they had seen could be a female figure similar to the Virgin Mary in her blue mantle, that they had probably seen in the many pictorial images that the missionaries carried around in their visits to the various tribes. Determined to meet her he left for Spain.[69] There, he was able to get the information he wanted, although initially she was rather reluctant to speak. Most importantly, he was able to give her some information which helped her to make sense of her trips. In particular he was able to tell her that the Indians had seen her, thus confirming her claims. From their first encounter on they began to construct the narrative of her miraculous travels. Surely, he thought that María and her experience amongst the Indians might boost the image and success of the Franciscan mission in America and maybe procure future support for it. His letter to the friars in Mexico, in which he reported on this encounter with her, was written in 1631, and gave the case notoriety. Benavides died a few years later on his way to Goa. The notoriety brought by his letter left María in some trouble, though only temporarily. She was examined by the Inquisition, but no accusation was ultimately made against her. Later, she would have become a personal confidante of King Philip IV, with whom she entertained a close epistolary relation, giving him spiritual advices.

María's fascinating story is interesting for a variety of reasons. The making of her visions and travels surely can be interpreted in many ways. The control exerted by men on female mysticism and on cloistered nuns, the opportunities spirituality offered to them, and the construction of femininine and masculine roles in the missionary enterprise reveal puzzling aspects of the participation of nuns in the colonization of the New World.

SEVEN

Open Communities for Women

Active Apostolate

As we have seen, the contemplative model of religious life—according to which women prayed and performed their spiritual duties withdrawn from the world—was enthusiastically promoted by the Church and exported to the colonies. However it was not the only model available to female religious. From the late Middle Ages onwards women practised a range of different forms of religious life, including the more flexible option of joining a community but taking simple vows only rather than the solemn vows taken by nuns. These simple vows were reversible and allowed women to maintain their secular status in the world. Although they often joined a religious order, dressed and prayed like nuns, and embraced chastity and poverty, these women practised a socially oriented form of commitment, fostering an active spirituality in direct contact with the world, rather than pure contemplation. They served God by praying as well as performing charitable service for the benefit of the most vulnerable members of society.[1] Because of this they were not bound by strict cloister rules. We find many groups of such women all over Europe, known as Tertiaries or *pinzochere* in Italy, beguines in Northern Europe, and *beatas* in the Iberian peninsula.[2]

The progressive attempt of the Catholic Church to strengthen enclosure—which was radicalized in the mid-sixteenth century by the universal legislation of Trent—challenged these forms of active commitment.[3]

Trent, however, did not result in a total transformation of all female religious into cloistered nuns. Active female communities and religious women working outside the walls persisted well after Trent. In late sixteenth-century Seville, for instance, some pious *beatas* were still living uncloistered and were active in the community. They rescued young women from the street, and gave them shelter, help, and advice. They also worked in the Royal Prison as carers and healers. Here they provided physical as well as spiritual care for its female inmates, telling them about exemplary lives of saints, and receiving monetary compensation for their services. *Beatas* embodied examples of perfection for women prisoners to follow, infusing them with religious fervour and encouraging them to enter asylums for contrite women. They offered support to a sector of the growing 'marginalized' female population of the city.[4]

Not only did active female communities survive at the time of the full fledging of the Catholic reformation, but brand new active orders and religious organizations were founded as well. There are examples of such active communities in Italy, the Low Countries, and above all in seventeenth-century France, where they flourished alongside the expansion of old, contemplative ones, such as the Carmelites.[5] These active communities promoted a model of piety based on chastity, penitence, and caring for others: the poor, the outcasts, and the dying.

By engaging in social work and education, the women who joined these active orders fulfilled social roles outside the cloister that Trent had reserved to married women only.[6] Indeed, in the wake of Trent, Catholic reformers recognized the importance of education, and of learning the principles and obligations of the Catholic faith. They saw the potential for women to contribute, and encouraged their involvement in teaching Christian lessons in the schools of their neighbourhood, offering help to the poor and the needy, and joining female congregations. But in addressing women-married women as well as widows-they did not include nuns. In his sermon on marriage, written toward the end of the sixteenth century, the Bolognese archbishop, Gabriele Paleotti, encouraged wealthy women to express their piety according to the devotional patterns established by the Catholic Church, and to 'commit to spiritual causes as attending the school of Christian

Doctrine to teach the little girls.... visit the sick and poor women of the parish...join a charitable congregation for women'.[7] According to Paleotti, charity was the preserve of laywomen, not nuns whose social role was to contemplate God in seclusion, rather than actively engaging in activities outside the cloister.

But although the active orders through which religious women took part in charity, departed from the Tridentine directives, one undeniable fact remained: the women who worked in these organizations filled a gap responding to specific social needs, and performed much-needed functions that ultimately explain their development. Indeed, the development of active communities, which we are about to observe, should be understood in the light of the broader social context and political climate of the sixteenth and seventeenth centuries. The French case is emblematic. Of the forty-eight new religious houses founded in Paris in the first half of the seventeenth century, only a small portion of them were active communities bound to simple vows and not subject to enclosure, a condition which allowed their members to perform services outside the house.[8] By the mid-seventeenth century, however, the number of such active and open organizations had increased, while the enthusiasm for the contemplative and enclosed model of religious life was beginning to fade. This rapid growth was likely caused, amongst other things, by the economic instability and social disruption which followed the Thirty Years War, bringing widespread misery and ever-increasing numbers of urban poor. In these conditions, the need to address social issues such as poor relief became pressing. Growing concern about these issues led benefactors to divert their efforts away from convents towards the support of more socially oriented religious communities.[9]

In France, the success of the active orders was reflected in the support they received, first of all from part of the Church establishment such as priests, sympathetic bishops, and—not least—the Jesuits, and secondly from the wealthy aristocracy who provided the funds. The funding they received was probably considered too much and from the 1690s the Crown sought to limit the wealth channelled into such organizations by aristocratic families, and in particular by widows making bequests and donations in their favour.[10] This support allowed these new organizations to establish a lasting presence, becoming active in hospitals, orphanages, and in the wider community, where they offered a variety of caring services. They became an 'integral part of modern France'.[11]

If we move away from France into the rest of Europe, we see however that the history of the new female religious organizations which emerged in the sixteenth and seventeenth centuries, is a history of their growing success as well as, in some cases, of their failure.[12] Indeed, their development was not always smooth. Some groups prospered, others faced hostile pressure and were obliged to redefine their original goals, or were ultimately dismantled. How did this happen? We can address these issues by looking at four different religious groups: the Ursulines, the English Ladies, the Visitandines, and the Sisters of Charity. These four groups shared common characteristics: the charismatic personality of their founders, their social concern to serve the community, and the invaluable support of influential patrons and skilful networking.[13] Whether or not they were successful, the women joining these newly formed groups stood at the forefront of the spiritual movements for Catholic reform and social change. More important still, their activities would leave their mark on the modern age.

Daughters of Saint Ursula

According to the legend, Ursula was a princess and early Christian from Britain, who consecrated her life to virginity. Wanted as a wife by a pagan prince, but determined neither to marry nor expose her country to the risk of his revenge should she decline, she found help in divine intervention. She had a vision: if she asked her perspective husband for three years' delay and a promise to convert to Christianity, she would win God's protection. Obediently, she put into practice God's will and then set off on a pilgrimage to Rome. She travelled in the company of no less than eleven thousand virgins. This massive army of women sailed the Rhine until Cologne, where Ursula received encouragement from an angel to proceed in her mission, and finally arrived in Rome. It was during the way back, in Cologne, that Ursula and her companions were assaulted by the Huns besieging the city, and found death in martyrdom. Their sacrifice had an immediate effect and brought the liberation of the city from the Huns.[14]

The cult of Saint Ursula was very strong in late medieval and Renaissance Europe. Great universities such as Paris, Coimbra, and Vienna adopted her as their patroness, and emperors and kings sponsored a growing number of confraternities named after her. Her legend was wonderfully visualized by Renaissance artists, such as Hans Memling, Vittore Carpaccio, and others, who narrated its crucial scenes: the virgins sailing on the boat, their arrival in Rome and meeting with the Pope and high dignitaries of the Church, and finally their martyrdom in Cologne, where they perished at the hands of soldiers armed with arches and arrows. The example of Ursula had a particular resonance for religious women. Not only had she refused marriage for the love of God, a recurring motive of saints' lives, but also her life reflected the theme of women's involvement in religious reform and missionary activity in the world, symbolized by the virgins' collective pilgrimage.[15]

Analogous virginal and missionary motives inspired the lives of the women who joined the early company of Saint Ursula, as we can see from the life of the founder of the company, the Italian Angela da Merici (1470/4–1540), and the subsequent development of the Ursulines, the very first female teaching order within the Catholic world.

Born to a humble family from Desenzano, a village in Venetian territory, not far from Lake Garda, Angela lost her parents at an early age, went to live with relatives, and eventually joined a group of Franciscan Tertiaries. Religious fervour, infused with mysticism and visions which she had from a very young age, drove her towards religious and charitable activities. In these years, in which the Franco-Italian wars had caused social distress and epidemics, Angela worked, together with a group of women many of whom were widows, in the female ward of the hospital for syphilis sufferers in Brescia. Her work extended to families of the ill women, which she and her companions frequently visited in the particular hope of supporting the young and most vulnerable female members, who needed protection. The idea of forming a female religious group grew out of her dedication to care work, in which she was joined by her female acquaintances, some of whom were her spiritual daughters. In 1532, one of these spiritual daughters established a house for orphans and repentant girls, the so-called Pietà orphanage,[16] providing them with refuge and catechism. In the following years, Angela—with a few other women— conceived and set up the informal first nucleus of the Ursulines, and then founded a formal group which took the name of the Company of Saint Ursula. In 1536 the company received episcopal approval. Angela was named superior and remained so for the rest of her life.[17] Her inspiration apparently came from a vision she had one day while praying, when

> she saw the sky open. A marvellous procession of angels and young virgins came forth, two by two, the angels playing various kinds of instruments and the virgins singing. . . . Once the procession had passed, there came a virgin, her sister [. . .] recently gone to paradise, who . . . predicted that God intended to make use of her, and that she would found a company of virgins that would grow, and similar things.[18]

Angela founded a company of virgins who renounced marriage in favour of dedication to God, and devoted their energies to the care and education of other women. Two aspects of her company reflect the innovative spirit of Angela's project. First of all, it challenged the traditional pattern of choice between either marriage or cloister, providing the women who joined with an alternative model of celibate life outside the ecclesiastical institutions. Ursulines lived in their family homes rather than a residential institution. They took private vows only, as opposed to the solemn vows taken by nuns. Ursulines had to be free from any commitments—or 'promises'—with religious communities, or indeed prospective husbands. The rule dictated by Angela was extremely clear in this respect:

> First of all, it must be remembered that anyone who wishes to enter or be admitted to this company must be a virgin. . . . Second, she must enter the company freely and happily, with the firm intention of serving God in this way of life. Third, she must not have made any promise to any monastery or, still less, to any man.[19]

Neither wives nor nuns, the Ursulines chose a third option that enabled them to remain in society. They looked after the children of the neighbourhood, they taught catechism in the parish church, and helped the poor and the ill in the hospitals, or orphans living in institutions. Aware of the vulnerability of single women living outside a religious community, Angela expected the Ursulines to watch out for each other. Those members who were orphans, or who were deprived of their families' support, could rely on the company to find them accommodation and pay for it. Similarly, those who were old, and in need of care, were to be looked after by the virgins of the company.[20] In Angela's mind therefore, the company acted as a substitute for, and at the same time an alternative to, the family.

Secondly, Angela recruited women from humble backgrounds usually excluded from convents, which as we have seen were mostly home to women from wealthy elite backgrounds. The Ursulines often came from families of artisans and humble professions, and moreover their educational activity was aimed at other young women of modest status, whose families could not afford to pay a convent dowry. Pious aristocratic widows from Brescian circles acted as governors of the company, acting as guides and protectors of its pupils.

Angela was not thinking—and perhaps never did think—of founding a religious institution, such as a congregation or a religious order. Although she borrowed motives from monastic rules and lifestyle, and wanted the Ursulines to opt for a life of prayer and penitence, as they would have done in a convent, she recognized that their social role was to be different from that of nuns. From the very beginning of her project, she sought a form of religious life which was alternative to the monastic model.

For instance, the ceremony for the entrance to the company was celebrated in a way quite similar to monastic profession, including singing the hymn 'Veni Sponsa Christi' usually sung for professing nuns, but this ceremony did not imply being bound to solemn vows as nuns were. Her rule recommended that the Ursulines should avoid too many direct contacts with male and female outsiders, and mundane occasions such as balls, marriages, and tournaments. But the Ursulines had to be able to properly interact with the world, whilst protecting their integrity and chastity. Ursulines could not withdraw from the community—like nuns—because of the care duties they performed. Significantly, not one chapter of her rule mentioned withdrawal, while the fourth chapter significantly discussed how to deal with the world. Angela rejected the monastic habit—one of the most visible signs of monastic state. Her rules prescribed that the Ursulines should dress appropriately, without wearing a recognizable habit. The girls who entered the company used their own clothing until it wore out. Their virginal clothing should be 'decorous and simple' and evoke the external mortification and chastity chosen by each woman joining the company. Ursulines were therefore to cover their bodies with clothing and headscarves and 'each should dress with closed bust and cover herself with veils ... made of linen or cotton, not too thin, and not transparent; ... the dress should be made of cloth or serge, and coloured black, or dark red, or russet or dark brown'.[21] Finally, the rule subjected the Ursulines to the authority of God, the Holy Church, the bishop, the spiritual director, and the male and female governors of the company. But it also placed them under the authority of their 'father and mother', as well as the laws and statutes of the state in which they lived. The family and the state therefore shadowed the Church in the guardianship of the women of Saint Ursula's, an unprecedented condition that signalled their radical difference from nuns.[22]

This model of religious life proved to be very popular and the Ursulines bloomed in a number of Catholic countries. In the late sixteenth century houses of Ursulines opened in Italy, France, Switzerland, and Germany, where rules for the Ursulines were rapidly printed. Their educational and charitable work was highly regarded and they gained the protection of the ecclesiastical elite. Judging from the number of new foundations and the status of their patrons, their success was spectacular. In Milan Carlo Borromeo—one of the great protagonists of the Catholic reformation—invited the Ursulines to come to the city to found a company on the model of the one founded in Brescia. Deeply impressed by these women's commitment to education, he saw them as important agents for the Catholic cause, and in particular the campaign of confessionalization launched by the Roman Church. Borromeo became head of the Ursulines and institutionalized their charitable and teaching functions by making these activities—that they already performed in parish churches and hospitals—a prescriptive role for members.[23]

It was more or less when the Ursulines began to attract this kind of attention that the first problems arose. Catholic ideals regarding nuns wanted them safely locked in their convents. Of course, the non-cloistered and socially oriented lifestyle of the Ursulines became an issue, and the company encountered more and more opposition from those who wanted to turn it into a proper religious order, kept behind convent walls. To a certain extent, this evolution towards a monastic model was also supported by the first Ursulines themselves. Many Ursulines who did not have a family, lived in houses with other members of the company. These small groups of women all belonging to the same religious company, inevitably bore some resemblance to the forms of micro-community life found in the traditional monastic setting. It was probably unavoidable therefore that the Ursulines experienced a process of progressive institutionalization. The move in this direction started soon after Angela's death. Virgins living in their houses did not fit in with the idea of social discipline sponsored by the Church and the Catholic states, where the rigid definition of gender roles relegated women either to marriage or the cloister. Families as well as the company's superiors were divided on this matter, and some of them were rather sceptical of the ideas of an illiterate woman like Angela. The first attempts to imposed enclosure on the company brought the expulsion of one of its first chancellors, Gabriele Cozzano—the author of a short *Answer* in which he spoke against cloistering.[24] What followed was the introduction—by the aristocrat general superior of the company, Lucrezia Lodrone—of a specific symbol to identify the Ursulines as a group: a black leather belt. Far from being only an exterior sign of interior chastity, this belt became the first step towards a formalized uniform along the lines of the monastic habit, which would eventually mark the transformation of the company into something more similar to a proper religious order.

Although some Ursulines retained—at least for the early decades after their foundation—their original form of life, and remained based in houses, living with their families, communities of Ursulines rapidly grew, sometimes adopting a variety of forms of collective life. Certain communities, for instance, willingly opted to become enclosed convents, bound to the three solemn vows. Others became congregations and were not bound to enclosure, although they eventually came under heavy pressure to adopt it.[25] In some case, the Ursulines accepted enclosure and all the other features pertaining to cloistered nuns, including grilles, turnstiles, walls, and doors with triple keys kept only by the superior and the two doorkeepers. But these barriers did not constitute real obstacles, and the Ursulines would continue to leave the convent for educational as well as devotional activities. In some communities—such as for instance in the Italian Ursuline houses founded in Parma and Piacenza—they were allowed to go out to hear mass and confess to their local parish church, or to the Jesuit church. Although not completely enclosed, they were praised and seen as vital to the work of the Church, not least by Jesuit priests who maintained that they offered examples of piety for other women to follow. One Jesuit priest, in 1623, defended the form of open enclosure adopted by the Ursulines in Parma, defining them as 'lights in the world'.[26]

The Ursulines made a particularly strong impact in France. Here their success much relied on the ascetic emphasis that marked the early years of the French Catholic revival. French Catholics, still recovering from the Wars of Religion, saw the Ursulines as a useful instrument to fight the spread of Protestantism, charging them with the task of educating young girls in the Catholic faith.[27] More than in Italy, however, the growth of the French Ursulines was characterized by a rapid shift which turned them into an enclosed order, under the aegis of Augustinian monastic rule. Although enclosed, they retained their educational vocation, obtaining permission to organize schools from within their enclosed communities.[28] By 1630 the country counted at least thirty-six teaching convents where the Ursulines instructed girls in the precepts of the Catholic credo. In these cloistered communities, the residential buildings had to serve both a monastic and an educational function, and were planned accordingly. The first Paris foundation, completed in 1610, was organized in a similar way to other cloistered convents. The nuns avoided contact with outsiders by placing grilles, curtains, and barriers in strategic places such as the parlour and the public church. The more residential and domestic spaces used and occupied by the nuns were separated from the student teaching areas. Students were confined to classrooms and dormitories, while nuns would retire into their protected inner cloister once their teaching duties were over. Teaching rooms were cloistered too in order to prevent the nuns coming into contact with any layperson but their pupils. In this way, education was provided within the enclosed space.[29]

Like other new female religious houses which flourished in France in the early seventeenth century, the Ursulines had the support of elite benefactors.[30] The Paris foundations took shape in close contact with contemplative Carmelite and Capuchin houses. The nuns enjoyed the protection of royal patrons who visited them often, and of many noble women who would accompany the future nuns on the day of the clothing ceremony, thus publicly acknowledging their patronage over the entire religious community. The establishment of the French Ursulines thus reflected the expectations of the wealthy and noble patrons who sponsored them, and who saw their activities as a way of improving their spiritual and social prestige.

Enclosure was no hindrance to their success, and by the end of the eighteenth century there were three hundred Ursuline houses in France. Nor was France an exception, as the order became omnipresent in the Low Countries, Germany, the Balkans, and across the Atlantic in New France and Brazil. The Ursulines became a durable feature of Western society, strictly associated to a female educational role.[31] In the end, Angela's idea of a company combining contemplation with social apostolate did not take complete hold in the way she had planned, but her creation survived. Yet the Ursulines' success lay in the leading role they were able to command in the crucial area of female education, at a time when the demand for female literacy had acquired greater significance.

'Jesuitesses', or the English Ladies

The winds of change sweeping from Italy through France and Europe also reached England where some women proved extremely receptive to the socially oriented model of collective religious life promoted by the Ursulines. Nearly a century after the birth of the Company of Saint Ursula, an English Catholic woman conceived a project which would become a thorn in the side of the Roman authorities for some time.

Mary Ward (1585–1645) was born into a family of the Catholic gentry from Yorkshire. Those were not easy times for Catholics in England. Henry VIII's Act of Supremacy (1534) separated the English Church from the Roman Catholic Church and marked the beginning of the English Reformation. Catholics who refused to embrace the new faith fled to the Continent to escape persecution, and wealthy families sent their children abroad in order to be educated in the Catholic credo, initially in the hope that it would be restored back home. The suppression of monasteries and convents also made it impossible for men and women to profess their Catholic faith by participating in community and monastic life, as some of their ancestors had done before them. Many left and joined religious communities in Flanders and France.[32] Mary Ward was one of them. Her first experience of convent life was in a community of Poor Clares in Saint-Omer, in Flanders—at that time part of the Spanish empire and called the Spanish Netherlands. In 1606, she entered as a lay sister, but left unimpressed after a couple of years, and soon embarked on a rather different adventure. With the support of a handful of other women she founded a school for Englishwomen, where they taught Catholic girls. This house opened in 1609 when Mary was 24 years old, and was the first in a long series of colleges for Catholic girls, which grew up all over Europe, under the name of the Institute of the Blessed Virgin Mary, or the English Ladies as it was commonly known.

Mary's plan was to found a religious order in which women would live together and devote their lives to God and the perfection of their own soul, as well as actively engaging in rescuing girls from Protestantism, by keeping them safely under the protection of the Roman Church though education and care. Like Angela Merici she too had a revelation regarding her plans. But while the Italian had a vision in which she saw her future spiritual sisters, Mary received, through divine intervention, more precise instructions concerning the rule her order should take. As she would recall, the extraordinary revelation took place while she was recovering from an illness

being alone, in some extraordinary repose of mind, I heard distinctly, not by the sound of voice, but intellectually understood, these words, '*Take the same* [rule] *of the Society*' [of Jesus]. So [I] understood as that we were to take the same both in matter and manner . . . These few words gave so great measure of light . . . , comfort, and strength, and change to the whole soul, as that [it was] impossible for me to doubt but that they came from Him, whose words are works.[33]

In a series of seventeenth-century paintings depicting the life of Mary Ward, we find the conceptualization of this vision associated with the origin of the English Ladies. Jesus appears to Mary and her companions, while they stand in a large room. As they stare at him, he points at a man standing beside them in the room, though slightly distant, inviting them to look at him. This man represents Ignatius de Loyola, the founder of the Jesuits.[34] As the scene suggests, God invites the women to look at Ignatius as an example to follow.

The Jesuit rule Mary intended to adopt was a problematic issue from the very beginning, for several reasons. The first was that the Jesuits, founded a few decades earlier, did not contemplate female membership. Their founder had obtained papal dispensation from the perpetual spiritual guidance of female religious communities. The rule of Ignatius was designed for men, and perceived as such, and Jesuits educated young men in rather exclusive colleges, preparing them for intellectual and political life, and for the missionary call to faraway places. Secondly, the difficulty of a female community adopting the Jesuits' rule lay in its non-cloistered condition, which—as in the case of the Ursulines—at that time was incompatible with the directives of the Church regarding religious women.

However, the non-cloistered condition was essential to Mary's project. As she wanted to teach girls how to be good Catholics, and not necessarily how to become nuns, she thought that this task was better performed in an open community than in a closed one. This is why although several existing rules were proposed to Mary and her first followers, they rejected them all: 'Diverse Institutes were drawn by several persons, some of which were approved and greatly commented by the last Bishop Blasius of St Omer, our great friend, and some other divines: these were offered us, there was no remedy, but refuse them, which caused infinite troubles.'[35] Mary saw the active missionary role of the Jesuits in the world as a model for her own mission, which would guarantee the fulfilment of her ambitions: 'In order to attain our end,' she wrote in a memorial to Pope Paul V in 1616, it is moreover necessary, for various and urgent important causes and for the needs of our Institute in these times,...that this our least and most unworthy Congregation should be allowed...to begin and exercise its duties without enclosure, as otherwise our Institute and method of life can neither be observed nor practiced with any hope of obtaining the fruit that we propose to draw from it.[36]

Many of Mary's contemporaries, including those who praised her work, knew only too well that this was a great impediment: 'Mrs Ward and her companions wishing to render to their country certain services which are more or less incompatible with the usual routine and strict enclosure of monastic rule, had resolved to devote themselves wholly to the teaching and education of girls whom their parents might send them from England.'[37] Furthermore, many also thought that the English Ladies were proposing an outrageous model of religious life, and that they had not the faintest intention of accepting the conventions and limits imposed on the presence of women in the Church. Not only were the English Ladies convinced of becoming nuns without being enclosed, they also wanted to take—on top of the three solemn vows—a fourth vow of obedience to the Pope, and serve as missionaries around the world. One of Mary's compatriots in Rome noted:

the Jesuitrices have exhibited ridiculous petitions which have scandalized the Court. They would take a fourth vow to be sent amongst the Turks and infidels to gain souls. Briefly, clausure [i.e. enclosure] they must embrace... else dissolved. But of clausure they will not hear,...and this they have not been ashamed of to answer to these great prelates, who think of them accordingly....I marvel what madmen advised them hither with these fooleries.[38]

In short, in the eyes of many contemporaries Mary and her sisters offered an appalling example.

It would be too reductive to think that the English Ladies' aspirations began and ended with the desire to escape enclosure, and that this explained their fascination for Ignatius de Loyola and his company. They had a much broader purpose: that of finding a way for women to participate in active spiritual renewal and fight for the Catholic faith through becoming an established religious order, like the Jesuits. In those very years, the development and power of the Jesuits was growing and Ignatius was made a saint by the Roman Church. Mary followed his spiritual teaching and found inspiration in the example of Ignatius, who had advised her to 'always walk in the presence of . . . God'.[39] She and her companions were committed to a rather strict spiritual discipline involving mental prayer, daily examinations of conscience, self-abnegation, and humility, and they regarded Ignatius as their protector and guide, whose 'counsels' had to be carefully heeded. Not surprisingly, given the Catholic emphasis on the cult for relics and holy corpses, the English Ladies jealously preserved some of Ignatius's bodily remains, which they used as powerful thaumaturgical tools. On more then one occasion, the saint's relics had saved the sisters from death. In 1614, Mary herself was amongst those to benefit from the saint's grace, being rescued when about to exhale her last breath:

> The same thing happened in the same house to another consecrated virgin of good family, Mary Ward, in the month of September. She was also reduced to death's door by a lingering consumption, and had piously received all last sacraments. At last they placed the reliquary containing the same particle of the cassock of the Blessed Ignatius upon her neck, and after a few days she had so far recovered her health beyond all expectation, as to be able to walk about the house and beyond it.

The determination of the English Ladies to engage in missionary work in the world was not the only matter to puzzle their contemporaries. They caused concern also because they were difficult to classify, and blurred the boundaries between the religious and secular spheres. They were religious women whose non-cloistered life made it unthinkable to associate them with nuns—as nuns should be enclosed. Yet their overtly devotional and religious attitude, as well as their external appearance, distinguished them from laywomen, and inevitably drew comparisons with nuns. Even their clothing declared their ambiguous and hybrid nature, and made it impossible for others to grasp their identity: they dressed in long black silk cloaks which covered their bodies entirely from head to toe, and a white linen band which covered their forehead, giving them an unmistakable resemblance to the traditional convent outfit of nuns.[40] The English Ladies were therefore a confusing mix: their presence outside the walls showed that they were not nuns, but their habits distinguished them from ordinary laywomen, revealing their deeply religious identity and group membership. This ambiguity, however, was precisely what Mary had in mind; by her own admission she wanted the English Ladies to pursue a 'mixed kind of life' that on the one hand consisted of contemplation and prayers, and on the other hand revolved around their social apostolate and missionary spirit, in the form of their active participation in female education.[41]

Public reaction to Mary's plans took a variety of forms. Rome— including Pope Urban VIII, who personally admired Mary and offered her some protection from her opponents—initially appreciated the educational potential of her project. The Jesuits themselves had mixed feelings and, in particular in the beginning, praised the work of Mary and her companions, although some of their adversaries soon became the enemies of the English Ladies too. But fortune was not on Mary's side, or perhaps her ideas were too radical for her times, and her treasured goal of wining the official approval of the Pope for her institute was not achieved, at least not in her lifetime. In 1631 Urban VIII abolished the English Ladies and ordered the dissolution of all communities founded in their name. Despite Urban's personal sympathy for Mary, he ultimately condemned her and her sisters as women who 'under the pretext of promoting the salvation of souls, [...] carried out many works that were least suitable to their sex, its mental weakness as well as womanly modesty, but [were unsuitable] in particular to the honour of virgins'.[42]

Abolition brought much pain and suffering to the English Ladies, and to Mary herself above all. Just one month after the formal papal condemnation of the institute, Mary was arrested, declared 'a heretic, a schismatic, an obstinate rebel against Holy Church...to be...thrown...into the jaws of death'.[43] At the time she was living in Munich, where with the enthusiastic support of the Wittelsbach ruling dynasty she had opened an institute with forty members. She was imprisoned, though not in an ordinary prison but in the convent of the Poor Clares of Munich, where she was detained for over two months under the strict surveillance of the cloistered nuns.[44] On her release she left Munich for Rome, where she continued her pedagogical activity in secular form, before returning to England where she died in 1645. The abolition of the English Ladies had dire consequences for her companions too. They were forced to abandon their communities, sometimes leaving them homeless and in poverty, forced to beg, enter another religious house, or return to their families.[45]

Mary's death failed to put an end to the English Ladies who survived but as secular institutions bound by simple vows. The idea of forming a religious order was abandoned. Although Mary had always feared this, she preferred secularization to enclosure. In her opinion, the recent example of the Ursulines, who had become a contemplative enclosed order, was to be avoided at all costs: the English Ladies should try to 'find another way to serve Him [God] than by becoming Ursulines'.[46] The English Ladies continued to pursue their teaching activity, and opened houses in Flanders, Germany, Italy, Austria, and later in Hungary, Ireland, and even Canada, where they provided their educational services to the community of Irish migrant women. In the eighteenth century, the Roman Church finally approved the Institute of English Ladies in its secular form— a decision that was probably motivated by the increasing popularity of the Institute, as well as the demand for institutions devoted to female education. In 1750 there were fourteen institutes and a hundred years later, in 1850, almost double that number.[47]

This rapid growth and geographical reach attested to the success and popularity of Mary's followers, which attracted increasing numbers of pupils. For instance, in Germany, in the second half of the seventeenth century, the Paradeiserhaus of Munich—which survived the 1631 abolition order, and maintained a constant presence through the following centuries—had forty teachers and twelve novices, serving three hundred pupils in the day school, and fifty boarders. Through a careful search for donations and dowries, the house accumulated enough wealth to pay for further foundations in Bavaria. The success of this school was due to at least two factors. First of all, the English Ladies offered a varied curriculum of study, which prioritized religious, moral, and intellectual education but valued practical skills too. Pupils were instructed in religious topics as well as reading, writing, and arithmetic.[48] The girls who reached the most advanced stages were able to study Latin, and also English, French, and Italian. Practical education included various domestic skills such as sewing, needlework, and cooking, good manners, and social skills, such as how to hold conversations, dance, and play musical instruments. Secondly, success also reflected the policy of welcoming women from an ever-expanding portion of society, including women in need, the poor, and orphans. The college hosted boarders from wealthy families, and organized a free day school for poorer girls. Nevertheless, the English Ladies remained less associated with the education of poor girls than with the education of wealthy young women. Future wives and mothers of prominent families came to them to master the female virtues— religious values, good manners, refined conversation, and house-making skills—according to the standards of their social class. Furthermore, inside the college, there existed rigid class distinctions: aristocratic girls dined at a separate table and were allowed chambermaids as servants in the school. Similar forms of discrimination were present in the curricula, which placed more emphasis on manual skills for the poorer girls in the day school. This stratification resembled the typical convent distinction between choir nuns and servant nuns. In the end, the institutes of the English Ladies prepared their charges for marriage and family life, following class divisions and reproducing the most stereotypical gender values. This was not what Mary had originally in mind. But one important feature of her initial ideal did remain: the chance for the unmarried women who joined the group and worked in it to pursue a teaching career living in an institution which was neither a convent nor a family. This opportunity represented a rather innovative path for women to follow, and eventually led to the female teaching profession of modern times.[49]

In the end Rome never granted Mary Ward the title of foundress of the institute, and she continued to be regarded as a 'rebel to the Holy Church', a stain that would only be removed as late as the twentieth century, when her name was finally rehabilitated.[50] The only 'Jesuit woman in the history of the [Catholic] Church' was not Mary—as she had so desired—but instead the Infanta Juana, the daughter of Emperor Charles V, and an early follower of Ignatius de Loyola.[51] Still, Mary's life and work reflect her early, almost heroic, strong-mindedness, which was echoed in her spiritual resolutions, written after her institute had taken first shape: 'I will endeavour that no sensible motions, nor occurrent accidents, change easily my inward composition nor external carriage, because freedom of mind and calmness of passions are so necessary both for my own profit in spirit and proceedings with others.'[52]

From Devout Women to Cloistered Nuns: The Visitandines

In the period in which Mary Ward and her English Ladies were fighting for acceptance, other women were experiencing similar troubles. We now move to France to follow these vicissitudes, intertwined with the spiritual life and activities of a rather exclusive portion of French society.

The origins of the Visitandines or, to use their full title, the order of the Visitation of Holy Mary, owed everything to the determination of one of the most famous pairs of 'friends' in the history of Western spirituality: François de Sales and Jeanne de Chantal. Spiritual friendships, as Jody Bilinkoff has recently shown, have been a constant feature of Catholic spirituality.[53] Priests served as confessors and spiritual advisers of pious and penitent women, both lay and religious, who laid bare their interior lives, mystic experiences, and visions, but also gave counsel in return, establishing with their confessors relationships of mutual spiritual exchange. These friendships were consummated within the written intimacy of epistolary communication as well as in periodical and personal encounters. In the case of Jeanne de Chantal and François de Sales, their relationship of spiritual and moral support nourished their devotion as well as creating the perfect environment to conceive a practical plan: the foundation of a new female religious order.

As the story goes, the two met in Dijon, and immediately recognized each other as ideal spiritual partners.[54] François de Sales, a member of an aristocratic family solidly connected to the French ecclesiastical elite, was the bishop of Geneva. Jeanne Françoise Fremyot de Chantal was the daughter of a high magistrate from Dijon, the mother of four children, and a widow at 29. After the death of her husband baron de Chantal in a hunting accident, her life came to a halt. Pain and mourning awakened in her the desire to withdraw and seek peace in spiritual life, rather than remarriage. She threw herself into deep religious introspection and charitable works. Her first meeting with François, on the occasion of his preaching in Dijon's ducal Sainte Chapelle, marked the start of their spiritual friendship and epistolary exchange. Theirs, as François contended, was the most perfect bond:

> I have never intended for there to be any connection between us that carries any obligation except that of love and true Christian friendship, whose binding force Saint Paul calls 'the bond of perfection'. And truly it is just that, for it is indissoluble and will not slacken. All other bonds are temporary, even that of vows of obedience which are broken by death and other occurrences.[55]

It was during one of their personal encounters that Jeanne secretly swore perpetual obedience to François, took the simple vows before him, and adopted him as her spiritual director. On assuming her spiritual direction he gave her some rules: chastity, charity, and interior freedom, including freedom from family ties. In deferring to his authority Jeanne was in turn aware of her own opportunity to enjoy a margin of autonomy in her actions, and indeed claimed that this was an opportunity available to all women: 'we show these confessors due respect, yet we explain to them very frankly our liberty of action'.[56] Women could use their relationship with their confessors in order to succeed in their spiritual as well as more practical and social goals. Jeanne had immense influence over François, although formally he was the spiritual director.[57] François's skilful support and intercession were crucial to her reaching her goal.

On the basis of this relationship François and Jeanne developed a shared project to found a new religious order in Annecy, which Jeanne would join. Jeanne was deeply attracted by religious life; François, for his part, saw the religious state as a state of 'perfection', particularly if this religious state was bound by vows. But Jeanne was a widow with children to care for, so the move to a religious house was replete with complications and in stark conflict to her family life. Nevertheless, she went ahead. As her biographers reported—reproducing a model narrated in the lives of many saintly women—her departure met with the opposition of her youngest child who vehemently disagreed with her decision. He tried to stop her physically from leaving him, obstructing her with his body, and imploring her not to go. In her writings, she described her move, projecting an image of herself as a woman in anguish, racked with guilt, and aware of the anger she had caused her relatives and children:

> I seemed to see my father and father-in-law, weighted down with the sorrows of age, crying out to God for Vengeance against me. On the other side my children were doing the same. It was as if a multitude of voices were speaking in my mind, accusing me of having committed a great fault. And what made me more miserable was that it was a reproach drawn from the Scriptures—that in the Church of God I would be taken for an infidel, since I had abandoned my children.[58]

Leaving aside her anxieties, in 1610 Jeanne travelled to Annecy. On Trinity Sunday, with three other women, she met François in the house of the local bishop, and received from him a copy of the rules and constitutions he had written for them. The report of the women's entrance into the convent, tells that after paying ritual homage by visiting all the churches in the city, they were escorted—though the night—to their new home on the shore of Lake Annecy, a house called 'la Galerie'. The town bore enthusiastic witness. When the ceremony concluded and everyone else had departed, the women knelt to pray and Jeanne assured them that 'This is the place of our delight and rest'.[59] Jeanne then became the superior and mistress of novices of the small community, and quickly engaged in an almost frantic organization of the house in the face of its rapid growth in vocations and the responsibilities of governing a community: 'I am overwhelmed with things to do', she wrote to François, 'but I do believe that everything will be all right. I have a great desire to fulfil God's will'.[60]

The Visitation was the result of a joint enterprise between Jeanne and François. They took decisions on important matters regarding the institute together, and the constitutions of the order were also a joint effort, written by François after discussions with Jeanne in Lyons. After his death in 1623, Jeanne drafted the final version of the text, and sent it to different houses for feedback. In 1624, all the mother superiors of Annecy approved it, and the constitutions were printed in 1628, revised in 1635, and a final edition produced in 1637.[61]

The two founders had conceived the Visitation as an open community of religious women, bound by simple vows, who ardently longed for spiritual experience, and who needed—at the same time—a refuge and a home to spend the rest of their lives. In particular, the community gave a home to women vulnerable because of their age, or physical condition. Widows, for example, could find that the open community of a Visitation convent was a protective residential environment which allowed them to continue to perform some of their family duties.[62] The same applied to those laywomen who retreated to the Visitation for brief periods of time. Moreover, the Visitandines did not follow a particularly harsh discipline of material deprivation, and were discouraged from enduring bodily mortifications in favour of simplicity and gentleness.[63] This made them particularly attractive to their members, who were often in a fragile condition.

By living uncloistered the Visitandines could immerse themselves in contemplative life while performing charitable activities at the same time. Jeanne maintained that 'A sick woman should be as precious as a pile of gold; it is a great treasure in the house of God to have people to provide holy charity and souls that take their suffering patiently. I have little or no repugnance in serving my neighbour in her most disgusting illnesses.'[64] Care work was not so demanding, however, and mainly consisted in monthly visits to poor and ill people which the Visitandines would take in turns.

But Annecy, and the new foundation, was only the beginning of a journey.[65] The Visitandines—like the Ursulines and the English Ladies—were placed under great pressure to become an enclosed order, with solemn vows, under the rule of Saint Augustine. This transformation into a fully enclosed contemplative order was a departure from the original project, and would have prevented the Visitandines from continuing their caring work outside. In spite of Jeanne's initial wish to remain faithful to their original project, and François's disappointment at the transformation, they did not resist for long. In 1618 the bishop of Lyons, Denis-Simon de Marquemont, obtained from Pope Paul V a declaration that changed the Visitation institute into a contemplative religion order, with perpetual vows. Such a transformation was perceived by the Visitandines as a very radical step which they sought to avert with great care and tact. Jeanne's letters to other sisters in France, written before they became enclosed, reveal that she exhorted them to be obedient and measure their words, in particular when speaking about enclosure: 'My very dear child', she wrote in 1616 to Mère Marie-Jacqueline Favre, in Lyons, 'when the good Archbishop [Marquemont] talks to you of enclosure or some other essential point of our rules, do not reply except with modesty and equanimity, with a little joyful laughter... as we are daughters of obedience, loving perfectly our institute, and this response should be all.'[66]

There are a number of reasons why enclosure was pushed through. Female contemplative orders bound to enclosure were flourishing in France in those years of Catholic revival, as attested by the boom of new Carmelite foundations. The Visitandines would therefore be adopting a common arrangement for the time. Furthermore, François—truly committed in his spiritual care of the community—did not regard the charitable impetus, which forcibly excluded enclosure, as a primary end of the Visitation, but rather as 'an exercise that conformed to the existing devotion of those who began the congregation and to the practices of the place where they were'.[67] Moreover, like Jeanne, he wished to contribute to spiritual renewal, and in his 'ladder' of perfection he valued solemnly vowed religious men and women more highly than those of only simple vows.[68] Solemn vows entailed enclosure. Lastly, François was a high prelate with an ecclesiastical career to nurture, and probably did not want to oppose and challenge the normative framework established for women by the Catholic Church. In short, the founders of the Visitandines probably did not regard the transformation—though important—as something which was going to be detrimental in spiritual, social, and political terms.

The enclosed Visitandines enjoyed remarkable success. Jeanne engaged in various activities surrounding the foundation of new communities, and died in 1641—nineteen years after François—leaving behind eighty-seven Visitation houses, a significant number for an order only 31 years old. She was buried in Annecy, in the church of the Visitation convent, besides François. Like him, she passed away in odour of sanctity.

The Visitandines' success was clearly related to the need for an honourable placement for the women of the urban elites, amongst which the Visitandines recruited the vast majority of their members. Together with the hunger for spiritual renewal, class was a crucial factor that explained the rapid expansion of Visitandines, a continual growth lasting until the French Revolution. They offered a convent, where noble and wealthy women lived in adoration of God, surrounded by peers and companions from similar rank, and where they found a substitute family to care for them. The Visitandines remained, however, a primarily French phenomenon, and—with the exception of a few foundations in Italy, Spain, Germany, and the north-east of Europe—lacked the international appeal of the Ursulines and English Ladies.[69]

Serving the Poor: The Daughters of Charity

If the Ursulines, the English Ladies, and the Visitandines had to come to terms—however willingly or reluctantly—with enclosure and the parameters of the Catholic reformation, another female group which took shape at the beginning of the seventeenth century managed to secure a long-term future whilst working around these restrictions. In order to follow the vicissitudes of this latter group, we turn our attention to another well-known French couple who, at the very time François de Sales and Jeanne de Chantal were founding their order, conceived a project that was structurally connected to theirs, but quite different in nature. Indeed, the formidable bond and charismatic friendship between Vincent de Paul and Louise de Marillac gave birth to a group of religious women that was to remain active in the world, notwithstanding the rigid framework that wanted them behind the walls.

Far from the exclusive and aristocratic circle of the baronesse de Chantal, we now move to a different social setting, in which an idea of active female apostolate was conceived that needed women who were

ready to immerse themselves in care of the poor, the ill, and the desti-
tute.[70]

Vincent de Paul (1581–1660) was a priest of rural origins, whose
ecclesiastical career had given him, and his family, the expected return:
connections with the court, the higher spheres of the capital's elite, and
circles of Catholic devotees, including such distinguished people as the
powerful Cardinal Pierre de Bérulle—the active supporter of Carmelite
foundations in France—as well as François de Sales and Jeanne de Chantal
themselves. Unlike some of his exclusive acquaintances, he was attracted
not by contemplative life, but by active engagement and missionary
activity for the benefit of the poor. This preference for ministering and
providing spiritual and physical care to the socially rejected was, for
Vincent de Paul, his calling and in his mind it was almost elevated to
the status of theory: 'It is written to search the kingdom of God . . . Search,
search, means care, means action.'[71] His ideal was to link contemplative
and active life by searching for God in missionary work: 'This care work
must be sanctified, searching God within it and finding him, rather than
seeing the work done.'[72]

Vincent de Paul was a man of action. He set up a number of
parish-based lay charities in Paris and the provinces to help the sick
and the poor in their homes, and in 1625 founded the Congregation of
the Mission. Then he began to develop the idea of a formalized all-female
group, under the protection and sponsorship of the high and middle
aristocracy. What he had seen in his work clearly suggested that the
time had come for this kind of all-female initiative: women far outnum-
bered men in their membership of charities. His encounter with Louise de
Marillac (1591–1660) provided him with the opportunity to realize his
plan. Louise de Marillac was the illegitimate daughter of Louis de Marillac,
a nobleman from an influential family in the court of Louis XIII. Educated
in a convent in Poissy, near Paris, Louise apparently manifested the desire
to remain for the rest of her life in permanent monastic retreat as a nun,
but was instead married to the personal secretary of the regent Marie de'
Medici, with whom she had one child. After the death of her husband
she engaged in pious and charitable works. Her encounter with Vincent de
Paul, who became her spiritual director, and her freedom from wifely

duties, allowed her to completely embrace a life in the service of the poor, working closely with de Paul and visiting charities in and outside Paris. In 1633, along with four other young women placed under her supervision, she founded the company of the Daughters of Charity, from her Parisian house.[73] Like her spiritual father, she too conceived of charity as a way of finding God, as well as a way of following the divine example: 'Souls who look for God find Him everywhere, but especially in the poor'. Her motto, 'The charity of Christ needs us', clearly expressed the purpose of her company, and this idea shone through in the first statement of the rules of the company—drafted by Louise in 1634 and then rewritten by Vincent de Paul in 1654 and 1655. These rules made missionary service compulsory, constituting the primary aim of the Daughters' lives:

> The principal end for which God has called and established the Daughters of Charity is to honour our Lord Jesus Christ as the source and model of all charity, serving him corporally and spiritually in the person of the poor, whether sick, children, prisoners, or others who through embarrassment, dare not make known their wants.[74]

The community of women brought together in de Marillac's house—for a while the first home of the Daughters of Charity—saw 'much coming and going'.[75] The company brought together young women from rural areas and the provinces who, under Louise's direction, received spiritual education as well as professional training with a view to becoming servants of the poor. The Daughters therefore were to live and work in direct contact with the community,

> their monastery being generally no other than the abode of the sick: their cell, a hired room; their chapel, the parish church; their cloister, the public street or the wards of hospitals; their enclosure, obedience; their grate, the fear of God; and their veil, holy modesty.[76]

The Daughters were required to lead a virtuous life 'as if they were professed in a religious order...and to give as much edification as nuns in the seclusion of their monasteries'.[77] They were to follow a monastic model—the basic prescriptions of which were poverty, chastity, and obedience—and their discipline was based on their own self-control. Bound to public charity, the sisters took private vows which they renewed annually, as opposed to the solemn and perpetual vows of the nuns. Furthermore, instead of religious habits they wore the humble clothes of rural women, who had been the first members of the company. Their main sign of distinction was a head-cover, completely hiding their hair, to which was later added a white rectangular piece of fabric. Louise de Marillac had a slightly different outfit from her companions, always covering her head with the black veil used by noble and respectable widows.

Although the Daughters were not classified as nuns, they were devout 'sisters' engaged in religious life. This association made them a quasi-secular group, and they had no aspiration to become a religious order. Marillac and de Paul had witnessed the vicissitudes of the Visitandines and their transformation into a cloistered comm-unity. They knew well that this was a thorny issue. Furthermore, Vincent de Paul had been personally involved in the spiritual care of these women, having succeeded François de Sales as superior of their house in Paris. But unlike the Visitandines, the Daughters managed to avoid enclosure, maintaining simple vows, and operating in the secular world. simple vows which operated in the secular world. They received their first official approval in 1645, from the archbishop of Paris, and the final approval of the Pope in 1668.[78] The official approval of the congregation allowed them to develop a strong sense of collective self within the group. This sense of collective identity was essential to fulfilling their charitable task, which for them was a constitu-tional part of their spiritual vocation. As Vincent de Paul claimed, 'Works pertaining to the service of God come to an end ordinarily with those who begin them, if there is no spiritual bond among the persons involved in them'.[79]

One important feature of the Daughters of Charity which distin-guished them from the Visitandines and the English Ladies, is that they recruited and trained women from the lower and middle social classes, and incorporated them into an almost professional career in the care of the vulnerable. In this they were similar to the first Italian Ursulines and followers of Angela Merici. The Daughters came mainly from humble, peasant families, though in the course of the years the company welcomed increasing numbers of women from artisan and professional families.[80]

To a certain extent, the two founders' interest in recruiting non-elite women may have been linked to the fact that they had themselves seen something of the precarious conditions of human life. Vincent de Paul, a priest from humble origins, undoubtedly had some direct knowledge of the living conditions of the lower classes. Louise de Marillac, an illegitimate and a widow, knew of the greater vulnerability of women without men. They were both sympathetic to the cause of lower-class women, whom they saw as the perfect force to recruit, and to whom they offered the opportunity to work for the community, alleviating the sufferings of other humans and ultimately gaining salvation for themselves.[81]

But the attempt to engage women from non-elite families was above all due to the fact that these women were prepared to do the type of heavy work that women from wealthy background had often proved unable and even unwilling to do. Caring for the poor and performing manual work such as washing and medicating diseased bodies, may have been a desirable option for particularly devout women willing to engage in penitence. But it contrasted starkly with the lifestyle and occupations of most high-ranked women, some of whom found these works repugnant.[82] The elite women in other charitable confraternities set up by Vincent de Paul had not proved so diligent in providing their services to the poor. These women, for instance the Ladies of Charity, tended to hand over their caring duties to their female domestic servants, who performed them out of obligation in the service of their mistress, rather than as a choice of care and piety.[83] The lower ranking Daughters of Charity were therefore a valuable labour force, providing a range of services that other women from wealthier origins were not prepared to deliver. Such an activity had its downside too, as they were valued mainly for their efforts at manual work. Although some of them may have had some basic education and literacy on entering, their daily employment excluded learning because this would distract them from their care work, with the exception of a few sisters who were given special and limited dispensation: 'Those who have permission to learn to write may devote to this purpose half an hour, at most, of the afternoon, at the time the superioress or Sister Servant shall think proper, and when they are entirely free from all necessary occupation.'[84]

The Daughters of Charity undoubtedly promoted a broad and inclusive model of charity. As was stated in their rules, they served the poor and the sick, as well as children and prisoners. This typology of the vulnerable perfectly represents the evolution of the group's activities in the years following its foundation. The Daughters opened primary schools for poor girls, entered hospital service in the Hôtel-Dieu and other hospitals, hosted abandoned children and orphans, and visited prisoners in galleys. They provided care to war refugees, served on the battlefields nursing wounded soldiers, ran soup kitchens and distributed clothing, alleviating the horror and devastation of French civil war of the 1650s. The sisters' services were invaluable: in Paris their motherhouse assisted as many as 1,300 poor. They fed 8,000 people a day in the parish of Saint-Paul alone.[85] The wide geographical reach of the sisters of Charity also attests to their durable success. At the time of Vincent and Louise's death in 1660 the group had fifty-one houses. By the eve of the French Revolution it had 439 houses, twenty of them in Poland and one in Spain. Abolished by the revolutionary authorities the company was re-established by Napoleon, and in 1805 it had 254 houses. In the following decades the daughters expanded all around the world, to Italy, Turkey, Algeria, Mexico, China, Lebanon, Madagascar, and the United States of America. According to one of the most recent surveys, in 1975 the Daughters had 3,718 houses and 39,856 members, making it one of the biggest female communities within the Catholic Church.[86]

This outcome poses interesting questions. Why did the enterprise launched by Vincent de Paul and Louise de Marillac encounter such lasting success, while other similar initiatives failed? Why were they the first women to survive without enclosure? These questions remain open, but one fact remains: the Daughters of Charity succeeded in promoting a type of charity rooted in the secular world, which was based on single women engaged in public service. This open formula of spiritual as well as social female commitment would remain in place for centuries, continuing into the modern age.[87] Other organizations were inspired by the Daughters and developed both in side and outside France. The Sisters of St Joseph, who were founded in the Massif Central in the 1640s, are a good example. They spread from France over the Atlantic and into America, where they ran orphanages, schools, and childcare services, educating generations of migrant men and women in the Catholic faith.[88] They remained active into the contemporary period. Like the Sisters of St Joseph, female secular congregations are now the vast majority, but it was the Daughters of Charity, centuries before, who first trod this path.

EPILOGUE

Can we provide a bridge from early modern convent life to the present? What happened to convent life in the meantime? In the eighteenth century convent numbers fell, although they seem to have risen again in the following century. The very appropriateness of life as a nun became a subject for discussion. In France convents and nuns became a topic debated vociferously in religious pamphlets, legal literature, and novels, in which nuns were portrayed in a variety of ways: as victims, religious fanatics, holy figures, and even as debauched women.[1] The French public's interest in nuns mainly concerned issues of political authority, and Church–State relations, economic matters and the problem of convent poverty, and, more generally, the purpose of convents. This was a time of monastic suppression which continued with the French Revolution's abolition of monastic vows.[2] Surprisingly, although a large number of studies have been concerned with the question of why women entered convents, very little has been written about why they left them, what happened to them after leaving and how they experienced the dissolution of their communities. In Italy, for instance, Napoleonic suppression brought great distress amongst religious women. Those who were allowed to stay in their community until it died out lamented that this situation would condemn them to a lifetime of poverty. Those who were supposed to return to their families did so, although some of them refused to leave, and appealed to the local authorities for permission to stay. Leaving the convent might be particularly difficult for nuns of poor social origin, for whom the convent—notwithstanding its restrictiveness and the voluntary shunning of material goods—had brought some degree of economic stability.[3] Even more important, nuns were not always welcomed back into their families. Exactly who was supposed to look after these single women, some of whom had passed marriageable age and were old or maybe ill? And could the mentality of eighteenth-century men and women cope with such a hybrid female identity as the ex-nun? These are questions that make us ponder not only the many meanings and implications of convent life, but also the rigidity of gender roles, and constraints placed on individuals by the society around them.

If we take a glance at the history of nuns after the eighteenth century, it is clear that active forms of female religious and social commitment grew in popularity, in parallel with the growth of secular communities such as those discussed in the last chapter of this book. Initiatives led by nuns in the nineteenth century involved participating in missionary work and taking on care and welfare activities, opening orphanages and nurseries. The nuns initiatives also included the organization of boarding houses for unmarried female labourers. In these residential establishments women lived within the secure surroundings of a quasi-monastic life, where their religious observance as well as their morality and sexuality were controlled. Prayers and psalms, holy communion, and catechism were part of their everyday life. In Italy, such expressions of 'corporate paternalism', whose counterparts existed in France, Spain, and in America, were supported by families, entrepreneurs, and parish priests, who had a keen appreciation of both the moral and the economic benefits of such arrangements.[4] Is this the idea of female religious life with which we are more familiar today? Maybe so, in which case it is quite different, on the whole, from the atmosphere of early modern convents that we have observed through the pages of this book.

The variety of forms of female religious life in the modern period suggests the intriguing possibility of developing other ways of thinking about this history, and looking at nuns outside the convent framework. The Catalan writer Antonio Rabinad recently published a novel—*Libertarias*—about a nun's experiences in the Spanish civil war.[5] Drawing on a variety of historical sources to compose his work of fiction, he made extensive use of the research of the historian Mary Nash in her poignant book *Mujeres libres* on women in the Spanish civil war.[6] Rabinad tells the captivating story of Juana, a young nun who at the outbreak of the civil war joined a group of women anarchists, together with other female workers and prostitutes, and took part in that euphoric chapter in Spanish history: the brief but heady anarchist revolution in Catalonia which flourished as state power collapsed under the pressure of the conflict. We do not know if nuns like Juana really existed, but this entirely plausible character invites us to speculate about the many sides of nuns' history that are still to be uncovered.

NOTES

INTRODUCTION

1. See the surveys of Amy E. Leonard, 'Female Religious Orders', in R. Po-chia Hsia (ed.), *A Companion to the Reformation World* (Oxford: Blackwell, 2004), 237–54; Olwen Hufton, *Whatever Happened to the History of the Nun?* (Royal Holloway University of London, Hayes Robinson Lecture Series 3, 2000). See also Jo Ann K. McNamara, *Sisters in Arms: Catholic Nuns through Two Millennia* (Cambridge, Mass.: Harvard University Press, 1996); Patricia Ranft, *Women and the Religious Life in Premodern Europe* (London: Palgrave Macmillan, 1996).

2. The bibliography on the topic is quite vast. See amongst others Gianna Pomata and Gabriella Zarri (eds.), *I monasteri femminili come centri di cultura fra Rinascimento e Barocco* (Rome: Edizioni di Storia e Letteratura, 2005); E. Ann Matter and John Coakley (eds.), *Creative Women in Medieval and Early Modern Italy* (Philadelphia: University of Pennsylvania Press, 1994); Craig. A. Monson (ed.), *The Crannied Wall: Women, Religion, and the Arts in Early Modern Europe* (Ann Arbor: University of Michigan Press, 1992); Electa Arenal and Stacey Schlau (eds.), *Untold Sisters: Hispanics Nuns in their Own Works* (Albuquerque, N. Mex.: University of New Mexico Press, 1989); Octavio Paz, *Sor Juana, or the Traps of Faith* (Cambridge Mass.: Belknap, 1988).

3. Natalie Zemon Davis, *Women on the Margins: Three Seventeenth-Century Lives* (Cambridge, Mass. and London: Harvard University Press, 1995). Luis Martín, *Daughters of the Conquistadores: Women of the Viceroyalty of Peru* (Albuquerque, N. Mex.: University of New Mexico Press, 1983).

4. Amy Leonard, *Nails in the Wall: Catholic Nuns in Reformation Germany* (Chicago: University of Chicago Press, 2005); Ulrike Strasser, *State of Virginity: Gender, Religion, and Politics in an Early Modern Catholic State* (Ann Arbor: University of Michigan Press, 2004); Claire Walker, *Gender and Politics in Early Modern Europe: English Convents in France and the Low Countries* (London: Palgrave

Macmillan, 2003); Craig E. Harline, *The Burden of Sister Margaret: Inside a Seventeenth-Century Convent* (New Haven: Yale University Press, 2000); Merry Wiesner-Hanks, *Convents Confront the Reformation: Catholic and Protestant Nuns in Germany* (Milwaukee: Marquette University Press, 1996).

5. Judith C. Brown, *Immodest Acts: The Life of a Lesbian Nun in Renaissance Italy* (New York: Oxford University Press, 1986).

6. Kathryn Burns, *Colonial Habits: Convents and the Spiritual Economy of Cuzco, Peru* (Durham, NC: Duke University Press, 1999): Elizabeth A. Lehfeldt, *Religious Women in Golden Age Spain: The Permeable Cloister* (Aldershot, Hants. and Burlington, Vt.: Ashgate, 2005), ch. 2.

7. R. Po-Chia Hsia, *The World of Catholic Renewal, 1540–1770* (Cambridge: Cambridge University Press, 2000); John W. O'Malley, *Trent and All That: Renaming Catholicism in the Early Modern Era* (Cambridge, Mass.: Harvard University Press, 2000).

8. Caroline Bynum Walker, *Holy Feast and Holy Fast: The Religious Significance of Food to Medieval Women* (Berkeley and Los Angeles: University of California Press, 1987), chs. 6–7.

9. Gabriella Zarri, 'Monasteri femminili e città', in ead., *Recinti: Donne, clausura e matrimonio nella prima metà moderna* (Bologna: Il Mulino, 2000), 43–143, at 53–6; Samuel K. Cohn Jr., 'Nuns and Dowry Funds: Women's Choice in the Renaissance', in id., *Women in the Streets: Essays on Sex and Power in Renaissance Italy* (Baltimore: The Johns Hopkins University Press, 1996), 76–97; Judith C. Brown, 'Monache a Firenze all'inizio dell'età moderna: Un'analisi demografica', *Quaderni storici*, 85 (1994), 117–52; Richard C. Trexler, 'Le Célibat à la fin du Moyen Âge: Les Religieuses de Florence', *Annales ESC* 27 (1972), 1329–50; R. Burr Lichtfield, 'Demographic Characteristics of Florentine Patrician Families, Sixteenth to Nineteenth Centuries', *Journal of Economic History*, 29 (1969), 191–205.

10. Dante E. Zanetti, 'La demografia del patriziato milanese nei secoli XVII, XVIII, XIX', *Annales cisalpines d'histoire sociale*, 2nd ser. 2 (1972).

11. Olwen Hufton, *The Prospect before Her: A History of Women in Western Europe 1500–1800* (London: HarperCollins, 1995), 64–5.

12. Francesca Medioli, *L' 'Inferno monacale' di Arcangela Tarabotti* (Turin: Rosemberg & Sellier, 1990).

13. Leonard, *Nails in the Wall*; Wiesner-Hanks, *Convents Confront the Reformation*.

14. Gabi Jancke-Leutzsch, 'Clara Staiger, la priora', in Giulia Calvi (ed.), *Barocco al femminile* (Rome: Laterza, 1992), 97–126.

15. Linda Lierheimer, 'Redefining Convent Space: Ideals of Female Community among Seventeenth-Century Ursuline Nuns', *Proceedings of the Western Society for French History*, 24 (1997), 211–20.

16. Daniela Solfaroli Camillocci, 'Ginevra, la Riforma e suor Jeanne de Jussie: La Petite Chronique di una clarissa intorno alla metà del cinquecento', in Pomata and Zarri (eds.), *I monasteri femminili*, 275–96.

17. Claire Walker, 'Combining Martha and Mary: Gender and Work in Seventeenth-Century English Cloisters', *Sixteenth Century Journal*, 30/2 (1999), 397–418.

18. Robert L. Kendrick, *Celestial Sirens: Nuns and their Music in Early Modern Milan* (Oxford: Oxford University Press, 1996); Craig A. Monson, *Disembodied Voices: Music and Culture in an Early Modern Italian Convent* (Berkeley and Los Angeles: University of California Press, 1995).

19. Elissa B. Weaver, *Convent Theatre in Early Modern Italy: Spiritual Fun and Learning for Women* (Cambridge: Cambridge University Press, 2002).

20. Jonathan Nelson (ed.), *Suor Plautilla Nelli (1523–1588): The First Woman Painter in Florence* (Florence: Cadmo, 2000).

21. P. Renée Baernstein, 'Vita pubblica, vita familiare e memoria storica nel monastero di San Paolo a Milano', in Pomata and Zarri (eds.), *I monasteri femminili*, 297–311; ead., *A Convent Tale: A Century of Sisterhood in Spanish Milan* (New York and London, Routledge, 2002); Sara Cabibbo and Marilena Modica, *La Santa dei Tomasi: Storia di suor Maria crocefissa (1645–1699)* (Turin: Einaudi, 1989).

22. Susan E. Dinan, *Women and Poor Relief in Seventeenth-Century France: The Early History of the Daughters of Charity* (Aldershot, Hants. and Burlington, Vt.: Ashgate, 2006); Hufton, *Prospect*, 381–91.

CHAPTER 1

1. See my 'Monastic Poverty and Material Culture in Early Modern Italian Convents', *Historical Journal*, 47/1 (2004), 1–20.

2. Arenal and Schlau (eds.), *Untold Sisters*, 402.

3. Ibid., 358.

4. Ranft, *Women and the Religious Life*, 1–14; 'Monachesimo', in *Dizionario degi Istituti di Perfezione* (Rome: Edizioni Paoline, 1978), coll. 1706–7.

5. André Vauchez, *The Laity in the Middle Ages: Religious Beliefs and Devotional Practices* (Notre Dame: University of Notre Dame Press, 1993); Herbert Grundmann, *Religious Movements in the Middle Ages: The Historical Links between Heresy, the Mendicant Orders, and the Women's Religious Movement in the Twelfth and Thirteenth Century, with the Historical Foundations of German Mysticism* (Notre Dame, Ind.: University of Notre Dame Press, 1995).

6. Jeffrey F. Hamburger, 'Art, Enclosure and the Cura Monialium: Prolegomena in the Guise of a Post-Script', *Gesta*, 31/2 (1992), 111.

7. On the contradiction between the desire for spiritual life and the rejection of family duties, in the lives of medieval holy women, see Walker Bynum, *Holy Feast and Holy Fast*, 219–44; Rudolph M. Bell, *Holy Anorexia* (Chicago: University of Chicago Press, 1985).

8. *Il Libro della Beata Angela da Foligno*, ed. Sergio Andreoli (Milan: San Paolo, 1996), 42–3.

9. Bynum, *Holy Feast*, 219; Bynum discussed these women widely on pp. 189–244.

10. Anna Scattigno, 'Jeanne de Chantal, la fondatrice', in Giulia Calvi (ed.), *Barocco al femminile* (Rome and Bari: Laterza, 1992), 175: Francis's letter to Jeanne,

August 1606; 'Giovanna Francesca di Chantal', in *Bibliotheca Sanctorum*, 6 (Rome: Città Nuova Editrice, 1996), col. 583; Wendy M. Wright, 'The Visitation of Holy Mary: The First Years (1610–1618)', in Richard L. DeMolen (ed.), *Religious Orders of the Catholic Reformation* (New York: Fordham University Press, 1994), 228.

11. Fernanda Sorbelli Bonfà, *Camilla Gonzaga Faá: Storia documentata* (Bologna: Zanichelli, 1918), 132–3; Valeria Finucci, 'Camilla Faá Gonzaga: The Italian Memorialist', in Katharina M. Wilson and Frank J. Warnke (eds.), *Women Writers of the Seventeenth Century* (Athens, Ga.: University of Georgia Press, 1989), 121–37.

12. Cabibbo and Modica, *La Santa dei Tomasi*, 49–81.

13. Grethe Jacobsen, 'Nordic Women and the Reformation', in Sherrin Marshall (ed.), *Women in Reformation and Counter-Reformation Europe: Public and Private Worlds* (Bloomington: Indiana University Press, 1989), 49–50.

14. Isabel dos Guimarães Sá, 'Between Spiritual and Material Culture: Male and Female Objects at the Portuguese Court, 1469–1580', in Sandra Cavallo and Silvia Evangelish (eds.), *Domestic and Institutional Interiors in Early Modern Europe* (Aldershot, Hants. and Burlington Vt.: Ashgate, forthcoming); Kate Lowe, 'Raina D. Leonor of Portugal's Patronage in Renaissance Florence and Cultural Exchange', in ead. (ed.), *Cultural Links between Portugal and Italy in the Renaissance* (Oxford: Oxford University Press, 2000), 225–48.

15. Magdalena S. Sánchez, *The Empress, the Queen, and the Nun: Women and Power at the Court of Philip III of Spain* (Baltimore: The Johns Hopkins University Press, 1998); Burns, *Colonial Habits*, 119–20 and 233.

16. Penelope D. Johnson, *Equal in Monastic Profession: Religious Women in Medieval France* (Chicago: University of Chicago Press, 1991), 13–34; Marilyn Oliva, *The Convent and the Community in Late Medieval England: Female Monasteries in the Diocese of Norwich, 1350–1540* (Woodbridge: The Boydell Press, 1998), 52–61; Lehfeldt, *Religious Women in Golden Age Spain*, 15–46; Leonard, *Nails in the Wall*, 20–21.

17. Mariló Vigil, *La vida de las mujeres en los siglos XVI y XVII* (Madrid: Siglo Veintiuno, 1986), 209.

18. Brown, 'Monache a Firenze', 117–52; Trexler, 'Le Célibate à la fin du Moyen Âge', 1329–38; Lichtfield Burr, 'Demographic Characteristics', 191–205; Jutta G. Sperling, *Convents and the Body Politic in Late Renaissance Venice* (Chicago: University of Chicago Press, 1999).

19. Medioli, *L' 'Inferno monacale'*, 120.

20. Ibid., 112.

21. Vigil, *La vida*, 210.

22. Denis Diderot, *The Nun* (Oxford: Oxford University Press, 2005); Georges May, 'Le modèle inconnu de 'La Religieuse' de Diderot: Marguerite Delamarre', *Revue d'histoire litteraire de la France* (1951), 273–87.

23. Francesca Medioli, 'Monacazioni forzate: donne ribelli al proprio destino', *Clio*, 3 (1994), 431–54.

24. Piet van Boxel, 'Dowry and the Conversion of the Jews in Sixteenth-Century Rome: Competition between the Church and the Jewish Community', in Trevor Dean and Kate J. P. Lowe (eds.), *Marriage in Italy, 1300–1650* (Cambridge: Cambridge University Press, 1998).

25. Concha Torres Sánchez, *La clausura imposible: conventualismo femenino y expansión contrar reformista* (Madrid: Asociación Cultural Almudayna, 2000), 149; *L'Art du* xvii*^me siècle dans les Carmels de France*, ed. Yves Rocher (Paris: Musée du Petit Palais, 1982), 101–6.

26. Silvia Evangelisti, 'Moral Virtues and Personal Goods: The Double Representation of Female Monastic Identity (Florence, 16th and 17th Centuries)', in Olwen Hufton (ed.), *Yearbook of the Department of History and Civilization: Women in Religious Life* (Florence: European University Institute, 1996), 39–40.

27. Sandra Cavallo, *Charity and Power in Early Modern Italy: Benefactors and their Motives in Turin, 1541–1789* (Cambridge: Cambridge University Press, 1995), 158–60; Sandra Cavallo and Lyndan Warner (eds.), *Widowhood in Medieval and Early Modern Europe* (Harlow: Longman, 1999).

28. Walker, 'Combining Martha and Mary', 397–418.

29. See my 'Monastic Poverty', 12.

30. Sherrill Cohen, *The Evolution of Women's Asylums since 1500: From Refuges for Ex-Prostitutes to Shelters for Battered Women* (Oxford: Oxford University Press, 1992), 13–21, and 127–41.

31. Ibid., 131.

32. Teresa of Avila, 'Costituzioni' chapter 'Sulla vita comunitaria', in *Regole per la vita conventuale* (Palermo: Sellerio, 1995), 39–42.

33. *Augustine of Hippo and his Monastic Rule*, ed. George Lawless (Oxford: Oxford University Press, 1987), 81.

34. Biblioteca Apostolica Vaticana (henceforth BAV), Vat. Lat. 11914, *Regulae et Constitutiones pro monasteriis ab ordinario episcopo compositae*, cc. 60^v–61^v, and 66^r. Archivio Segreto Vaticano (henceforth ASV), *Prattica del governo spirituale e temporale de Monasteri delle Monache secondo le regole et constitutioni de Santi Padri loro fondatori et del Sacro Conciliodi Trento e di Sommi Pontefici* [1604], cc. 119^r–120^v and 129^v.

35. BAV, *Regulae*, c. 33; ASV, *Prattica*, c. 132; Teresa of Avila, *Regole*, pp. 33–6.

36. See my 'Monastic Poverty', 4–7.

37. Gabriella Zarri, 'Monasteri feminili e città', 82–94.

38. Paolo Richiedei, *Regola data dal Padre S. Agostino alle monache* (Brescia: Domenico Grommi, 1687), test. 57, 1.

39. M. Barrio Gozalo, 'La población religiosa de la Corona de Castilla entre el barroco y la ilustración (1591–1768)', *Bollettino di demografia storica SIDES*, 22 (1995), 11–21; C. Buccianti, 'Monasteri femminili a Siena nel seicento: note di demografia storica', ibid. 23–42; E. Montagut Contreras, 'Servicio doméstico y educación en los conventos femeninos del antiguo régimen (siglo XVIII)', *Torre de los Lujanes*, 15 (1990), 156–66; Burns, *Colonial Habits*, 112–20; Ofelia Rey

Castelao and Raquel Iglesias Estepa, 'Domestic Service in Spain, 1750–1836: The Domestic Servants of the Clergy', in A. Fauve-Chamoux (ed.), *Domestic Service and the Formation of European Identity: Understanding the Globalization of Domestic Work, 16th–21st Centuries* (Berne and Berlin: Peter Lang, 2004), 127–40.

40. See my 'Ricche e povere: Classi di religiose nelle comunità monastiche femminili tra cinque e seicento', in Margareth Larzinger and Raffaella Sari (eds.), *Nubili e celibi tra scielta e costrizione (secoli XVI–XIX)* (forthcoming Udine: Forum, 2007).

41. Archivio di Stato di Firenze (henceforth ASF), *Corporazioni religiose soppresse dal governo francese* (henceforth *CRS*), 133, S. Giovannino, 60, cc. 122–6.

42. Paolo Richiedei, *Pratica di coscienza per tutte le religiose claustrali divisa in ventidue trattati* (Bologna, Longhi, 1710), 3, n. 48.

43. Teresa of Avila, *Regole*, 43.

44. ASV, *Prattica*, cc. 164.^{v}–200.^{r}.

45. *Classi di religiosi*, in *Dizionario*, ii (1975), coll. 1154–5.

46. Merry E. Wiesner, 'Nuns, Wives, and Mothers: Women and the Reformation in Germany', in *Women in Reformation*, p. 11.

47. Wiesner Hanks (ed.), *Convents Confront the Reformation*, 12–17. Merry E. Wiesner, 'Ideology Meets the Empire: Reformed Convents and the Reformation', in ead., *Gender, Church, and State in Early Modern Germany* (London and New York: Longman, 1988), 47–62; *Luther on Women: A Sourcebook*, ed. Susan Karant-Nunn and Merry E. Wiesner-Hanks (Cambridge: Cambridge University Press, 2003); Patricia Crawford, *Women and Religion in England 1500–1720* (London and New York: Routledge, 1993), 26–31 and 46; Jacobsen, 'Nordic Women', 47–51.

48. Crawford, *Women and Religion*, 28–9.

49. Jacobsen, 'Nordic Women', 56.

50. Leonard, *Nails in the Wall*, 64.

51. Gwendolyn Bryant, 'The Nuremberg Abbess: Caritas Pirkheimer', in Katharina M. Wilson (ed.), *Women Writers of the Renaissance and Reformation* (Athens, Ga.: University of Georgia Press, 1987), 287–303, esp. 297.

52. Wiesner, 'Ideology', 51–2; Olwen Hufton and Frank Tallett, 'Communities of Women, the Religious Life, and Public Service in Eighteenth-Century France', in Marylin J. Boxer and Jean H. Quataert (eds.), *Connecting Spheres: Women in the Western World, 1500 to the Present* (Oxford: Oxford University Press, 1987).

53. Crawford, *Women and Religion*, 84.

54. Wlesner Hanks (ed.), *Convents*, 17.

55. Ibid. 14; Crawford, *Women and Religion*, 26–31; Marie B. Rowlands, 'Recusant Women 1560–1640', in Mary Prior (ed.), *Women in English Society 1500–1800* (London: Routledge, 1985), 167.

56. Crawford, *Women and Religion*, 27–30.

57. Leonard, *Nails in the Wall*, 74.

58. Wiesner Hanks (ed.), *Convents*, 83.

59. Ibid. 87–9.

60. Ibid. 99.

61. Ibid. 17.
62. Monica Chojnacka and Merry E. Wiesner-Hanks (eds.), *Ages of Woman, Ages of Man: Sources in European Social History, 1400–1750* (London: Pearson Education, 2002), 243–4.

CHAPTER 2

1. Stendhal, *Croniques italiennes* (Paris: Flammarion, 1977), 100–1, translation mine.
2. Rule of Saint Benedict, chapter 66, quoted in Eileen Power, *Medieval English Nunneries c.1275 to 1535* (New York: Biblo and Tannen: 1922), 341.
3. Elizabeth Makowski, *Canon Law and Cloistered Women: Periculoso and its Commentators, 1298–1545* (Washington DC: Catholic University of America Press, 1997), 1–20; McNamara, *Sisters in Arms*, 472–81; Jane Tibbetts Schulenburg, 'Strict Active Enclosure and its Effects on the Female Monastic Experience (ca.500–1100)', in John A. Nichols and M. Thomas Shank (eds.), *Distant Echoes: Medieval Religious Women* (Kalamazoo, Mich.: Cistercian Publications, 1984), 51–86.
4. Quoted in Schulenburg, 'Strict Active Enclosure', 53.
5. Quoted ibid. 54.
6. Francesco Pellizzari, *Trattato delle principali obbligazioni delle monache* (Ferrara: Gioseppe Gironi, 1647), ch. 4: 'On the obligation of enclosure for nuns', pt. 1, answer 5.
7. Penelope Johnson, 'La Théorie de la clôture et l'activité réelle des moniales françaises du *xie* au *xiiie* siècle', in *Les Religieuses dans le cloître et dans le monde des origines à nos jours* (Saint-Étienne: Publication de l'Université de Saint-Étienne, 1994), 491–506.
8. Schulenburg, 'Strict Active Enclosure', 61–3.
9. Ibid. 63.
10. Ibid. 56–8.
11. Makowski, *Canon Law*, 135.
12. Pellizzari, *Trattato*, ch. 4, introd.
13. H. J. Schroeder (ed.), *Canons and Decrees of the Council of Trent* (St Louis, Mo. and London: Herder, 1960), ch. 5, pp. 220–1; Gabriella Zarri, 'Gender, Religious Institutions and Social Discipline: The Reform of the Regulars', in Judith C. Brown and Robert C. Davis (eds.), *Gender and Society in Renaissance Italy* (London and New York: Longman, 1998), 193–212.
14. See Ruth P. Liebowitz, 'Virgins in the Service of Christ: The Dispute over an Active Apostolate for Women during the Counter-Reformation', in Rosemary Ruether and Eleanor McLaughlin (eds.), *Women of Spirit: Female Leadership in the Jewish and Christian Traditions* (New York: Simon and Schuster, 1979), 132–51; Craig Harline, 'Actives and Contemplatives: The Female Religious of the Low Countries Before and after Trent', *Catholic Historical Review* 81/4 (1995), 541–67.

15. Zarri, 'Gender', 193–212.

16. Elizabeth A. Lehnfeldt, 'Discipline, Vocation, and Patronage: Spanish Religious Women in a Tridentine Microclimate', *Sixteenth Century Journal*, 30/4 (1999), 1009–30.

17. Sperling, *Convents and the Body Politic*, 115–169; Mary Laven, *Virgins of Venice: Enclosed Lives and Broken Vows in the Renaissance Convent* (London: Penguin, 2002), 79–98. See also my ' "We do not have it, and we do not want it": Women, Power, and Convent Reform in Florence', *Sixteenth Century Journal*, 34/3 (2003), 677–700. On Naples see Elisa Novi Chavarria, *Monache e gentildonne, un labile confine: Poteri politici e identità religiose nei monasteri napoletani, secoli XVI–XVII* (Milan: Franco Angeli, 2001).

18. Ulrike Strasser, 'Bones of Contention: Cloistered Nuns, Decorated Relics, and the Contest over Women's Place in the Public Sphere of Counter-Reformation Munich', *Archiv for Reformation History*, 90 (1999), 255–88, and ead., *State of Virginity*, 70–85.

19. Elizabeth Rapley, *The Dévotes: Women and the Church in Seventeenth-Century France* (London and Montreal: McGill-Queens's University Press, 1990).

20. Makowski, *Canon Law*, 129, n. 9; Francesca Medioli, 'An Unequal Law: the Enforcement of Clausura Before and After the Council of Trent,' in Christine Meek (ed.), *Women in Renaissance and Early Modern Europe* (Dublin: Four Courts Press, 2000), 136–52; Harline, 'Actives and Contemplatives', 555–63. On medieval lay nuns in the Low Countries see Walter Simons, *Cities of Ladies: Beguine Communities in the Medieval Low Countries, 1200–1565* (Philadelphia: University of Pennsylvania Press, 2001).

21. Hamburger, 'Art, Enclosure and the Cura Monialium', 111.

22. Bernardette Barrière, 'The Cistercian Convent of Coytoux in the Twelfth Century: Anxiety, Authority and Architecture in the Female Spiritual Life', *Gesta*, 31/2 (1992), 76–82, at 77–9.

23. Suzanne Fonay Wemple, S.'Salvatore/S.Giulia: A Case Study in the Endowement and Patronage of a Major Female Monastery in Northern Italy', in J. Kirshner and S. Fonay Wemple (eds.), *Women of the Medieval World* (Oxford: Oxford University Press, 1985), 85–102; G. Pasquali, 'S. Giulia di Brescia', in Andrea Castagnetti (ed.), *Inventari altomedieval: di terre, coloni e redditi (secc. IX–X)* (Rome: Istituto Storico Italiano pe il Medio Evo, 1979), 41–94.

24. Carlo Borromeo, 'Regole appartenenti alle monache, cavate dai Concilii Provinciali di Milano, fatte volgari, e ridotte in un corpo, sotto i titoli del primo', in *Acta Ecclesiae Mediolanensis* (Mediolani: Ex Officina Typographica quon. Pacifici Pontijs, 1599). See also George J. Wigley, *St Charles Borromeo's 'Instructions on Ecclesiastical Buildings'* (London, 1857).

25. Baernstein, *A Convent Tale*, ch. 3; Zarri, 'Monasteri feminili e città', 119.

26. ASF, CRS, 133, San Giovannino, 60, c. 113.

27. ASF, CRS, 106, Santa Caterina da Siena, 35, c. 220[r].

28. Barrière, 'Cistercian Convent of Coyroux', 79–80.

29. Borromeo, *Regole*.

30. Quoted in Gabriella Zarri, 'Recinti sacri: Sito e forma dei monasteri femminili a Bologna tra '500 e '600', in S.fia Boesch Gajano and Lucetta Scaraffia (eds.), *Luoghi sacri e spazi della santitá* (Turin, 1990), 385–6.

31. Lehfeldt, 'Discipline, Vocation, and Patronage', 1015.

32. Zarri, 'Recinti sacri', 385.

33. Burns, *Colonial Habits*, 107.

34. Lorraine N. Simmons, 'The Abbey Church at of Fontevraud in the Later Twelfth Century: Anxiety, Authority and Architecture in the Female Spiritual Life', *Gesta*, 31/2 (1990), 103.

35. Borromeo, *Regole.*

36. Sandrina Bandera and Maria Teresa Fiorio (eds.), *Bernadino Luini e la pittura del Rinascimento a Milano: Gli affreschi di San Maurizio al Monastero Maggiore* (Milan: Skira, 2000), 117–305.

37. Caroline A. Bruzelius, 'Hearing is Believing: Clarissan Architecture, ca.1213–1340', *Gesta*, 31/2 (1990), 83–91, at 88.

38. Helen Hills, 'Cities and Virgins: Female Aristocratic Convents in Early Modern Naples and Palermo', *Oxford Art Journal* (1999), 48–50; ead., *Invisible City: The Architecture of Devotion in Seventeenth-Century Neapolitan Convents* (Oxford: Oxford University Press, 2004). It is not clear to what extent this architectural model was typical of countries such as Italy or Spain or it was found in other Catholic countries too; on this see Mafalda Magalhaes Barros et al. (eds.), *Struggle for Synthesis: The Total Work of Art in the 17th and 18th Centuries* (Lisbon: Ministério da Cultura, 1999). I would like to thank Helen Hills for this suggestion.

39. Burns, *Colonial Habits*, 115.

40. Helen Hills, 'Housing Institutional Architecture: Searching for a Domestic Holy in Post-Tridentine Italian Convents', in Sandra Cavallo and Silvia Evangelisti (eds.), *Domestic and Institutional Interiors in Early Modern Europe* (Ashgate, forthcoming).

41. On the material and dynastic aspects of convents' interiors see Helen Hills, 'Enamelled with the Blood of a Noble Lineage: Tracing Noble Blood and Female Holiness in Early Modern Neapolitan Convents and their Architecture', *Church History*, 73/1 (2004), 1–40. Sánchez, *La Clausura Imposible*, at 109–10; Guimarães Sá, 'Between Spiritual and Material Culture'.

42. Hills, 'Housing Institutional Architecture'.

43. On Saint Clare see Elizabeth A. Petroff, 'A Medieval Woman's Utopian Vision: The Rule of Saint Clare of Assisi', in *Body and Soul: Essays on Medieval Women and Mysticism* (New York and Oxford: Oxford University Press, 1994), 66–79; Rosalind B. Brooke and Christopher N. L. Brooke, *St Clare*, in Derek Baker (ed.), *Medieval Women* (Oxford: Blackwell, 1978), 275–87.

44. Bilinkoff, *The Avila*, 115.

45. Ibid. 122.

46. From Saint Teresa's *Constitutions*, 'Of enclosure', in Teresa of Avila, *The Complete Works of Saint Teresa of Jesus*, trans. and ed. E. Allison Peers (London: Sheed and Ward, 1946), iii. 224.

47. Bilinkoff, *The Avila*, 132.

48. Ibid. 134–6. Alison Weber, 'Spiritual Administration: Gender and Discernment in the Carmelite Reform', *Sixteenth Century Journal*, 31/1 (2000), 123–46, in part 124.

49. Bilinkoff, *The Avila*, 136.

50. Weber, 'Spiritual Administration', 124.

51. Ibid. 131–2.

52. On Teresa's interpretation of the third religious vow, that of obedience, see Bilinkoff, *The Avila*, 133–4.

53. Penelope Johnson, 'La Théorie de la clôture', 491–505.

54. Claire Walker, 'Combining Martha and Mary', 397; ead., *Gender and Politics in Early Modern Europe*.

55. Walker, 'Combining Martha', 408–15.

56. Ibid. 405.

57. Burns, *Colonial Habits*, 108.

58. Francesca Medioli, 'La clausura delle monache nell'amministrazione della Congregazione Romana sopra i Regolari', in Gabriella Zarri (ed.), *Il monachesimo femminile in Italia dall'alto medioevo al secolo XVII a confronto con l'oggi* (Verona: Il Segno, 1997), 249–282; ead., 'Monacazioni forzate: Donne ribelli al proprio destino', *Clio*, 3 (1994), 431–54; Katherine Gill, '*Scandala*: Controversies Concerning *Clausura* and Women's Religious Communities in Late Medieval Italy', in Scott L. Waugh and Peter D. Diehl (eds.), *Christendom and its Discontents: Exclusion Persecution, and Rebellion, 1000–1500* (Cambridge: Cambridge University Press, 1996), 177–203; Sperling, *Convents and the Body Politic*, 115–69.

59. Monson, *Disembodied Voices*, 163–4.

60. Medioli, 'La clausura', 249.

61. Lehfeldt, *Religious Women*, 105–74.

62. Gill, '*Scandala*', 188–91.

63. See my 'Art and the Advent of *Clausura*: The Convent of Saint Catherine of Siena in Tridentine Florence', in Jonathan Nelson (ed.), *Suor Plautilla Nelli (1523–1588): The First Woman Painter of Florence* (Florence: Cadmo, 2000), 69–79.

64. Ibid., app. II, pp. 113–14.

65. Ibid. 114.

66. Marie A. Thomas, 'Muscovite Convents in the Seventeenth Century', *Russian History*, 10/2 (1983), 230–42.

67. Renata Ago, *Carriere e clientele nella Roma barocca* (Rome and Bari: Laterza, 1990), 64–5.

68. Magdalena S. Sánchez, *The Empress, the Queen, and the Nun: Women and Power at the Court of Philip III of Spain* (Baltimore: The Johns Hopkins University Press, 1998), 137–55.

69. Sanchez, *The Empress*, 141–8.

70. Strasser, 'Bones of Contention', 273–86.

71. Colleen Reardon, *Holy Concord within Sacred Walls: Nuns and Music in Siena, 1575–1700* (New York and Oxford: Oxford University Press, 2002), 46–7.

72. Strasser, 'Bones of Contention', 281.

73. Ibid. 269 and 264.

74. Ibid. 268. See also Gill, '*Scandala*', 201.

CHAPTER 3

1. Emily James Putnam, *The Lady: Studies in Certain Significant Phases of her History* (1910), quoted in Electa Arenal and Stacey Schlau (eds.), *Untold Sisters*, 5.

2. Margareth L. King, 'Book-Lined Cells: Women and Humanism in the Early Italian Renaissance', in Patricia H. Labalme (ed.), *Beyond their Sex: Learned Women of the European Past* (New York and London: New York University Press, 1984), 66–90, at 80–1.

3. Benedetto Croce, 'Donne letterate nel seicento', in *Nuovi saggi sulla letteratura italiana del seicento* (Bari, 1968), 158, quoted in Elissa B. Weaver, 'Spiritual Fun: A Study of Sixteenth-Century Tuscan Convent Theater', in Mary Beth Rose (ed.), *Women in the Middle Ages and Renaissance: Literary and Historical Perspectives* (Syracuse, NY: Syracuse University Press, 1986), 173.

4. Saint Paul, Letters (1 Cor 14: 34–7), quoted in Alison Weber, *Teresa of Avila and the Rhetoric of Femininity* (Princeton: Princeton University Press, 1990), 19.

5. Natalie Zemon Davis, 'Women on Top', in Lorna Hutson (ed.), *Feminism and Renaissance Studies* (Oxford: Oxford University Press, 1999), 157; Merry E. Wiesner, *Women and Gender in Early Modern Europe* (Cambridge: Cambridge University Press, 2000), ch. 5; Margaret L. King and Albert Rabil Jr. (eds.), *Her Immaculate Hand: Selected Works by and about the Women Humanists of Quattrocento Italy* (Binghamton NY: State University of New York, 1981).

6. On convent education see Sharon Strocchia, 'Learning the Virtues: Convent Schools and Female Culture in Renaissance Florence', in Barbara Whitehead (ed.), *Women's Education in Early Modern Europe, 1500–1800* (New York: Garland, 1999), 3–46. See also ead., 'Taken into Custody: Girls and Convent Guardianship in Renaissance Florence', *Renaissance Studies*, 17 (2003), 177–200. On convent libraries in Italy see Serena Spanó Martinelli, 'La biblioteca del Corpus Domini bolognese: L'inconsueto spaccato di una cultura monastica femminile', *La Bibliofilia*, 88 (1986), 1–23; Maria Dolores Perez Baltasar, 'Saber y Creación Literaria: Los Claustros Femeninos en la Edad Moderna', *Cuadernos de Historia Moderna*, 20 (1998), 129–43; Elizabeth Rapley, *A Social History of the Cloisters: Daily Life in the Teaching Monasteries of the Old Regime* (Montreal: McGill-Queen's University Press, 2001).

7. Natalie Zemon Davis, 'Gender and Genre: Women as Historical Writers, 1400–1820', in Labalme (ed.), *Beyond their Sex*, 153–82.

8. Teresa of Avila, *The Complete Works*, ii. 201.

9. Ibid. 220.

10. See e.g. Petroff, *Medieval Women Visionary Literature.*

11. Isabelle Poutrin, *Le voile et la plume: autobiographie et sainteté feminine dans l'Espagne moderne* (Madrid: Casa de Velázquez, 1995).

12. Mary E. Giles, *The Book of Prayer of Sor Maria of Santo Domingo* (Albany, NY: State University of New York Press, 1990); Marit E. Monteiro, *Geestelijke Maagden: Leven Tussen Klooster en Wereld in Noord-Nederland Gedurende de Zeventiende Eeuw* (Hilversum: Verloren, 1996), chs. 4 and 5.

13. Poutrin, *Le Voile,* 13–26.

14. Ibid. 318. Ronald E. Surtz, *Writing Women in Late Medieval and Early Modern Spain* (Philadelphia: University of Pennsylvania Press, 1995).

15. *Tutte le opere di Santa Maria Maddalena de Pazzi, dai manoscritti originali* (Florence: Centro Internazionale del Libro, 1960–6); Giovanni Pozzi and Claudio Leonardi (eds.), *Scrittrici mistiche italiane* (Genoa: Marietti, 1988), 419–46.

16. Jody Bilinkoff, *Related Lives: Confessors and their Female Penitents, 1450–1750* (Ithaca, NY: Cornell University Press, 2005), 17–20.

17. *Scrittrici mistiche italiane,* 306–7; Camilla Battista Varano, *Le opere spirituali,* ed. G. Boccanegra (Jesi: Scuola Tipografica Francescana, 1958).

18. Adriano Prosperi, 'Diari femminili e discernimento degli spiriti: Le mistiche della prima età moderna in Italia', *Dimensioni e problemi della ricerca storica,* 2 (1994), 77–103; id., 'Lettere spirituali', in *Donne e fede* (Rome and Bari: Laterza, 1994), 227–51 (trans. *Women and Faith: Catholic Religious Life in Italy from Late Antiquity to the Present* (Cambridge, Mass.: Harvard University Press, 1999); Stephen Haliczer, *Female Mystics in the Golden Ages of Spain: Between Exaltation and Infamy* (Oxford and New York: Oxford University Press, 2002).

19. Arenal and Schlau (eds.), *Untold Sisters,* 383.

20. Haliczer, *Between Exaltation and Infamy,* 196–7; Gerardo da Brescia, *L'autobiografia della beata suor Maria Maddalena Martinengo di Barco Clarissa Cappuccina* (Milan: Centro Studi Cappuccini Lombardi, 1964), 72.

21. *Un tesoro nascosto ossia il Diario di S. Veronica Giuliani,* ed. P. Pizzicaria (Prato: Tipografica Giachetti, Figlio & C., 1895–1905); Pozzi and Leonardi (eds.), *Scrittrici mistiche italiane,* 505–42.

22. Pozzi and Leonardi (eds.), *Scrittrici mistiche italiane,* 263; Joseph R. Berrigan, 'Saint Catherine of Bologna: Franciscan Mystic', in Katarina M. Wilson (ed.), *Women Writers of the Renaissance and Reformation* (Athens, Ga.: University of Georgia Press, 1987), 81–95.

23. Caterina Vigri, *Le sette armi spirituali,* ed. Cecilia Foletti (Padua: Antenore, 1985), 162.

24. Arenal and Schlau (eds.), *Untold Sisters,* 57.

25. Teresa of Avila, *Complete Works,* i. 130.

26. Quoted from her letters in Vera Fortunati (ed.), *Vita artistica nel monastero femminile: Exempla* (Bologna: Compositori, 2002), 185; Raymond Jonas, *France and the Cult of the Sacred Heart: An Epic Tale for Modern Times* (Berkeley and Los

Angeles: University of California Press, 2000). See *Bibliotheca Sanctorum*, viii (Rome: Città Nuova Editrice, 1996), 804–9.

27. Pozzi and Leonardi (eds.), *Scrittrici mistiche italiane*, 382–6; Massimo Firpo, 'Paola Antonia Negri, monaca angelica (1508–1555)', in Ottavia Niccoli (ed.), *Rinascimento al femminile* (Rome and Bari: Laterza, 1991), 35–82.

28. Anna Scattigno, ' "Carissimo figliolo in Cristo": Direzione spirituale e mediazione sociale nell'epistolario di Caterina de'Ricci (1542–1590)', in Lucia Ferrante, Maura Palazzi, and Gianna Pomata (eds.), *Ragnatele di rapporti: Patronage e reti di relazione nella storia delle donne* (Turin: Rosember & Sellier, 1988), 219–39; Id., 'Lettere dal convento', in Gabriella Zarri (ed.), *Per lettera: La scrittura epistolare femminile tra archivio e tipografia, Secoli XV–XVIII* (Rome: Viella, 1999), 347–8.

29. Cabibbo and Modica, *La santa dei Tomasi*, 133–4.

30. Poutrin, *Le Voile*, 353.

31. Pozzi and Leonardi (eds.), *Scrittrici mistiche italiane*, 447–61.

32. Arenal and Schlau (eds.), *Untold Sisters*, 199–227.

33. Ibid. 293–410; Asunción Lavrin, 'Women and Religion in Spanish America', in Ruether and Keller (eds.), *Women and Religion in America*, 42–78; Elisa Sampson, *Colonial Angels: Narratives of Gender and Spirituality in Mexico, 1580–1750* (Austin: University of Texas Press, 2000); Kathryn J. McKnight, *The Mystic of Tunja: The Writings of Madre Castillo, 1671–1742* (Amherst, Mass.: University of Massachusetts Press, 1997).

34. Arenal and Schlau (eds.), *Untold Sisters*, 384–5.

35. Natalie Zemon Davis, 'Genre and Gender', 157.

36. Illuminata Bembo, 'Specchio di Illuminazione', in Caterina Vigri, *Le armi necessarie alla battaglia spirituale* (Bologna: Lelio dalla Volpe, 1787), 3–4. See also Illuminata Bembo, *Specchio di illuminazione*, ed. Silvia Mostaccio (Florence: Sismel Edizioni del Galluzzo, 2001), 3–4.

37. Arenal and Schlau (eds.), *Untold Sisters*, 276.

38. Ibid. 273.

39. ASF, S. Jacopo di Ripoli, 23, *Libro di Croniche segnato A* (1508–1778), c. 137^{v}.

40. Kate J. P. Lowe, 'History Writing from within the Convent in Cinquecento Italy: The Nuns' Version', in Letizia Panizza (ed.), *Women in Italian Renaissance Culture and Society* (Oxford: Oxford University Press, 2000), 113 and n. 38.

41. Jaqueline Pascal, *A Rule for Children and other Writings*, ed. John J. Conley, SJ. (Chicago: University of Chicago Press, 2003), 124–7; Ranft, *Women and the Religious Life*, 122–4.

42. See Kate J. P. Lowe, *Nuns' Chronicles and Convent Culture in Renaissance and Counter-Reformation Italy* (Cambridge: Cambridge University Press, 2003); Charlotte Woodford, *Nuns as Historians in Early Modern Germany* (Oxford: Oxford University Press, 2002).

43. Michele Catalano (ed.), *La leggenda della beata Eustochia da Messina* (Messina and Florence: G. D'Anna, 1950).

44. *Ricordanze del monastero di S. Lucia osc. in Foligno* (Assisi: Porziuncola, 1987), 4.

45. Maria de San José Salazar, *Book for the Hour of Recreation*, ed. Alison Weber and Amanda Powell (Chicago: University of Chicago Press, 2002), 43.

46. *Founding of the Ancient Convent de Santa Teresa* and *An Account of the Origin and Foundation of the Monastery of San Joaquin, of Discalced Carmelite Nazarene nuns* (Lima, 1793), both in Arenal and Schlau (eds.), *Untold Sisters*, 325–30 and 368–74; Poutrin, *Le Voile*, 455.

47. Davis, 'Genre and Gender', 177 n. 17.

48. Angelica Baitelli, *Annali Historici dell'edificatione Erettione et Dotatione del Serenissimo Monasterio di S. Salvatore, et S. Giulia di Brescia* (Brescia: Antonio Rizzardi, 1657).

49. Woodford, *Nuns as Historians*, 106–43.

50. Amedeo Quondam, 'Lanzichenecchi in convento: Suor orsola e la storia tra archivio e devozione', *Schifanoia*, 6 (1988), 93.

51. Woodford, *Nuns as Historians*, 109.

52. Ibid. 106–84.

53. Bryant, 'Caritas Pirckheimer', 297.

54. Ibid. 301.

55. Woodford, *Nuns as Historians*, 44.

56. Natalie Zemon Davis, 'Women's History in Transition: The European Case', *Feminist Studies*, 3 (Spring–Summer, 1976), 83–103.

57. Teresa de Jesús, *Camino de perfección* (Madrid: Collección Austral, 1997), 81, refers to chs. 3 and 7 of *Way to Perfection*, trans. Jonathan Hopkin. My deepest thanks to Jim Casey for finding this quotation for me.

58. Medioli, *L' 'Inferno monacale'*, 147.

59. Ibid., quotation at 143.

60. Ibid. 148.

61. Ibid. 152 Medioli offers an excellent and insightful analysis of Tarabotti's work and underlines its connection to the *Querelle des femmes*. See also Letizia Panizza's introductory essay in Arcangela Tarabotti, *Che le donne siano della spezie degli uomini: Women are no less rational than men*, ed. Letizia Panizza (London: Institute of Roman Studies, 1994), pp. vii–xxx.

62. Medioli, *L' 'Inferno'*, 149.

63. Ibid. 154.

64. Ibid. 185.

65. Ibid. 150.

66. Tarabotti, *Che le donne*, pp. vii–xxx.

67. Ibid. 3–4.

68. Medioli, *L' 'Inferno'*, 157.

69. Juana Inés de la Cruz, *The Answer/La Respuesta: Including a Selection of Poems*, trans. and ed. Electa Arenal and Amanda Powell (New York: Feminist Press at the City University of New York, 1994), 1–17; Pamela Kirk, *Sor Juana Inés de la Cruz: Religion, Art, and Feminism* (New York: Continuum, 1998).

70. Juana Inés de la Cruz, *The Answer*, 7.

71. Ibid. 18–9, and 31–7.
72. Ibid. 53–5.
73. Ibid. 91.
74. Ibid. 77.
75. Ibid. 85–7.
76. Kirk, *Sor Juana*, 108.
77. Ibid. 147–50.

CHAPTER 4

1. Arenal and Schlau (eds.), *Untold Sisters*, 72–3.
2. Ibid. 148.
3. From Saint Teresa's constitutions, quoted in Maria de San José Salazar, *Book for the Hour of Recreation*, 13.
4. On convert playwrights see Su Roswitha and Hildegard of Bingen see Peter Dronke, *Women Writers of the Middle Ages: A Study of Texts from Perpetua (d.203) to Marguerite Porete (d.1310)* (Cambridge: Cambridge University Press, 1984), 55–83 and 144–201; *The Dramas of Hrotswitha of Gandersheim*, ed. Katharina M. Wilson (Saskatoon: Peregrina Publishing Co., 1985); Nancy Cotton, *Women Playwrights in England 1363–1750* (Lewisburg, Pa.: Bucknell University Press; London and Toronto: Associated University Presses, 1980); Marcela de San Felix, *Obra Completa: Coloquios Espirituales, Loas Y otro Poemas*, ed. Electa Arenal and Georgina Sabat Rivers (Barelona: PPU, 1988).
5. Arenal and Schlau (eds.), *Untold Sisters*, 148–51.
6. Frank J. Warnke (ed.), *Three Women Poets, Renaissance and Baroque: Louise Labé, Gaspara Stampa, and Sor Juana Inés de la Cruz* (London and Toronto: Associated University Press, 1987), 16.
7. Elissa B. Weaver, *Convent Theatre in Early Modern Italy: Spiritual Fun and Learning for Women* (Cambridge: Cambridge University Press, 2002).
8. Ibid. chs. 3–5.
9. Ibid. 59–69.
10. Ibid. 79, 244.
11. Ibid. 62.
12. Ibid. 63.
13. Ibid. 61–75.
14. Arenal and Schlau (eds.), *Untold Sisters*, 157–8.
15. Weaver, *Convent Theatre*, 97–101.
16. Ibid. 144.
17. Ibid. 220–1.
18. Arenal and Schlau (eds.), *Untold Sisters*, 229–81.
19. Ibid. 230–50.
20. Ibid. 244.

21. Ibid. 243.

22. *A Spiritual Drama, Entitled the Death of Desire*, quoted ibid. 253.

23. Weaver, *Convent Theatre*, 128–51.

24. Elissa Weaver, 'Suor Maria Clemente Ruoti, Playwright and Academician', in Matter and Coakley (eds.), *Creative Women, 290.*

25. Elissa Weaver, 'The Convent Wall in Tuscan Convent Drama', in Monson (ed.), *The Crannied Wall, 76. Weaver, 'Suor Maria Clemente', 286.*

26. Weaver, *Convent Theatre*, 179–92.

27. Ibid. 1–2.

28. Beatrice del Sera, *Amor di Virtù: Commedia in cinque atti, 1548*, ed. Elissa Weaver (Ravenna: Longo Editore, 1990).

29. Weaver, 'The Convent Wall', 76–7.

30. Arenal and Schlau (eds.), *Untold Sisters*, 149.

31. Weaver, *Convent Theatre*, 246.

32. Ibid. 83.

33. Ibid. 86.

34. Weaver, 'Suor Maria Clemente', 286.

35. Weaver, *Convent Theatre*, 84, quoting Alessandro de Medici's treatise for governing nuns (1601); Alessandro was the prefect of the Sacred Congregation of Bishops and Regular Orders in Rome.

36. Laven, *Virgins of Venice*, 135.

37. Arenal and Schlau (eds.), *Untold Sisters*, 244.

38. Weaver, *Convent Theatre*, 232.

39. Ibid. 88–9.

40. Laven, *Virgins of Venice*, 17.

41. Weaver, *Convent Theatre*, 49–95; Arenal and Schlau (eds.), *Untold Sisters*, 148.

42. Colleen R. Baade, 'La "musica sutil" del monasterio de la madre de Dios de Constantinopla: aportaciones para la historia de la musica en los monasteries femeninons de Madrid a finales del siglo XVI–siglo XVII', *Revista de Musicologia*, 20/1 (2002), 221–30.

43. Walter Salmen, 'Tanzen in Klostern wahrend des Mittelalters', in *Die Kloster als Pflegestatten von Musik und Kunst* (850 Jahre Kloster Michaelstein), 67–74. In the Middle Ages sacred dancing was common in churches too. My warmest thanks to Pedro Memelsdorff, musician, musicologist, and friend, for discussing aspects of the history of early music which were completely unknown to me.

44. '"A Garden of Delights": Medieval Sacred Music', *Women of Note Quarterly: The Magazine of Historical and Contemporary Women Composers*, 8 (2000), 9–26.

45. Maria Rosa Cesari, '"Per encomiar le donzelle ch'entran, nel chiostro": Pubblicazioni celebrative per monacazioni femminili tra sei e settecento', *Il Carrobbio*, 19/20 (1993), 203–22; Anne Bagnall Yardley, 'The Marriage of Heaven and

Earth: A Late Medieval Source of the Consecration Virginum, *Current Musicology* 45–7 (Fall 1988), 305–24.

46. Robert L. Kendrick, 'Four Views of Milanese Nuns' Music', in Matter and Coakley (eds.), *Creative Women*, 326; id., *Celestial Sirens: Nuns and their Music in Early Modern Milan* (Oxford: Oxford University Press, 1996), 329.

47. Colleen R. Baade, 'Music and Misgiving in Female Monasteries in Early Modern Castile', unpublished conference paper presented at *Female Monasticism in Early Modern Europe*, Cambridge, Wolfson College, 23–4 July 2003.

48. Teresa of Avila, *Complete Works*, iii. 248.

49. Hans Ryschawy, ' "Am Ende Wurde Sie Zur Pein" Musik in Oberschwabischen Frauenklostern am Beispiel der Zisterze Baindt', *Musik in Baden-Wurttemberg*, 2 (1995), 167–92; Georg Gunther, 'Ad Chorum Bonacellensem: The Practice of Music in the Cistercian Nunnery of Gutenzell at the End of the 18th Century', *Cistercienser Chronik: Forum fur Geschichte, Kunst, Literatur und Spiritualitat des Monchtums*, 105/3 (1998), 453–77.

50. Craig A. Monson, 'The Making of Lucrezia Orsina Vizzana's Componimenti Musicali (1623)', in Matter and Coakley (eds.), *Creative Women*, 304; Monson, *Disembodied Voices*, 17–91.

51. Kendrick, 'Four Views', 326.

52. Jonathan E. Glixon, 'Images of Paradises or Worldly Theaters? Toward a Taxonomy of Musical Performances at Venician Nunneries', in *Essays on Music and Culture in Honour of Herbert Kellman* (Paris and Tours: Minerve, 2001), 442; id., *Honoring God and the City: Music at the Venetian Confraternities, 1260–1807* (New York and Oxford: Oxford University Press, 2003).

53. Carmen Julia Gutierrez Gonzalez, 'De Monjas y Tropos: Musica Tardomedieval en un convento Mallorquin', *Anuario Musical: Revista de Musicologia del CESIC*, 53 (1998), 29–60.

54. Kelley Harness, 'The "Perfect Model of the Union between the Spiritual and Temporal": La Crocetta and the Medici', unpublished conference paper presented at *Female Monasticism in Early Modern Europe*, Cambridge, Wolfson College, 23–4 July 2003.

55. Reardon, *Holy Concord*, 21.

56. Robert L. Kendrick, 'The Traditions of Milanese Convent Music and the Sacred Dialogues of Chiara Margarita Cozzolani', in Monson (ed.), *The Crannied Wall*, 215.

57. Monson, 'The Making', 305.

58. Baade, 'La "musica sutil" ', 224.

59. Monson, 'The Making', 306–14.

60. On Milan see Kendrick, *Celestial Sirens*. Chiara Margarita Cozzolani, *Motets*, ed. Robert L. Kendrick (Madison: A-R Editions, 1998); Paolo Monticelli, *Isabella Leonarda, la musa novarese* (Turin: Centro di Studi Piemontesi, Instituto per i beni musicali in Piemonte, 1998), 15–27.

61. *Rime d'Isabella Andreini Padovana Comica Gelosa* (Milan: Girolamo Bordone, 1601).

62. Monson, 'The Making', 301.

63. Ibid.

64. Robert Stevenson, 'Mexico City Cathedral Music 1600–1675', *Inter-American Music Review*, 9/1 (1987), 75–114.

65. Dinko Fabris, ' "Le Chant de Trois Notes": Une tradition musicale du xviie siècle chez les Sœurs de l'Ordre de la Visitation de Marie', in Jean Duron (ed.), *Plain-Chant et Liturgie en France au xviie siècle* (Paris: Éditions du Centre de Musique Bocoque de Versailles, Éditions Klincksieck, 1997), 265–83.

66. Gerlinde Haas, 'Pauken und Trompeten . . . im Frauenkloster: "Komponistinnen", Chorregentinnen und andere Musikerinnen des Ursulines-Klosters in Graz in der Zeit 1686–1755/65', *Musicologia Austriaca*, 18 (1999), 141–50.

67. Jean-Pierre Pinson, 'Le Plain-Chant en Nouvelle-France aux xviie at xviiie siècles: vers une première sintèse', in Duron (ed.), *Plain-Chant et liturgie en France au xviie siècle*, 249–64; Elisabeth Gallat-Morin, 'La Presence en Nouvelle-France de la musique du temps de Louis XIV', *Ostinato Rigore: Revue internationale d'études musicales*, 8–9 (1997), 21–34.

68. Deborah Ann Kauffman, '*Chants and Motets* (1733): Nivers, Clerambault, and Changing Musical Style at the *Maison Royal de Saint-Louis* at Saint-Cyr', Ph.D. thesis, Stanford University, 1994, 8.

69. Reardon, *Holy Concord*, 48.

70. Ibid. 46–7.

71. Kimberlyn Montford, 'L'*Anno santo* and Female Monastic Churches: The Politics, Businness and Music of the Holy Year in Rome (1675)', *Journal of Seventeenth-Century Music*, 6/1 (2000), electronic resource.

72. Reardon, *Holy Concord*, 44–7; Kendric, 'Celestial Sirens', 160.

73. Juan Carlos Estenssoro, 'Música y fiestas en los Monasterios de Monjas Limenas. Siglos XVII y XVIII', *Revista Musical de Venezuela*, 34 (1997), 127–35, at 134–5.

CHAPTER 5

1. Stefania Biancani, 'La leggenda di un'artista monaca: Caterina Vigri'; Irene Graziani, 'L'iconografia di Caterina Vigri: Dalla clausura alla città'; and Alessandro Zacchi, 'Giulio Morina al Corpus Domini: Nuove proposte per due problemi ancora irrisolti', all in *Vita artistica*, Fortunati (ed.), 203–19, 221–44, 245–90 respectively. On Caterina Vigri, see *La Santa nella storia nelle lettere e nell'arte* (Bologna: Alfonso Garagnani, 1912); Jeryldene Wood, *Women, Art, and Spirituality: The Poor Clares of Early Modern Italy* (Cambridge: Cambridge University Press, 1996), 130. See also Gabriella Zarri, *Le sante vive: Profezie di corte e devozione femminile tra '400 e '500* (Turin: Rosemberg & Sellier, 1990), 87–163; Caterina Vigri, *Pregare con le immagini: il Breviario di Caterina Vigri*, ed. Vera Fortunati and Claudio Leonardi (Florence: Sismel Edizioni del Galluzzo; Bologna: Compositori; 2004).

2. Marilyn Dunn, 'Spaces Shaped for Spiritual Perfection: Convent Architecture and Nuns in Early Modern Rome', in Helen Hills (ed.), *Architecture and the Politics of Gender in Early Modern Europe* (Aldershot, Harts. and Burlington Vt. Ashgate 2003), 151–76.

3. Yves Rocher (ed.), *L'Art du xviime siècle dans les Carmels de France* (Paris: Musée du Petit Palais, 1982), 101–6.

4. On Roman laywomen as patrons see Carolyn Valone, 'Roman Matrons as Patrons: Various Views of the Cloister Wall', in Monson (ed.), *Crannied Wall*, 49–72; ead, 'Piety and Patronage: Women and the Early Jesuits', in Matter and Coakley (eds.), *Creative Women*, 157–84.

5. Marilyn R. Dunn, 'Spiritual Philanthropists: Women as Convent Patrons in Seicento Rome', in Cynthia Lawrence (ed.), *Women and Art in Early Modern Europe: Patrons, Collectors, and Connoisseurs* (University Park, Pa.: The Pennsylvania State University Press, 1997), 154–88.

6. Ibid. 157–63.

7. Ibid. 158.

8. Ibid. 159.

9. Ibid. 166–75.

10. Ibid. 167–8.

11. Ibid. 172–5.

12. Olwen Hufton, 'Altruism and Reciprocity: The Early Jesuits and their Female Patrons', *Renaissance Studies*, 15/3 (2001), 328–53.

13. *Memoriale di Monteluce: Cronaca del monastero delle clarisse di Perugia dal 1448 al 1838*, ed. Ugolino Nicolini (Assisi: Porziuncola, 1983), 85–6.

14. Geryldene Wood, 'Breaking the Silence: The Poor Clares and the Visual Arts in Fifteenth-Century Italy', *Renaissance Quarterly*, 48/2 (1995), 262–286, at 270.

15. Ibid. 268.

16. Ibid. 271–2.

17. Kate Lowe, 'Nuns and Choice: Artistic Decision-making in Medicean Florence' in Eckart Marchand and Alison Wright (eds.), *With and Without the Medici: Studies in Tuscan Art and Patronage 1434–1530* (Aldershot, Hants. and Burlington Vt.: Ashgate, 1998).

18. Mary-Ann Winkelmes, 'Taking Part: Benedictine Nuns as Patrons of Art and Architecture', in *Picturing Women in Renaissance and Baroque Italy* (Cambridge: Cambridge University Press, 1997), 102–9.

19. Ibid. 98–101; Regina Stefaniak, 'Correggio's *Camera di San Paolo*: An Archaeology of the Gaze', *Art History*, 12 (1993), 203–38.

20. On nuns as individual patrons see Marilyn R. Dunn, 'Nuns as Patrons: The Decorations of S. Marta at the Collegio Romano', *Art Bulletin*, 70/3 (1988), 451–77.

21. Gary M. Radke, 'Nuns and their Art: The Case of San Zaccaria in Renaissance Venice', *Renaissance Quarterly* (2001), 431–59.

22. Ibid. 450.

23. Simona Brighetti, 'La "perfetta monaca": Creanza cristiana in convento tra letteratura, precettistica e iconografia', in Fortunati (ed.), *Vita artistica*, 54.

24. Anabel Thomas, *Art and Piety in the Female Religious Communities of Renaissance Italy* (Cambridge: Cambridge University Press, 2003), 114–50.

25. Christiane Klapisch-Zuber, 'Holy Dolls: Play and Piety in Florence in the Quattrocento', in ead., *Women, Family, and Ritual in Renaissance Italy* (Chicago: University of Chicago Press, 1985), 310–29.

26. Ibid. 324. See also Arenal and Schlau (eds.), *Untold Sisters*: two Christ dolls are reproduced on pp. 190 and 284, although it is not specified whether these dolls were used for display in the convent or individually by nuns (or both).

27. Rocher (ed.), *L'Art du XVIIme siècle*, 40.

28. Martha J. Egan, 'Escudos de Monjas: Religious Miniatures of New Spain', *Latin American Art*, 5/4 (1994), 43–6; Cabibbo e Modica, *La Santa dei Tomasi*, portraits of Rosalia Traina and Isabella Tomasi, n. 3 and 4; Arenal and Schlau (eds.), *Untold Sisters*, portrait of a crowned nun, 291, and 'The Costumes of the Nuns of the Convents of Mexico' no number.

29. Egan, 'Escudos de Monjas', 45.

30. Ibid. 46.

31. Arenal and Schlau (eds.), *Untold Sisters*, 153–4.

32. Vita Fortunati, 'Ruolo e funzione delle imagini dei monasteri femminili', in ead. (ed.), *Vita artistica*, 25–7.

33. Andrea G. Pearson, 'Nuns, Images, and the Ideals of Women's Monasticism: Two Paintings from the Cistercian Convent of Flines', *Renaissance Quarterly*, 54 (2001), 1356–1402; ead., *Envisioning Gender in Burgundian Devotional Art, 1350–1530: Experience, Authority, Resistance* (Aldershot, Hants. and Burlington, Vt.: Ashgate, 2005).

34. Pearson, 'Nuns, Images, and the Ideals of Women's Monasticism', 1366–71.

35. Ibid. 1374–5.

36. Ibid. 1386–90.

37. Pia F. Cuneo, 'The Basilica Cycle of Saint Katherine's Convent: Art and Female Community in Early-Renaissance Augsburg', *Woman's Art Journal*, 19/1 (1998), 21–5.

38. Ibid. 22.

39. Ibid. 25 n. 1.

40. Arenal and Schlau (eds.), *Untold Sisters*, 132 and 174–5.

41. Ibid. 175.

42. Jeffrey F. Hamburger, *Nuns as Artists: The Visual Culture of a Medieval Convent* (Berkeley and Los Angeles: University of California Press, 1997), 17.

43. From Johannes Meyer—a fifteenth-century Dominican from Basle who translated from Latin into German the *Instructiones de officiis ordinis*, a set of instructions for nuns—quoted in Delia Gaze (ed.), *Dictionary of Women Artists* (London and Chicago: Fitzroy Dearborn Publishers, 1997), 21–3.

44. Jane L. Carroll, 'Woven Devotions: Reform and Piety in Tapestries by Dominican Nuns', in ead. and Alison G. Stewart (eds.), *Saints, Sinners, and Sisters: Gender*

and Northern Art in Medieval and Early Modern Europe (Aldershot, Hants. and Burlington Vt.: Ashgate, 2003), 182–201.

45. Jeffrey F. Hamburger, ' "To Make Women Weep": Ugly as "Feminine" and the Origins of Modern Aesthetics', *Res*, 31 (Spring, 1997), 9–33; id., *The Visual and the Visionary: Art and Female Spirituality in Late Medieval Germany* (New York: Zone Books, 1998).

46. Images created by nuns possessed 'a distinctive visual rhetoric closely geared to monastic audience', Hamburger, ' "To Make Women Weep" ', 27.

47. Hamburger, *Nuns as Artists*, 46.

48. From Maria de San Alberto unpublished work, 'Mercies Bestowed by Our Lord' (1633), quoted in Arenal and Schlau (eds.), *Untold Sisters*, 153.

49. See Vigri, 'Pregare cor le immagini'.

50. Franca Trinchieri Camiz ' "Virgo-non sterilis...": Nuns as Artists in Seventeenth-Century Rome', in *Picturing Women*, 140.

51. Arenal and Schlau (eds.), *Untold Sisters*, 131–8.

52. Nancarrow, 'Picturing Intimacy in a Spanish Golden Age Convent', *Oxford Art Journal*, 1 (2000), 97–111.

53. Ibid. 103–5.

54. Nancarrow, 'The Artistic Activity of Spanish Nuns During the Golden Age' in Liana De Girolemi Cheney (ed.), *Essays on Women Artists: 'The Most Excellent'* i (Lewinston, NY: Edwin Mellen 2003), 41–51, 42.

55. Nancarrow, 'Picturing Intimacy', 105–7.

56. Trinchieri Camiz, ' "Virgo-non sterilis" ', 140–51.

57. Ibid. 149.

58. Jonathan Nelson (ed.), *Suor Plautilla Nelli (1523–1588): The First Woman Painter in Florence* (Florence: Cadmo, 2000).

59. See my 'Art and the Advent of Clausura', ibid. 78.

60. Catherine Turrill, 'Compagnie and Discepole: The Presence of Other Women Artists at Santa Caterina da Siena', ibid. 90–7, at 84–5.

61. Ibid. 91–7.

62. Ibid., app., 103–10.

63. Quoted ibid. 112.

64. Caroline Murphy, 'Plautilla Nelli, between Cloister and Client: A Study in Negotiation', ibid. 57–65.

65. Ibid. 61.

66. Nancarrow, 'The Artistic Activity of Spanish Nuns', 44.

67. Ann Sutherland Harris and Linda Nochlin (eds.), *Women Artists: 1550–1950* (New York: Alfred Knopf, 1976), 125–30.

68. Molly Bourne, 'From Court to Cloister and Back Again: The Circulation of Objects in the Clarissan Convent of Sant'Orsola in Mantua', in Cavallo and Evangelisti (eds.), *Domestic and Institutional Interiors*. On Lucrina Fetti see Cynthia A. Gladen, 'Suor Lucrina Fetti: Pittrice in una corte monastica seicentesca', in Pomata and Zarri (eds.), *Monasteri femminili*, 123–41.

69. Gladen, 'Suor Lucrina', 138–41; the attribution of some of these portraits to Lucrina is still a matter of debate among scholars. The portrait of Eleonora I is

the only one which is signed by Lucrina. Harris and Nochlin (eds.), *Women Artists*, 125–30.

70. Angela Ghirardi, 'Dipingere in lode del cielo: Sour Orsola Maddalena Caccia e la vocazione artistica delle Orsoline di Moncalvo', in Fortunati (ed.), *Vita artistica*, 128.

71. Ibid. 129.

72. Silvia Urbini, 'Sul ruolo della donna "incisore" nella storia del libro illustrato', in Gabriella Zarri (ed.), *Donna, disciplina, creanza cristiana dal XV al XVII secolo: Studi e testi a stampa* (Rome: Edizioni di Storia e Letteratura, 1996), 367–91.

73. Ana Garcia Sanz y Leticia Sánchez Hernandez, 'Iconografia de monjas, santas y beatas en los monasterios reales espanoles', in *La mujer en el arte espanol: VII jornadas de arte* (Madrid: Alpuerto, 1997), 131–42.

74. On nuns' portraits in Mexico see Elisa Garcia Barragan, 'Mistica y esplendor barrocos en Mexico colonial: Retratos de monjas coronadas', *Boletin del Museo e Instituto 'Camon Aznar'*, 48–9 (1992), 61–82.

75. Fortunati, 'Ruolo e funzione', 22–4.

76. Ibid. 24–5.

77. Ibid. 39.

78. Diane Owen Hughes, 'Representing the Family: Portraits and Purposes in Early Modern Italy', *Journal of Interdisciplinary History*, 17 (1986), 7–38.

79. Garcia Barragan, 'Mistica y esplendor barrocos', 64.

80. Ibid. 76, picture n. 4.

81. Ibid. 77–9.

CHAPTER 6

1. See for instance, Concepción Torres, *Ana de Jesús: Cartas (1590–1621)* (Salamanca: Ediciones Universidad de Salamanca, 1995), 26–9; Walker, *Gender and Politics*, 74–101; Dominique Deslandres, 'In the Shadow of the Cloister: Representations of Female Holiness in New France', in Allan Greer and Jody Bilinkoff (eds.), *Colonial Saints: Discovering the Holy in the Americas, 1500–1800* (New York and London: Routledge, 2003), 129–52.

2. 'Carmelitane Scalze', in *Dizionario degli istituti di perfezione*, ii (1975), col. 423.

3. Torres, *Ana de Jesús*, 33–8; Torres Sánchez, *La clausura imposible*, 128–38.

4. Torres, *Ana de Jesús*, 34.

5. Arenal and Schlau (eds.), *Untold Sisters*, 19.

6. Ibid. 27–30.

7. Ibid. 111.

8. Torres, *Ana de Jesús*, 9–13.

9. Torres Sánchez, *La clausura imposible*, 17, 19–51.

10. Ibid. 52–3.

11. Torres, *Ana de Jesús*, 48–9.

12. Torres Sánchez, *La clausura imposible*, 61–2.

13. Barbara B. Diefendorf, *From Penance to Charity: Pious Women and the Catholic Reformation in Paris* (Oxford and New York: Oxford University Press, 2004), 101–18.

14. Ibid. 136–7.

15. Torres Sánchez, *La clausura imposible*, 43–50; Diefendorf, *From Penance to Charity*, 77–8.

16. Diefendorf, *From Penance to Charity*, 77–100.

17. Ibid. 77.

18. Torres Sánchez, *La clausura imposible*, 57.

19. Ibid. 66; Diefendorf, *From Penitence to Charity*, 105–18.

20. Torres Sánchez, *La clausura imposible*, 58.

21. Ibid. 51.

22. Ibid. 150.

23. Torres, *Ana de Jesús*, 93–4.

24. Ibid. 76.

25. Tim Coates, *Convicts and Orphans: Forced and State-Sponsored Colonizers in the Portuguese Empire (1550–1755)* (Stamford: Stamford University Press, 2001).

26. The life of Marie de l'Incarnation has been thoroughly discussed by Davis, *Women on the Margins*, 63–139, on which this section of my chapter is based. See also 'Guyart, Marie', in *Dizionario degli istituti di perfezione*, iv (1977), 1501–3.

27. Davis, *Women*, 65–73.

28. Marie-Florine Bruneau, *Women Mystics Confront the Modern World: Marie de l'Incarnation (1599–1672) and Madame Guyon (1648–1717)* (Albany. NY: State University of New York Press, 1998), 61.

29. Davis, *Women*, 78.

30. Ibid.

31. Ibid.

32. Christine Allen, 'Women in Colonial French America' in Rosemary Radford Ruether and Rosemary Skinner Keller (eds.), *Women and Religion in America: The Colonia and Revolutionary Period*, ii (New York, Harper & Row, 1983), 95.

33. Davis, *Women*, 83.

34. Ibid. 84–94.

35. Ibid. 98–9.

36. Ibid. 96.

37. Bruneau, *Women Mystics*, 102; Davis, *Women*, 114–15.

38. Bruneau, *Women Mystics*, 96.

39. Ibid. 100.

40. Davis, *Women*, 96–7.

41. Bruneau, *Women Mystics*, 90.

42. Davis, *Women*, 98–9.

43. Ibid. 115–16.
44. Bruneau, *Women Mystics*, 115.
45. Ibid. 116.
46. Ibid.
47. William Henry Foster III, 'Women at the Centers, Men at the Margins: The Wilderness Mission of the Secular Sisters of Early Montreal Reconsidered', in Susan E. Dinan and Debra Meyers (eds.), *Women and Religion in Old and New Worlds* (London and New York: Routledge, 2001), 93–112; Patricia Simpson, *Marguerite Bourgeoys and Montreal, 1640–1665* (Montreal and Kingston: McGill-Queens University Press, 1997).
48. Bruneau, *Women Mystics*, 117.
49. See ibid. 116 and 119–22.
50. On Spanish American convents see Asunción Lavrin, 'Female Religious', in Louisa Schell Hoberman and Susan Midgen Socolow (ed.), *Cities and Society in Colonial Latin America* (Albuquerque, N. Mex.: University of New Mexico Press, 1986), 165–95; ead., 'Values and Meaning of Monastic Life for Nuns of Colonial Mexico', *Catholic Historical Review* 16/3 (1983), 75–92; ead., 'Women and Religion in Spanish America' in Ruether and Keller (eds.), *Women and Religion in America*, 42–78; ead. (ed.), *Latin American Women: Historical Perspectives* (Westport, Conn.: Greenwood Press, 1978); Martín, *Daughters of the Conquistadores*; Josefina Muriel, *Cultura femenina novohispana* (Mexico: Universidad Nacional Autónoma de México, 1982). On Brazilian convents see Susan Soeiro, 'The Social and Economic Role of the Convent: Women and Nuns in Colonial Bahia, 1677–1800', *Hispanic American Historical Review*, 54 (1974), 209–32.
51. Arenal and Schlau (eds.), *Untold Sisters*, 337.
52. Ibid. 296.
53. Lavrin, 'Female Religious', 166–72.
54. Ibid. 189.
55. Ibid. 175.
56. 'Carmelitane Scalze', col. 446.
57. Lavrin, 'Female Religious', 176–9.
58. Ibid. 169–70.
59. Arenal and Schlau (eds.), *Untold Sisters*, 301.
60. Elisa Sampson, 'Writing in the New Spanish Cloister', in Olwen Hufton (ed.), *Yearbook of the Department of History and Civilization: Women in the Religious Life* (Florence: European University Institute, 1996), 72.
61. Ibid. 73–4.
62. Ibid. 75.
63. Burns, *Colonial Habits*, 119–20.
64. Ibid. 15–8.
65. Lavrin, 'Female Religious', 176.
66. Arenal and Schlau (eds.), *Untold Sisters*, 293.
67. Sampson, 'Writing in the New Spanish Cloister', 63.

68. Thomas D. Kendrick, *Mary of Agreda: The Life and Legend of a Spanish Nun* (London: Routledge and Kegan Paul, 1967), 31–45. On Maria de Agreda see Clark A. Colahan, *The Visions of Sor Maria de Agreda: Writing, Knowledge, and Power* (Tucson: University of Arizona Press, 1994).

69. Kendrick, *Mary of Agreda*, 51.

CHAPTER 7

1. On such religious women see Grundmann, *Religious Movements*; Vauchez, *The Laity*; Simons, *Cities of Ladies*.

2. These distinctions are not to be taken too rigidly as there existed—as in the medieval Netherlands for instance—religious houses where women did not take vows at all, Harline, 'Actives and Contemplatives', 551; Florence Koorn, 'Women without Vows: The Case of the Beguines and the Sisters of the Common Life in the Northern Netherlands', in Elisja Schulte van Kessel (ed.), *Women and Men in Spiritual Culture, XIV–XVII Centuries: A Meeting of North and South*, (The Hague: Netherlands Government Publishing Office, 1986), 135–47.

3. Liebowitz, 'Virgins', 136–7.

4. Mary Elizabeth Perry, *Gender and Disorder in Early Modern Seville* (Princeton: Princeton University Press, 1990), 102–3.

5. Harline, 'Actives and Contemplatives', 548 and 557–9; Diefendorf, *From Penitence to Charity*, 173–238; Thomas Worcester, ' "Neither Married Nor Cloistered": Blessed Isabelle in Catholic Reformation', *Sixteenth Century Journal*, 30/2 (1999), 457–72.

6. Olwen Hufton, *Prospect*, 373–4. See also Olwen Hufton and Frank Tallett, 'Communities of Women, the Religious Life, and Public Service in Eighteenth-Century France', in Marylin J. Boxer and Jean H. Quataert (eds.), *Connecting Spheres: Women in the Western World, 1500 to the Present* (Oxford: Oxford University Press, 1987), 75–85; Olwen Hufton, *Whatever Happened to the History of the Nun?* (Royal Holloway University of London, Hayes Robinson Lecture Series 3 (2000)).

7. Quoted in Hufton, *Prospect*, 359.

8. Diefendorf, *From Penitence to Charity*, 136–7.

9. Ibid. *Charity* 171. On charity and welfare, in a comparative European perspective, see Brian Pullan, *Poverty and Charity: Europe, Italy, Venice, 1400–1700* (Aldershot: Variourum, 1994); Ole Peter Grell, Andrew Cunningham, and Jon Arrizabalaga (eds.), *Health Care and Poor Relief in Counter-Reformation Europe* (London and New York: Routledge, 1999).

10. Hufton, *Whatever Happened*, 20.

11. Elizabeth Rapley, *The Dévotes: Women and Church in Seventeenth-Century France* (Montreal: McGill-Queen's University Press, 1990); Susan E. Dinan, 'Motivations for Charity in Early Modern France', in Thomas Max Safley (ed.),

The Reformation of Charity: The Secular and the Religious in Early Modern Poor Relief (Boston and Leiden: Brill, 2003), 191.

12. Hufton, *Prospect*, 375; Liebowitz, 'Virgins', 137–47.

13. Walker, *Gender and Politics*, 132.

14. 'Orsola' in *Bibliotheca Sanctorum*, ix (Rome: Città Nuova Editrice, 1967), coll. 1252–71.

15. Danielle Culpepper, ' "Our Particular Cloister": Ursulines and Female Education in Seventeenth-Century Parma and Piacenza', *Sixteenth Century Journal*, 4 (2005), 1017–37; Querciolo Mazzonis, 'A Female Idea of Religious Perfection: Angela Merici and the Company of St. Ursula (1535–1540)', *Renaissance Studies*, 18 (2004), 391–411; Charmarie J. Blaisdell, 'Angela Merici and the Ursulines', in Richard L. De Molen (ed.), *Religious Orders of the Counter-Reformation* (New York: Fordham University Press, 1994), 98–136; Gabriella Zarri, 'Ursula and Catherine: The Marriage of Virgins in the Sixteenth Century', in Matter and Coackley (eds.), *Creative Women*, 245; Thérèse Ledochowska, *Angèle Merici et la Compagnie de Ste-Ursule* (Rome and Milan: Ancora, 1967).

16. 'Orsoline', in *Dizionario degli Istituti di Perfezione*, vi (1980), coll. 841–3.

17. Ibid. 834–57.

18. Zarri, 'Ursula and Catherine', 238.

19. Luciana Mariani, Elisa Tarolli, and Marie Seynaeve, *Angela Merici: Contributo per una biografia* (Milan: Ancora, 1986), 494.

20. 'Orsoline', coll. 841–2.

21. Mariani, *Angela Merici*, 494.

22. Ibid. ch. 9; 'Orsoline', col. 840.

23. Blaisdell, 'Angela Merici', 117–20.

24. Ibid. 115–16.

25. Ibid. 120–1.

26. Culpepper, ' "Our Particular Cloister" ', 1025.

27. Hufton, *Prospect*, 374; Diefendorf, *From Penitence to Charity*, 125.

28. Diefendorf, *From Penitence to Charity*, 126–30; Lierheimer, 'Redefining Convent Space', 211–20; ead., 'Preaching or Teaching? Defining the Ursuline Mission in Seventeenth-Century France' in Beverly Mayne Kienzle and Pamela J. Walker (eds.), *Women Preachers and Prophets through Two Millennia of Christianity* (Berkeley and Los Angeles: University of California Press, 1998), 212–26. On the teaching orders see Rapley, *Social History of the Cloister*.

29. Diefendorf, *From Penitence to Charity*, 126.

30. Ibid. 130–3.

31. Hufton, *Prospect*, 374; 'Orsoline', coll. 847–51.

32. Crawford, *Women and Religion in England*, 26–7.

33. Mary C. E. Chambers, *The Life of Mary Ward (1585–1645)* (London: Burns and Oates, 1882), i. 283.

34. See picture in 'Ward, Mary', in *Dizionario degli istituti di perfezione*, x (2003), coll. 583–86.

35. Chambers, *The Life of Mary Ward*, i. 291.

36. Ibid. 377.

37. Ibid. 296.

38. Ibid. ii. 60.

39. Ibid. i. 377.

40. Ibid. 357–62.

41. Ibid. 376.

42. Quoted in Strasser, *State of Virginity*, 159.

43. Quoted in Ranft, *Women and the Religious Life*, 126–7.

44. Strasser, *State of Virginity*, 159–60.

45. Ibid. 161.

46. Quoted ibid. 215 n. 63.

47. 'Istituto della Beata Vergine Maria', in *Dizionario degli istituti di perfezione*, v (1978), coll. 129–33.

48. Strasser, *State of Virginity*, 162–72.

49. Ibid. 166.

50. 'Istituto', coll. 131–3.

51. 'Gesuitesse', in *Dizionario degli istituti di perfezione*, iv (1977), coll. 1146–49.

52. Chambers, *Life of Mary Ward*, i. 357.

53. Bilinkoff, *Related Lives*, 12–31.

54. 'Giovanna Francesca Fremyot de Chantal', in *Dizionario degli istituti di perfezione*, iv (1977), coll. 1200–9.

55. Wendy M. Wright, *Bond of Perfection: Jeanne de Chantal and François de Sales* (New York: Paulist Press, 1985), 103–4.

56. Quoted in Ranft, *Women and the Religious Life*, 116.

57. Ibid. 117.

58. Wright, *Bond of Perfection*, 131.

59. Ibid. 131–2.

60. Ibid. 158.

61. Marie Patricia Burns, 'Jeanne de Chantal et la tradition', in Bernard Dompnier et Dominique Julia (eds.), *Visitation et Visitandines aux xviie et xviiie siècles* (Saint-Étienne: Publication de l'Université de Saint-Étienne, 2001), 37–51, at 43.

62. Wendy M. Wright, 'The Visitation of Holy Mary: The First Years (1610–1618)', in De Molen (ed.), *Religious Orders of the Catholic Reformation*, 227.

63. Ibid., 233–4.

64. *Il Direttore delle religiose estratto dalle Opere della Santa Madre Giovanna Francesca Fremiot di Chantal* (Venice: Gianmaria Bassaglia, 1785), 185–6.

65. 'Giovanna Francesca Fremyot de Chantal', coll. 1200–9. Francis of Sales and Jeanne-Françoise de Chantal, *Letters of Spiritual Direction* (New York: Paulist Press, 1988).

66. Sainte Jeanne-Françoise Fremyot de Chantal, *Correspondances*, vol. i (Paris: Cerf, 1986), 135.

67. Wright, 'Visitation', 248 n. 54.

68. Harline, 'Actives and Contemplatives', 551 n. 23.

69. Dominique Julia, 'L'expansion de l'ordre de la Visitation des origines à la Révolution française', in *Visitation et Visitandines aux xviie et xviiie siècles*, 115–76.

70. Hufton and Tallet, 'Communities of Women', 78–82.

71. On the Daughters of Charity see Susan E. Dinan, *Women and Poor-Relief in Seventeenth Century France: The Early History of the Daughters of Charity* (Aldershot; Hants. and Burlington, Vt.: Ashgate, 2006); ead., 'Confraternities as a Venue for Female Activism during the Catholic Reformation', in John P. Donnelly and Michael W. Maher (eds.), *Confraternities and Catholic Reform in Italy, France, and Spain* (Kirksville, Mo.: Jefferson University Press, 1999), 191–214; 'Vincenzo de Paoli' in *Dizionario degli istituti di perfezione*, x, coll. 79–89.

72. 'Vincenzo de Paoli', coll. 85–6.

73. 'Luisa de Marillac', in *Dizionario degli istituti di perfezione*, v (1978), coll. 764–8.

74. 'Rules', ch. 1.1., in *Vincent de Paul and Louise de Marillac: Rules, Conferences, and Writings*, ed. Frances Ryan, DC, and John E. Rybolt, CM (New York: Paulist Press, 1995), 169.

75. Louise Sullivan, DC, 'Louise de Marillac: A Spiritual Portrait', in *Vincent de Paul and Louise de Marillac*, 41.

76. 'Rules', ch. 1.2., ibid. 169.

77. Ibid. 169.

78. Dinan, 'Confraternities', 204–7.

79. Sullivan, 'Louise de Marillac', 50.

80. Susan E. Dinan, 'Public Charity and Public Piety: The Missionary Vocation of the Daughters of Charity', *Proceedings of the Western Society for French History*, 27 (Spring 2001), 207–8 n. 7.

81. Sullivan, 'Louise de Marillac', 46.

82. 'Figlie della Carità di San Vincenzo de Paoli', in *Dizionario degli istituti di perfezione*, iii (1976), coll. 1539–48.

83. Dinan, 'Confraternities', 200.

84. 'Rules', ch. 9.11., 190.

85. Dinan, 'Public Charity', 203–5; Sullivan, 'Louise de Marillac', 52–7.

86. 'Figlie della Carità', coll. 1546–7.

87. On the innovative impetus of the Daughters see Rapley, *The Dévotes*, 114, and Dinan, 'Confraternities', 208–9.

88. Hufton, *Whatever Happened*, 24–8; M. Vacher, *Des régulières dans le siècle: Les Sœurs de Saint Joseph de Père Médaille aux xviie et xviiie siècles* (Paris: Clermont Ferrand, 1991).

EPILOGUE

1. Mita Choudhury, *Convents and Nuns in Eighteenth-Century French Political Culture* (Ithaca, NY: Cornell University Press, 2004).
2. Hufton and Tallett, 'Communities of Women', 77; Olwen Hufton, *Women and the Limits of Citizenship in the French Revolution: The Donald G. Creighton Lectures 1989* (Toronto: University of Toronto Press, 1992).
3. Evangelisti, 'Ricche e povere'.
4. Alice Kelikian, 'Nuns, Entrepreneurs, and Church Welfare in Italy', in Hufton (ed.), *Yearbook of the Department of History and Civilization*, 119–38.
5. Antonio Rabinad, *La suora anarchica* (Vetere CE: Edizioni Spartaco, 2006).
6. Mary Nash, *Mujeres Libres: Espana, 1936–1939* (Barcelona. Tusquets, 1975); ead., *Defying Male Civilization: Women in the Spanish Civil War* (Denver, Colo.: Arden Press, 1995).

BIBLIOGRAPHY

Manuscript Sources

Archivio Segreto Vaticano (ASV), *Prattica del governo spirituale e temporale de Monasteri delle Monache secondo le regole et constitutioni de Santi Padri loro fondatori et del Sacro Concilio di Trento e di Sommi Pontefici* [1604].
Archivio di Stato di Firenze (ASF), *Corporazioni soppresse dal governo francese* (CRS), 133, S. Giovannino, 60.
—— CRS, 106, Santa Caterina da Siena, 35.
—— S. Jacopo di Ripoli, 23, *Libro di Croniche segnato A* (1508–1778).
Biblioteca Apostolica Vaticana (BAV), Vat. Lat. 11914, *Regulae et Costitutiones pro monasteriis ab ordinario episcopo compositae.*

Published Sources

Ago, Renata, *Carriere e clientele nella Roma barocca* (Rome and Bari: Laterza, 1990).
Allen, Christine, 'Women in Colonial French America', in Rosemary Radford Ruether and Rosemary Skinner Keller (eds.), *Women and Religion in America: The Colonial and Revolutionary Period*, ii (New York: Harper and Row, 1983), 79–31.
Angela da Foligno, *Il Libro della Beata Angela da Foligno*, ed. Sergio Andreoli (Cinisello Balsamo: San Paolo, 1996).
Arenal, Electa, and Schlau, Stacey (eds.), *Untold Sisters: Hispanics Nuns in their Own Words* (Albuquerque, N. Mex.: University of New Mexico Press, 1989).

Baade, Colleen R., 'La "musica sutil" del monasterio de la madre de Dios de Constantinopla: Aportaciones para la historia de la musica en los monasteries femeninons de Madrid a finales del siglo XVI–siglo XVII', *Revista de Musicologia*, 20/1 (2002), 221–30.

Baade, Colleen R., 'Music and Misgiving in Female Monasteries in Early Modern
    Castile', unpublished conference paper presented at *Female Monasticism in Early
    Modern Europe*, Cambridge, Wolfson College, 23–4 July 2003.

Baernstein, P. Renée, 'Vita pubblica, vita familiare e memoria storica nel monastero di
    San Paolo a Milano', in Pomata and Zarri (eds.), *I monasteri femminili*, 297–311.

—— *A Convent Tale: A Century of Sisterhood in Spanish Milan* (New York and
    London: Routledge, 2002).

—— 'In Widow's Habit: Women between Convent and Family in Sixteenth-Century
    Milan', *Sixteenth Century Journal*, 24 (1994), 787–807.

Baitelli, Angelica, *Annali Historici dell'Edificatione Erettione et Dotatione del Serenis-
    simo Monasterio di S. Salvatore, et S.Giulia di Brescia* (Brescia: Antonio Rizzardi,
    1657).

Bandera, Sandrina, and Fiorio, Maria Teresa (eds.), *Bernadino Luini e la pittura del
    Rinascimento a Milano: Gli affreschi di San Maurizio al Monastero Maggiore* (Milan:
    Skira, 2000).

Barragan, Elisa Garcia, 'Mistica y esplendor barrocos en Mexico colonial: Retratos de
    monjas coronadas', *Boletin del Museo e Instituto 'Camon Aznar'*, 48–9 (1992), 61–82.

Barrière, Bernardette, 'The Cistercian Convent of Coytoux in the Twelfth Century:
    Anxiety, Authority and Architecture in the Female Spiritual Life', *Gesta*, 31/2 (1992),
    76–82.

Barros, Mafalda Magalhaes et al. (eds.), *Struggle for Synthesis: The Total Work of Art in
    the 17th and 18th Centuries* (Lisbon: Ministério da Cultura, 1999).

Bell, Rudolph M., *Holy Anorexia* (Chicago: University of Chicago Press, 1985).

Bembo, Illuminata, *Specchio di Illuminazione*, ed. Silvia Mostaccio (Florence: Sismel
    Edizioni del Gralluzzo, 2001).

Berrigan, Joseph R., 'Saint Catherine of Bologna: Franciscan Mystic', in Katarina M.
    Wilson (ed.), *Women Writers of the Renaissance and Reformation* (Athens, Ga.:
    University of Georgia Press, 1987), 81–95.

Biancani, Stefania, 'La leggenda di un'artista monaca: Caterina Vigri', in Pomata and
    Zarri (eds.), *I monasteri femminili*, 203–19.

Bibliotheca Sanctorum, 12 vols. (Rome: Città Nuova Editrice, 1961–9).

Bilinkoff, Jodi, *The Avila of Saint Teresa: Religious Reform in a Sixteenth-Century City*
    (Ithaca, NY: Cornell University Press, 1990).

—— *Related Lives: Confessors and their Female Penitents, 1450–1750* (Ithaca, NY:
    Cornell University Press, 2005).

Blaisdell, Charmarie J., 'Angela Merici and the Ursulines', in Richard L. De Molen
    (ed.), *Religious Orders of the Counter-Reformation* (New York: Fordham University
    Press, 1994).

Bonfà, Fernanda Sorbelli, *Camilla Gonzaga Faá: Storia documentata* (Bologna:
    Zanichelli, 1918).

Borromeo, Carlo, 'Regole appartenenti alle monache, cavate dai Concilii Provinciali di
    Milano, fatte volgari, e ridotte in un corpo, sotto i titoli del primo', in *Acta Ecclesiae
    Mediolanensis* (Mediolani: ex officina Typografica quon. Pacifici Pontijs, 1599).

Bourne, Molly, 'From Court to Cloister and Back Again: The Circulation of Objects in the Clarissan Convent of Sant'Orsola in Mantua', in Cavallo and Evangelisti (eds.), *Domestic and Institutional Interiors* (forthcoming).

Boxer, Marylin J., and Quataert, Jean H. (eds.), *Connecting Spheres: Women in the Western World, 1500 to the Present* (Oxford: Oxford University Press, 1987).

Brighetti, Simona, 'La "perfetta monaca": Creanza cristiana in convento tra letteratura, precettistica e iconografia', in Fortunati (ed.), *Vita artistica nel monastero femminile*, 46–69.

Brooke, Rosalind B., and Brooke, Christopher N. L., 'St Clare', in Derek Baker (ed.), *Medieval Women* (Oxford: Blackwell, 1978), 275–87.

Brown, Judith C., *Immodest Acts: The Life of a Lesbian Nun in Renaissance Italy* (New York: Oxford University Press, 1986).

—— 'Monache a Firenze all'inizio dell'età moderna: Un'analisi comparata', *Quaderni storici*, 85 (1994), 117–52.

—— and Davis, Robert C. (eds.), *Gender and Society in Renaissance Italy* (London and New York: Longman, 1998).

Bruneau, Marie-Florine, *Women Mystics Confront the Modern World: Marie de l'Incarnation (1599–1672) and Madame Guyon (1648–1717)* (Albany, NY: State University of New York Press, 1998).

Bruzelius, Caroline A., 'Hearing is Believing: Clarissan Architecture, ca.1213–1340', *Gesta*, 31/2 (1990), 83–91.

Bryant, Gwendolyn, 'The Nuremberg Abbess: Caritas Pirkheimer', in Katharina M. Wilson (ed.), *Women Writers of the Renaissance and Reformation* (Athens, Ga.: University of Georgia Press, 1987), 287–303.

Buccianti, C., 'Monasteri femminili a Siena nel seicento: Note di demografia storica', *Bollettino di demografia storica SIDES*, 22 (1995), 23–42.

Burns, Kathryn, *Colonial Habits: Convents and the Spiritual Economy of Cuzco, Peru* (Durham, NC: Duke University Press, 1999).

Burns, Marie Patricia, 'Jeanne de Chantal et la tradition', in Bernard Dompnier and Julia Dominique (eds.), *Visitation et Visitandines aux xviie et xviiie siècles* (Saint-Étienne: Publication de l'Université de Saint-Etienne, 2001).

Burr, R. Lichtfield, 'Demographic Characteristics of Florentine Patricians' Families, Sixteenth to Nineteenth Centuries', *Journal of Economic History*, 29 (1969), 191–205.

Bynum, Caroline Walker, *Holy Feast and Holy Fast: The Religious Significance of Food to Medieval Women* (Berkeley and Los Angeles: University of California Press, 1987).

Cabibbo, Sara, and Modica, Marilena, *La Santa dei Tomasi: Storia di suor Maria crocefissa (1645–1699)* (Turin: Einaudi, 1989).

Camiz, Franca Trinchieri, '"Virgo-non sterilis...": Nuns as Artists in Seventeenth-Century Rome', in *Picturing Women in Renaissance and Baroque Italy* (Cambridge: Cambridge University Press, 1997), 139–64.

Carroll, Jane L., 'Woven Devotions: Reform and Piety in Tapestries by Dominican Nuns', in Jane L. Carroll and Alison G. Stewart (eds.), *Saints, Sinners, and Sisters: Gender and Northern Art in Medieval and Early Modern Europe* (Aldershot, Hants. and Burlington Vt.: Ashgate, 2003), 182–201.

Castelao, Ofelia Rey, and Estepa, Raquel Iglesias, 'Domestic Service in Spain, 1750–1836: The Domestic Servants of the Clergy', in Antoinette Fauve-Chamoux (ed.), *Domestic Service and the Formation of European Identity: Understanding the Globalization of Domestic Work, 16th-21st Centuries* (Berne and Berlin: Peter Lang, 2005), 127–40.

Catalano, Michele (ed.), *La leggenda della beata Eustochia da Messina* (Messina and Florence: G. D'Anna, 1950).

Cavallo, Sandra, *Charity and Power in Early Modern Italy: Benefactors and their Motives in Turin, 1541–1789* (Cambridge: Cambridge University Press, 1995).

—— and Warner, Lyndan (eds.), *Widowhood in Medieval and Early Modern Europe* (Harlow: Longman, 1999).

—— and Evangelisti, Silvia (eds.), *Domestic and Institutional Interiors in Early Modern Europe* (Aldershot, Hants. and Burlington Vt.: Ashgate forthcoming).

Cesari, Maria Rosa, ' "Per encomiar le donzelle ch'entran nel chiostro": Pubblicazioni celebrative per monacazioni femminili tra sei e settecento', *Il Carrobbio*, 19/20 (1993), 203–22.

Chambers, Mary C. E., *The Life of Mary Ward (1585–1645)* (London: Burns and Oates, 1882).

Chavarria, Elisa Novi, *Monache e gentildonne, un labile confine: Poteri politici e identità religiose nei monasteri napoletani, secoli XVI–XVII* (Milan: Franco Angeli, 2001).

Chojnacka, Monica, and Wiesner-Hanks, Merry E. (eds.), *Ages of Woman, Ages of Man: Sources in European Social History, 1400–1750* (London: Pearson Education, 2002).

Choudhuri, Mita, *Convents and Nuns in Eighteenth-Century French Political Culture* (Ithaca, NY: Cornell University Press, 2004).

Coates, Tim, *Convicts and Orphans: Forced and State-Sponsored Colonizers in the Portuguese Empire (1550–1755)* (Stamford: Stamford University Press, 2001).

Cohen, Sherrill, *The Evolution of Women's Asylums since 1500: From Refuges for Ex-Prostitutes to Shelters for Battered Women* (Oxford: Oxford University Press, 1992).

Cohn, Samuel K. Jr., 'Nuns and Dowry Funds: Women's Choices in the Renaissance' in id., *Women in the Streets: Essays on Sex and Power in Renaissance Italy* (Baltimore: The Johns Hopkin University Press, 1996), 76–97.

Colahan, Clark A., *The Visions of Sor Maria de Agreda: Writing, Knowledge, and Power* (Tucson: University of Arizona Press, 1994).

Contreras, E. Montagut, 'Servicio doméstico y educación en los conventos femeninos del antiguo régimen (siglo XVIII)', *Torre de los Lujanes*, 15 (1990), 156–66.

Cotton, Nancy, *Women Playwrights in England 1363–1750* (Lewisburg, Pa.: Bucknell University Press; London and Toronto: Associated University Presses, 1980).

Cozzolani, Chiara Margarita, *Motets,* ed. Robert L. Kendrick (Madison: A-R Editions, 1998).

Crawford, Patricia, *Women and Religion in England 1500–1720* (London and New York: Routledge, 1993).

Croce, Benedetto, 'Donne letterate nel seicento', in *Nuovi saggi sulla letteratura italiana del seicento* (Bari: Laterza, 1968).

Culpepper, Danielle, '"Our Particular Cloister": Ursulines and Female Education in Seventeenth-Century Parma and Piacenza', *Sixteenth Century Journal,* 4 (2005), 1017–37.

Cuneo, Pia F., 'The Basilica Cycle of Saint Katherine's Convent: Art and Female Community in Early-Renaissance Augsburg', *Woman's Art Journal,* 19/1 (1998), 21–5.

da Brescia, Gerardo, *L'autobiografia della beata suor Maria Maddalena Martinengo di Barco Clarissa Cappuccina* (Milan: Centro Studi Cappuccini Lombardi, 1964).

Davis, Natalie Zemon, 'Women's History in Transition: The European Case', *Feminist Studies, 3* (Spring–Summer 1976), 83–103.

—— 'Gender and Genre: Women as Historical Writers, 1400–1820', in Patricia H. Labalme (ed.), *Beyond their Sex: Learned Women of the European Past* (New York: New York University Press, 1984), 153–82.

—— *Women on the Margins: Three Seventeenth-Century Lives* (Cambridge, Mass.: Harvard University Press, 1995).

—— 'Women on Top', in Lorna Hutson (ed.), *Feminism and Renaissance Studies* (Oxford: Oxford University Press, 1999).

Dean, Trevor, and Lowe, Kate J. P. (eds.), *Marriage in Italy, 1300–1650* (Cambridge: Cambridge University Press, 1998).

de Chantal, Sainte Jeanne-Françoise Fremyot, *Correspondance,* i (Paris: Cerf, 1986).

de la Cruz, Juana Inés, *The Answer/La Respuesta: Including a Selection of Poems,* trans. and ed. Electa Arenal and Amanda Powell (New York: The Feminist Press at the City University of New York, 1994), 1–17.

de San José Salazar, Maria, *Book for the Hour of Recreation,* ed. Alison Weber and Amanda Powell (Chicago: University of Chicago Press, 2002).

del Sera, Beatrice, *Amor di Virtù: Commedia in cinque atti, 1548,* ed. Elissa Weaver (Ravenna: Longo Editore, 1990).

Deslandres, Dominique, 'In the Shadow of the Cloister: Representations of Female Holiness in New France', in Allan Greer and Jody Bilinkoff (eds.), *Colonial Saints: Discovering the Holy in the Americas, 1500–1800* (New York and London: Routledge, 2003), 129–52.

Diderot, Denis, *The Nun* (Oxford: Oxford University Press, 2005).

Diefendorf, Barbara B., *From Penitence to Charity: Pious Women and the Catholic Reformation in Paris* (Oxford and New York: Oxford University Press, 2004).

Dinan, Susan E., 'Confraternities as a Venue for Female Activism during the Catholic Reformation', in John P. Donnelly and Michael W. Maher (eds.), *Confraternities and*

Catholic Reform in Italy, France, and Spain (Kirksville, Mo.: Thomas Jefferson University Press, 1999), 191–214.

Dinan, Susan E., 'Public Charity and Public Piety: The Missionary Vocation of the Daughters of Charity', *Proceedings of the Western Society for French History*, 27 (Spring 2001), 200–9.

—— 'Motivations for Charity in Early Modern France', in Thomas Max Safley (ed.), *The Reformation of Charity: The Secular and the Religious in Early Modern Poor Relief* (Boston and Leiden: Brill, 2003), 176–92.

—— *Women and Poor Relief in Seventeenth-Century France: The Early History of the Daughters of Charity* (Aldershot, Hants. and Burlington, Vt.: Ashgate, 2006).

Dizionario degli istituti di perfezione, 10 vols., ed. Guerrino Pelliccia and Giancarlo Rocca (Milan: Edizioni Paoline, 1973–2003).

Dronke, Peter, *Women Writers of the Middle Ages: A Study of Texts from Perpetua (d.203) to Marguerite Porete (d.1310)* (Cambridge: Cambridge University Press, 1984).

Dunn, Marilyn R., 'Nuns as Patrons: The Decorations of S. Marta at the Collegio Romano', *Art Bulletin*, 70/3 (1988), 451–77.

—— 'Spiritual Philanthropists: Women as Convent Patrons in Seicento Rome', in Cynthia Lawrence (ed.), *Women and Art in Early Modern Europe: Patrons, Collectors, and Connoisseurs* (Pennsylvania, Pa.: Pennsylvania State University Press, 1997), 154–88.

—— 'Spaces Shaped for Spiritual Perfection: Convent Architecture and Nuns in Early Modern Rome', in Helen Hills (ed.), *Architecture and the Politics of Gender in Early Modern Europe* (Aldershot, Hants. and Burlington Vt.: Ashgate, 2003), 151–76.

Egan, Martha J., 'Escudos de Monjas: Religious Miniatures of New Spain', *Latin American Art*, 5/4 (1994), 43–46.

Estenssoro, Juan Carlos, 'Música y fiestas en los Monasterios de Monjas Limenas: Siglos XVII y XVIII', *Revista Musical de Venezuela*, 34 (1997), 127–35.

Evangelisti, Silvia, ' "Farne ciò che pare e piace": l'uso e la trasmissione delle celle nel monastero di Santa Giulia di Brescia (1597–1688)', *Quaderni storici*, 88 (1995), 85–110.

—— 'Moral Virtues and Personal Goods: The Double Representation of Female Monastic Identity (Florence, 16th and 17th Centuries)', in Hufton (ed.), *Yearbook of the Department of History and Civilization: Women in Religious Life* (1996), 27–54.

—— ' "Art and the Advent of *Clausura*": The Convent of Saint Catherine of Siena in Tridentine Florence', in Jonathan Nelson (ed.), *Suor Plautilla Nelli (1523–1588): The First Woman Painter of Florence* (Florence: Cadmo, 2000), 67–82.

—— ' "We do not have it, and we do not want it": Women, Power, and Convent Reform in Florence', *Sixteenth Century Journal*, 34/3 (2003), 677–700.

—— 'Monastic Poverty and Material Culture in Early Modern Italian Convents', *Historical Journal*, 47/1 (2004), 1–20.

—— 'Ricche e povere: Classi di religiose nelle comunità monastiche femminili tra cinque e seicento', in Margareth Lanzinger and Raffaella Sarti (eds.), *Nubili e celiti tra scelta e costruzione (secoli XVI–XIX)* (Udine: Forum, forthcoming 2007).

Fabris, Dinko, ' "Le Chant de trois notes": Une tradition musicale du XVIIe siecle chez les Sœurs de l'Ordre de la Visitation de Marie', in Jean Duron (ed.), *Plain-chant et liturgie en France au XVIIe Siecle* (Paris: Éditions du Centre de Musique Baroque de Versailles, Éditions Klincksieck, 1997).

Fanti, Mario, *Abiti e lavori delle monache di Bologna* (Bologna: Tamari, 1972).

Fauve-Chamoux, A., and Sarti, R. (eds.), *Domestic Service and the Formation of European Identity: Understanding the Globalization of Domestic Work, 16th–21st Centuries* (Berne and Berlin: Peter Lang, 2005).

Ferguson, Moira, *First Feminists: British Women Writers 1578–1799* (Bloomington: Indiana University Press, 1985).

Finucci, Valeria, 'Camilla Faá Gonzaga: The Italian Memorialist', in Katharina M. Wilson and Frank J. Warnke (eds.), *Women Writers of the Seventeenth Century* (Athens, Ga.: University of Georgia Press, 1989), 121–37.

Firpo, Massimo, 'Paola Antonia Negri, monaca angelica (1508–1555)', in *Rinascimento al femminile* (Rome and Bari: Laterza, 1991), 35–82.

Fonay Wemple, Suzanne, 'S. Salvatore/S. Giulia: A Case Study in the Endowement and Patronage of a Major Female Monastery in Northern Italy', in J. Kirshner and S. Fonay Wemple (eds.), *Women of the Medieval World* (Oxford: Oxford University Press, 1985), 85–102.

Fortunati, Vera (ed.), *Vita artistica nel monastero femminile: Exempla* (Bologna: Compositori, 2002).

Foster III, William Henry, 'Women at the Centers, Men at the Margins: The Wilderness Mission of the Secular Sisters of Early Montreal Reconsidered', in Susan E. Dinan and Debra Meyers (eds.), *Women and Religion in Old and New Worlds* (London and New York: Routledge, 2001), 93–112.

Gajano, Sofia Boesch, and Scaraffia, Lucetta (eds.), *Luoghi sacri e spazi della santità* (Turin: Rosemberg & Sellier, 1990).

Gallat-Morin, Elisabeth, 'La Presence en Nouvelle-France de la musique du temps de Louis XIV', *Ostinato Rigore: Revue internationale d'études musicales*, 8–9 (1997), 21–34.

Gaze, Delia, (ed.), *Dictionary of Women Artists* (London and Chicago: Fitzroy Dearborn Publishers, 1997).

Ghirardi, Angela, 'Dipingere in lode del cielo: Suor Orsola Maddalena Caccia e la vocazione artistica delle Orsoline di Moncalvo', in Fortunati (ed.), *Vita artistica nel monastero femminile*, 114–32.

Giles, Mary E., *The Book of Prayer of Sor Maria of Santo Domingo* (Albany, NY: University of New York Press, 1990).

Gill, Katherine, '*Scandala*: Controversies Concerning *Clausura* and Women's Religious Communities in Late Medieval Italy', in Scott L. Waugh and Peter D. Diehl (eds.), *Christendom and Its Discontents: Exclusion, Persecution, and Rebellion, 1000–1500* (Cambridge: Cambridge University Press, 1996), 177–203.

Giuliani, Veronica, *Un tesoro nascosto ossia il diario di S.Veronica Giuliani*, ed. P. Pizzicaria (Prato: Tip. Giachetti, Figlio & C, 1895–1905).

Gladen, Cynthia A., 'Suor Lucrina Fetti: Pittrice in una corte monastica seicentesca', in Pomata Gianna e Gabriella Zarri (eds.), *I monasteri femminili come centri di cultura fra Rinascimento e Barocco* (Rome: Edizioni di Storia e Letteratura, 2005), 123–41.

Glantz, Margo, *Sor Juana Ines de la Cruz: Saberes y Placeres* (Mexico: Toluca, 1996).

Glixon, Jonathan E., 'Images of Paradises or Worldly Theaters? Toward a Taxonomy of Musical Performances at Venetian Nunneries', in *Essays on Music and Culture in Honour of Herbert Kellman* (Paris and Tours: Minerve, 2001).

—— *Honoring God and the City: Music at the Venetian Confraternities, 1260–1807* (New York and Oxford: Oxford University Press, 2003).

Gonzalez, Carmen Julia Gutierrez, 'De Monjas y Tropos: Musica Tardomedieval en un convento Mallorquin', *Anuario Musical: Revista de Musicologia del CESIC*, 53 (1998), 29–60.

Gozalo, M. Barrio, 'La población religiosa de la Corona De Castilla entre el barroco y la ilustración (1591–1768)', *Bollettino di demografia storica SIDES*, 22 (1995)), 11–21.

Graziani, Irene, 'L'iconografia di Caterina Vigri: dalla clausura alla città', in Fortunati (ed.), *Vita artistica nel monastero femminile*, 221–44.

Grell, Ole Peter, Cunningham, Andrew, and Arrizabalaga, Jon, *Health Care and Poor Relief in Counter-Reformation Europe* (London and New York: Routledge, 1999).

Greer, Allan, and Bilinkoff, Jody (eds.), *Colonial Saints: Discovery the Holy in the Americas* (New York and London: Routledge, 2003).

Grundmann, Herbert, *Religious Movements in the Middle Ages: The Historical Links between Heresy, the Mendicant Orders, and the Women's Religious Movement in the Twelfth and Thirteenth Century, with the Historical Foundations of German Mysticism* (Notre Dame, Ind.: University of Notre Dame Press, 1995).

Guimarães Sa, Isabel dos, 'Between Spiritual and Material Culture: Male and Female Objects at the Portuguese Court, 1469–1580' (in Cavallo and Silvia Evangelisti (eds.), *Domestic and Institutional Interiors* forthcoming).

Gunther, Georg, 'Ad Chorum Bonacellensem: The Practice of Music in the Cistercian Nunnery of Gutenzell at the End of the 18th Century', *Cistercienser Chronik: Forum fur Geschichte, Kunst, Literatur und Spiritualitat des Monchtums*, 105/3 (1998), 453–77.

Haas, Gerlinde, 'Pauken und Trompeten…im Frauenkloster: "Komponistinnen", Chorregentinnen und andere Musikerinnen des Ursulines-Klosters in Graz in der Zeit 1686–1755/65', *Musicologia Austriaca*, 18 (1999), 141–50.

Haliczer, Stephen, *Between Exaltation and Infamy: Female Mystics in the Golden Age of Spain* (Oxford: Oxford University Press, 2002).

Hamburger, Jeffrey F., 'Art, Enclosure and the Cura Monialium: Prolegomena in the Guise of a Post-Script', *Gesta*, 31/2 (1992).

—— *Nuns as Artists: The Visual Culture of a Medieval Convent* (Berkeley and Los Angeles: University of California Press, 1997).

—— '"To Make Women Weep": Ugly as "Feminine" and the Origins of Modern Aesthetics', *Res*, 31 (Spring 1997), 9–33.

—— The Visual and the Visionary: Art and Female Spirituality in Late Medieval Germany (New York: Zone Books, 1998).

Harline, Craig, 'Actives and Contemplatives: The Female Religious of the Low Countries Before and After Trent', Catholic Historical Review, 81/4 (1995), 541–67.

—— The Burden of Sister Margaret: Inside a Seventeenth-Century Convent (New Haven: Yale University Press, 2000).

Harness, Kelley, 'The "Perfect Model of the Union between the Spiritual and Temporal": La Crocetta and the Medici', unpublished conference paper presented at Female Monasticism in Early Modern Europe, Cambridge, Wolfson College, 23–4 July 2003.

Harris, Ann Sutherland, and Nochlin, Linda (eds.), Women Artists: 1550–1950 (New York: Alfred Knopf, 1976).

Hernandez, Ana Garcia Sanz and Sanchez, Leticia, 'Iconografia de monjas, santas y beatas en los monasteries reales espanoles', in La mujer en el arte espanol: VII jornadas de arte (Madrid: Alpuerto, 1997), 131–42.

Hills, Helen, 'Cities and Virgins: Female Aristocratic Convents in Early Modern Naples and Palermo', Oxford Art Journal (1999), 48–50.

—— 'Enamelled with the Blood of a Noble Lineage: Tracing Noble Blood and Female Holiness in Early Modern Neapolitan Convents and their Architecture', Church History, 73/1 (2004), 1–40.

—— Invisible City: The Architecture of Devotion in Seventeenth-Century Neapolitan Convents (Oxford: Oxford University Press, 2004).

—— 'Housing Institutional Architecture: Searching for a Domestic Holy in Post-Tridentine Italian Convents', in Cavallo and Evangelisti (eds.), Domestic and Institutional Interiors (forthcoming).

Hsia, R. Po-Chia, The World of Catholic Renewal, 1540–1770 (Cambridge: Cambridge University Press, 2000).

Hufton, Olwen, The Prospect before Her: A History of Women in Western Europe (London: HarperCollins, 1995).

—— 'Altruism and Reciprocity: The Early Jesuits and their Female Patrons', Renaissance Studies, 15/3 (2001), 328–53.

—— 'Whatever Happened to the History of the Nun?', Royal Holloway University of London, Hayes Robinson Lecture Series 3 (2000).

—— Women and the Limits of Citizenship in the French Revolution: The Donald G. Creighton Lectures 1989 (Toronto: University of Toronto Press, 1992).

—— (ed.), Yearbook of the Department of History and Civilization: Women in Religious Life (Florence: European University Institute, 1996).

—— and Tallett, Frank, 'Communities of Women, the Religious Life, and Public Service in Eighteenth-Century France', in Marylin J. Boxer and Jean H. Quataert (eds.), Connecting Spheres: Women in the Western World, 1500 to the Present (Oxford: Oxford University Press, 1987), 75–85.

Hughes, Diane Owen, 'Representing the Family: Portraits and Purposes in Early Modern Italy', Journal of Interdisciplinary History, 17 (1986), 7–38.

Jacobsen, Grethe, 'Nordic Women and the Reformation', in Sherrin Marshall (ed.), *Women in Reformation and Counter-Reformation Europe: Public and Private Worlds* (Bloomington: Indiana University Press, 1989), 49–50.

Jancke-Leutzsch, Gabi, 'Clara Staiger, la priora', in Giulia Calvi (ed.), *Barocco al femminile* (Rome: Laterza, 1992), 97–126.

Jonas, Raymond, *France and the Cult of the Sacred Heart: An Epic Tale for Modern Times* (Berkeley and Los Angeles: University of California Press, 2000).

Johnson, Penelope D., *Equal in Monastic Profession: Religious Women in Medieval France* (Chicago: University of Chicago Press, 1991).

—— 'La Théorie de la clôture et l'activité réelle des moniales françaises du xie au xiiie siècle', in *Les Religieuses dans le cloître et dans le monde des origines à nos jours* (Saint-Étienne: Publication de l'Université de Saint-Étienne, 1994), 491–506.

Julia, Dominique, 'L'Expansion de l'ordre de la Visitation des origins à la Révolution française', in Dompnier and Julia (eds.), *Visitation et Visitandines aux xviie et xviiie siècles*, 37–51.

Karant-Nunn, Susan, and Wiesner-Hanks, Merry E., *Luther on Women: A Sourcebook* (Cambridge: Cambridge University Press, 2003).

Kauffman, Deborah Ann, '*Chants and Motets* (1733): Nivers, Clerambault, and Changing Musical Style at the *Maison Royal de Saint-Louis* at Saint-Cyr', Ph.D. thesis, Stanford University, 1994.

Kelikian, Alice, 'Nuns, Entrepreneurs, and Church Welfare in Italy', in Hufton (ed.), *Yearbook of the Department of History and Civilization* (1996), 119–38.

Kendrick, Thomas D., *Mary of Agreda: The Life and Legend of a Spanish Nun* (London: Routledge and Kegan Paul, 1967).

Kendrick, Robert L., 'The Traditions of Milanese Convent Music and the Sacred Dialogues of Chiara Margarita Cozzolani', in Monson (ed.), *Crannied Wall*, 211–33.

—— 'Four Views of Milanese Nuns' Music', in Matter and Coakley (eds.), *Creative Women* 324–42.

—— *Celestial Sirens: Nuns and their Music in Early Modern Milan* (Oxford: Oxford University Press, 1996).

Kirk, Pamela, *Sor Juana Inés de la Cruz: Religion, Art, and Feminism* (New York: Continuum, 1998).

King, Margaret L., 'Book-Lined Cells: Women and Humanism in the Early Italian Renaissance', in Labalme (ed.), *Beyond their Sex*, 66–90.

—— and Rabil Jr., Albert (eds.), *Her Immaculate Hand: Selected Works by and about the Women Humanists of Quattrocento Italy* (Binghamton, NY: State University of New York, 1981).

Klapisch-Zuber, Christiane, 'Holy Dolls: Play and Piety in Florence in the Quattrocento', in ead., *Women, Family, and Ritual in Renaissance Italy* (Chicago: University of Chicago Press, 1985), 310–29.

Koorn, Florence, 'Women without Vows: The Case of the Beguines and the Sisters of the Common Life in the Northern Netherlands', in Elisja Schulte van Kessel (ed.), *Women and Men in Spiritual Culture: XIV–XVII Centuries: A Meeting of North and South* (The Hague: Netherlands Government Publishing Office, 1986), 135–47.

—— 'Elizabeth Strouven, la donna religiosa', in Giulia Calvi (ed.), *Barocco al femminile* (Rome and Bari: Laterza, 1992), 127–52.

Laven, Mary, *Virgins of Venice: Enclosed Lives and Broken Vows in the Renaissance Convent* (London: Penguin, 2002).

Lavrin, Asunción, 'Women and Religion in Spanish America', in Rosemary Radford Ruether and Rosemary Skinner Keller (eds.), *Women and Religion in America: The Colonial and Revolutionary Period*, ii (New York: Harper & Row, 1983), 42–78.

—— (ed.), *Latin American Women: Historical Perspectives* (Westport, Conn.: Greenwood Press, 1978).

—— 'Values and Meaning of Monastic Life for Nuns of Colonial Mexico', *Catholic Historical Review*, 16/3 (1983).

—— 'Female Religious', in Louisa Schell Hoberman and Susan Midgen Socolow (ed.), *Cities and Society in Colonial Latin America* (Albuquerque, N. Mex.: University of New Mexico Press, 1986).

Lawless, George (ed.), *Augustine of Hippo and his Monastic Rule* (Oxford: Oxford University Press, 1987).

Ledochowska, Thérèse, *Angèle Merici et la Compagnie de Ste-Ursule* (Rome and Milan: Ancora, 1967).

Lehfeldt, Elizabeth A., *Religious Women in Golden Age Spain: The Permeable Cloister* (Aldershot, Hants. and Burlington, Vt.: Ashgate, 2005).

—— 'Discipline, Vocation, and Patronage: Spanish Religious Women in a Tridentine Microclimate', *Sixteenth Century Journal*, 30/4 (1999), 1009–30.

Leonard, Amy, *Nails in the Wall: Catholic Nuns in Reformation Germany* (Chicago: University of Chicago Press, 2005).

—— 'Female Religious Orders' in R. Po-chia Hsia (ed.), *A Companion to the Reformation World* (Oxford: Blackwell, 2004), 237–54.

Liebowitz, Ruth P., 'Virgins in the Service of Christ: The Dispute over an Active Apostolate for Women During the Counter-Reformation', in Ruether and McLaughlin (eds.), *Women of Spirit*, 132–51.

Lierheimer, Linda, 'Redefining Convent Space: Ideals of Female Community among Seventeenth-Century Ursuline Nuns', *Proceedings of the Western Society for French History*, 24 (1997), 211–20.

—— 'Preaching or Teaching? Defining the Ursuline Mission in Seventeenth-Century France', in Beverly Mayne Kienzle and Pamela J. Walker (eds.), *Women Preachers and Prophets through Two Millennia of Christianity* (Berkeley and Los Angeles: University of California Press, 1998), 212–26.

Litchfield, R. Burr, 'Demographic Characteristics of Florentine Patrician Families, Sixteenth to Nineteenth Centuries', *Journal of Economic History*, 29 (1969), 191–205.

Lowe, Kate, 'Nuns and Choice: Artistic Decision-Making in Medicean Florence', in Eckart Marchand and Alison Wright (eds.), *With and Without the Medici: Studies in Tuscan Art and Patronage 1434–1530* (Aldershot, Hants. and Burlington Vt.: Ashgate, 1998), 129–53.

—— 'History Writing from within the Convent in Cinquecento Italy: The Nuns' Version', in Letizia Panizza (ed.), *Women in Italian Renaissance Culture and Society* (Oxford: Oxford University Press, 2000), 105–21.

—— 'Raina D. Leonor of Portugal's Patronage in Renaissance Florence and Cultural Exchange', in ead. (ed.), *Cultural Links between Portugal and Italy in the Renaissance* (Oxford: Oxford University Press, 2000), 225–48.

—— *Nuns' Chronicles and Convent Culture in Renaissance and Counter-Reformation Italy* (Cambridge: Cambridge University Press, 2003).

Lux Sterritt, Laurence, *Redefining Female Religious Life: French Ursulines and English Ladies in Seventeenth-Century Catholicism* (Aldershot Hants. and Burlington Vt.: Ashgate, 2005).

McKnight, Kathryn J., *The Mystic of Tunja: The Writings of Madre Castillo, 1671–1742* (Amherst, Mass: University of Massachusetts Press, 1997).

McLaughlin, Eleanor Commo, 'Equality of Souls, Inequality of Sexes: Women in Medieval Theology', in Rosemary Ruether (ed.), *Religion and Sexism* (New York: Simon & Schuster, 1974), 213–66.

McNamara, Jo Ann K., *Sisters in Arms: Catholic Nuns through Two Millennia* (Cambridge, Mass.: Harvard University Press, 1996).

Makowski, Elizabeth, *Canon Law and Cloistered Women: Periculoso and its Commentators, 1298–1545* (Washington DC: Catholic University of America Press, 1997).

Marcela de San Felix, *Obra Completa: Coloquios Espirituates, Loas y otro Poemas*, ed. Electa Arenal and Georgina Sabàt Rivers (Barcelona: PPU, 1988).

Maria Maddalena de Pazzi, *Tutte le opere di Maria Maddalena de Pazzi dai manoscritti originali* (Florence: Centro Internazionale del Libro, 1960–60).

Mariani, Luciana, Tarolli, Elisa, and Seynaeve, Marie, *Angela Merici: Contributo per una biografia* (Milan: Ancora, 1986).

Marshall, Sherrin (ed.), *Women in Reformation and Counter-Reformation Europe: Public and Private Worlds* (Bloomington: Indiana University Press, 1989).

Martín, Luis, *Daughters of the Conquistadores: Women of the Viceroyalty of Peru* (Albuquerque, N. Mex.: University of New Mexico Press, 1983).

Matter, E. Ann, and Coakley, John (eds.), *Creative Women in Medieval and Early Modern Italy* (Philadelphia: University of Pennsylvania Press, 1994).

May, Georges, 'Le Modèle inconnu de "La Religieuse" de Diderot: Marguerite Delamarre', *Revue d'histoire litteraire de la France* (1951), 273–87.

Mazzonis, Querciolo, 'A Female Idea of Religious Perfection: Angela Merici and the Company of St. Ursula (1535–1540)', *Renaissance Studies*, 18 (2004), 391–411.

Medioli, Francesca, *L' 'Inferno monacale' di Arcangela Tarabotti* (Turin: Rosemberg & Sellier, 1990).

—— 'Monacazioni forzate: Donne ribelli al proprio destino', *Clio*, 3 (1994), 431–54.

—— 'La clausura delle monache nell'amministrazione della Congregazione Romana sopra i Regolari', in Gabriella Zarri (ed.), *Il monachesimo femminile in Italia dall'alto medioevo al secolo XVII a confronto con l'oggi* (Verona: Il Segno, 1997), 249–82.

—— 'An Unequal Law: The Enforcement of Clausura Before and After the Council of Trent', in Christine Meek (ed.), *Women in Renaissance and Early Modern Europe* (Dublin: Four Courts Press, 2000), 136–52.

Memoriale di Monteluce: Cronaca del monastero delle Clarisse di Perugia dal 1448 al 1838, ed. Ugolino Nicolini (Assisi: Porziuncola, 1983).

Monson, Craig A., 'The Making of Lucrezia Orsina Vizzana's Componimenti Musicali (1623)', in Matter and Coakley (eds.), *Creative Women in Medieval and Early Modern Italy*, 297–323.

—— *Disembodied Voices: Music and Culture in an Early Modern Italian Convent* (Berkeley and Los Angeles: University of California Press, 1995).

—— (ed.), *The Crannied Wall: Women, Religion, and the Arts in Early Modern Europe* (Ann Arbor: University of Michigan Press, 1992).

Monteiro, Marit E., *Geestelijke Maagden: Leven Tussen Klooster en Wereld in Noord-Nederland Gedurende de Zeventiende Eeuw* (Hilversum: Verloren, 1996).

Montford, Kimberlyn, 'L'anno santo and Female Monastic Churches: The Politics, Businness and Music of the Holy Year in Rome (1675)', *Journal of Seventeenth-Century Music*, 6/1 (2000), (electronic resource).

Monticelli, Paolo, *Isabella Leonarda, la musa novarese* (Turin: Centro di Studi Piemontesi, Instituto per i beni musicali in Piemonte, 1998).

Muriel, Josefina, *Cultura femenina novohispana* (Mexico: Universidad Nacional Autónoma de México, 1982).

Murphy, Caroline, 'Plautilla Nelli, between Cloister and Client: A Study in Negotiation', in Nelson (ed.), *Suor Plautilla Nelli*, 57–65.

Nancarrow, Mindy Taggard, 'Picturing Intimacy in a Spanish Golden Age Convent', *Oxford Art Journal*, 1 (2000), 97–111.

—— 'The Artistic Activity of Spanish Nuns during the Golden Age', in Liana De Girolami Cheney (ed.), *Essays on Women Arists: 'The Most Excellent'*, i (Lewinston, NY: Edwin Mellen, 2003), 41–51.

Nash, Mary, *Mujeres libres: España, 1936–1939* (Barcelona: Tusquets, 1975).

Nelson, Jonathan (ed.), *Suor Plautilla Nelli (1523–1588): The First Woman Painter in Florence* (Florence: Cadmo, 2000).

Oliva, Marilyn, *The Convent and the Community in Late Medieval England: Female Monasteries in the Diocese of Norwich, 1350–1540* (Woodbridge: The Boydell Press, 1998).

O'Malley, John W., *Trent and All That: Renaming Catholicism in the Early Modern Era* (Cambridge, Mass.: Harvard University Press, 2000).

Pascal, Jaqueline, *A Rule for Children and other Writings*, ed. John J. Conley, SJ (Chicago: University of Chicago Press, 2003).

Pasquali, G., 'S. Giulia di Brescia', in Andrea Castagnetti (ed.), *Inventari altomedieval di terre, coloni e redditi (secc. IX–X)* (Rome: Istituto Storico Italiano per il Medio Evo, 1979), 41–94.

Paz, Octavio, *Sor Juana, or the Traps of Faith* (Cambridge, Mass.: Belknap, 1988).

Pearson, Andrea G., 'Nuns, Images, and the Ideals of Women's Monasticism: Two Paintings from the Cistercian Convent of Flines', *Renaissance Quarterly*, 54 (2001), 1356–1402.

—— *Envisioning Gender in Burgundian Devotional Art, 1350–1530: Experience, Authority, Resistance* (Aldershot, Hants. and Burlington, Vt.: Ashgate, 2005).

Pellizzari, Francesco, *Trattato delle principali obbligazioni delle monache* (Ferrara: Giuseppe Gironi, 1647).

Perez Baltasar, Maria Dolores, 'Saber y Creación Literaria: Los Claustros Femeninos en la Edad Moderna', *Cuadernos de Historia Moderna*, 20 (1998), 129–43.

Perry, Mary Elizabeth, *Gender and Disorder in Early Modern Seville* (Princeton: Princeton University Press, 1990).

Petroff, Elizabeth A., 'A Medieval Woman's Utopian Vision: The Rule of Saint Clare of Assisi', in *Body and Soul: Essays on Medieval Women and Mysticism* (New York and Oxford: Oxford University Press, 1994), 66–79.

—— *Medieval Women Visionary Literature* (Oxford: Oxford University Press, 1986).

Pinson, Jean-Pierre, 'Le Plain-Chant en Nouvelle-France aux xviie at xviiie siecles: Vers une première sintèse', in Jean Duron (ed.), *Plain-Chant et liturgie en France au xviie siècle* (Paris: Klincksieck Editions, 2000), 249–64.

Pioppi, Suor Lucia, *Diario (1541–1612),* ed. Rolando Bussi (Modena: Panini, 1982).

Pomata, Gianna, and Zarri, Gabriella (eds.), *I monasteri femminili come centri di cultura tra Rinascimento e Barocco* (Rome: Edizioni di Storia e Letteratura, 2005).

Poutrin, Isabelle, *Le Voile et la plume: Autobiographie et sainteté feminine dans l'Espagne moderne* (Madrid: Casa de Velázquez, 1995).

Power, Eileen, *Medieval English Nunneries c.1275 to 1535* (New York: Biblo and Tannen, 1922).

Pozzi, Giovanni, and Leonardi, Claudio (eds.), *Scrittrici mistiche italiane* (Genoa: Marietti, 1988).

Prior, Mary (ed.), *Women in English Society 1500–1800* (London: Routledge, 1985).

Prosperi, Adriano, 'Diari femminili e discernimento degli spiriti: Le mistiche della prima età moderna in Italia', *Dimensioni e problemi della ricerca storica*, 2 (1994), 77–103.

—— 'Lettere spirituali', in Scaraffia Lucetta and Gabriella Zarri (eds.), *Donne e fede: Santità e vita religiosa in Italia* (Rome: Laterza, 1994), 227–51.

Pullan, Brian, *Poverty and Charity: Europe, Italy, Venice, 1400–1700* (Aldershot: Variourum 1994).

Quondam, Amedeo, 'Lanzichenecchi in convento: Suor orsola e la storia tra archivio e devozione', *Schifanoia*, 6 (1988), 37–125.

Rabinad, Antonio, *La suora anarchica* (Vetere: Edizioni Spartaco, 2006).

Radke, Gary M., 'Nuns and their Art: The Case of San Zaccaria in Renaissance Venice', *Renaissance Quarterly* (2001), 431–59.

Rapley, Elizabeth, *The Dévotes: Women and the Church in Seventeenth-Century France* (London and Montreal: McGill-Queen's University Press, 1990).

—— *A Social History of the Cloister: Daily Life in the Teaching Monasteries of the Old Regime* (Montreal: McGill-Queens University Press, 2001).

Ranft, Patricia, *Women and the Religious Life in Premodern Europe* (London: Palgrave Macmillan, 1996).

Reardon, Colleen, *Holy Concord within Sacred Walls: Nuns and Music in Siena, 1575–1700* (New York and Oxford: Oxford University Press, 2002).

Richiedei, Paolo, *Regola data dal Padre S. Agostino alle monache* (Brescia: Domenico Grommi, 1687).

—— *Pratica di coscienza per tutte le religiose claustrali divisa in ventidue trattati* (Bologna: Longhi, 1710).

Roberts, Ann, 'Plautilla Nelli's "Last Supper" and the Tradition of Dominican Refectory Decorations', in Nelson (ed.), *Suor Plautilla Nelli*, 45–55.

Rocher, Yves (ed.), *L'Art du XVIIe siècle dans les Carmels de France* (Paris: Musée du Petit Palais, 1982).

Rowlands, Marie B., 'Recusant Women 1560–1640', in Prior (ed.), *Women in English Society*, 149–80.

Ruether, Rosemary, and McLaughlin, Eleanor (eds.), *Women of Spirit: Female Leadership in the Jewish and Christian Traditions* (New York: Simon and Schuster, 1979).

Ryschawy, Hans, '"Am Ende Wurde Sie Zur Pein" Musik in Oberschwabischen Frauenklostern am Beispiel der Zisterze Baindt', *Musik in Baden-Wurttemberg*, 2 (1995), 167–92.

Sales, François de, and de Chantal, Jeanne-Françoise, *Letters of Spiritual Direction* (New York: Paulist Press, 1988).

Salmen, Walter, 'Tanzen in Klostern wahrend des Mittelalters', in *Die Kloster als Pflegestatten von Musik und Kunst* (850 Jahre Kloster Michaelstein), 67–74.

Sampson, Elisa, 'Writing in the New Spanish Cloister', in Hufton (ed.), *Yearbook of the Department of History and Civilization* (1996), 55–95.

—— *Colonial Angels: Narratives of Gender and Spirituality in Mexico, 1580–1750* (Austin: University of Texas Press, 2000).

Sánchez, Concha Torres, *Ana de Jesus: Cartas (1590–1621): Religiosidad y vida cotidiana en la clausura femenina del Siglo de Oro* (Salamanca: Ediciones Universidad de Salamanca, 1995).

—— *Ana de Jesús (1545–1621)* (Madrid: Ediciones del Orto, 1999).

—— *La clausura imposible: Conventualismo femenino y expansión contrarreformista* (Madrid: Asociación Cultural Almudayna, 2000).

Sánchez, Magdalena S., *The Empress, the Queen, and the Nun: Women and Power at the Court of Philip III of Spain* (Baltimore: The Johns Hopkins University Press, 1998).

La Santa nella storia nelle lettere e nell'arte (Bologna: Alfonso Garagnani, 1912).

Scandella, Angela Emmanuela, and Bocciali, Giovanni (eds.), *Ricordanze del monastero di S.Lucia osc. in Foligno* (Assisi: Porziuncola, 1987).

Scaraffia, Lucetta, and Zarri, Gabriella (ed.), *Donne e fede: Santità e vita religiosa in Italia* (Rome: Laterza, 1994).

Scattigno, Anna, '"Carissimo figliolo in Cristo": Direzione spirituale e mediazione sociale nell'epistolario di Caterina de'Ricci (1542–1590)', in Lucia Ferrante, Maura Palazzi, and Gianna Pomata (eds.), *Ragnatele di rapporti: Patronage e reti di relazione nella storia delle donne* (Turin: Rosember & Sellier, 1988), 219–39.

—— 'Jeanne de Chantal, la fondatrice', in Giulia Calvi (ed.), *Barocco al femminile* (Rome and Bari: Laterza 1992), 153–90.

—— 'Lettere dal convento', in Gabriella Zarri (ed.), *Per lettera: La scrittura epistolare femminile tra archivio e tipografia secoli XV–XVIII* (Rome: Viella, 1999), 347–8.

Schroeder, H. J. (ed.), *Canons and Decrees of the Council of Trent* (St Louis, Mo. and London: Herder, 1960).

Schulenburg, Jane Tibbetts, 'Strict Active Enclosure and its Effects on the Female Monastic Experience (ca.500–1100)', in John A. Nichols and Lilian T. Schank (eds.), *Distant Echoes: Medieval Religious Women* (Kalamazoo, Mich.: Cistercian Publications, 1984), 51–86.

Simmons, Lorraine N., 'The Abbey Church at of Fontevraud in the Later Twelfth Century: Anxiety, Authority and Architecture in the Female Spiritual Life', *Gesta*, 31/2 (1990), 103.

Simons, Walter, *Cities of Ladies: Beguine Communities in the Medieval Low Countries, 1200–1565* (Philadelphia: University of Pennsylvania Press, 2001).

Simpson, Patricia, *Marguerite Bourgeoys and Montreal, 1640–1665* (Montreal and Kingston: McGill-Queens University Press, 1997).

Soeiro, Susan, 'The Social and Economic Role of the Convent: Women and Nuns in Colonial Bahia, 1677–1800', *Hispanic American Historical Review*, 54 (1974), 209–32.

Solfaroli Camillocci, Daniela, 'Ginevra, la Riforma e sour Jeanne de Jussie: La *petite chronique* di una clarissa intorno alla metà del cinquecento', in Pomata and Zarri (eds.), *I monasteri femminili*, 275–96.

Spanó Martinelli, Serena, 'La biblioteca del Corpus Domini bolognese: L'inconsueto spaccato di una cultura monastic femminile' *La Bibliofilia*, 88 (1986), 1–23.

Sperling, Jutta G., *Convents and the Body Politic in Late Renaissance Venice* (Chicago: University of Chicago Press, 1999).

Stefaniak, Regina, 'Correggio's *Camera di San Paolo*: An Archaeology of the Gaze', *Art History*, 12 (1993), 203–38.

Stendhal, *Croniques italiennes* (Paris: Flammarion, 1977).

Stevenson, Robert, 'Mexico City Cathedral Music 1600–1675', *Inter-American Music Review*, 9/1 (1987), 75–114.

Strasser, Ulrike, 'Bones of Contention: Cloistered Nuns, Decorated Relics, and the Contest over Women's Place in the Public Sphere of Counter-Reformation Munich', *Archive for Reformation History*, 90 (1999), 255–88.

—— *State of Virginity: Gender, Religion, and Politics in an Early Modern Catholic State* (Ann Arbor: University of Michigan Press, 2004).

Strocchia, Sharon, 'Learning the Virtues: Convent Schools and Female Culture in Renaissance Florence', in Barbara Whitehead (ed.), *Women's Education in Early Modern Europe, 1500–1800*, (New York: Garland, 1999), 3–46.

—— 'Taken into Custody: Girls and Convent Guardianship in Renaissance Florence', *Renaissance Studies*, 17 (2003), 177–200.

Sullivan, Louise, 'Louise de Marillac: a Spiritual Portrait', in Frances Ryan and John E. Rybolt (eds.), *Vincent de Paul and Louise de Marillac: Rules, Conferences, and Writings* (New York: Paulist Press, 1995).

Surtz, Ronald E., *Writing Women in Late Medieval and Early Modern Spain* (Philadelphia: University of Pennsylvania Press, 1995).

Tarabotti, Arcangela, *Che le donne siano della spezie degli uomini: Women are no less rational than men*, ed. Letizia Panizza (London: Institute of Roman Studies, 1994).

Teresa of Avila, *The Complete Works of Saint Teresa of Avila*, trans. and ed. E. Allison Peers (London: Sheed and Ward, 1946).

Thomas, Anabel, *Art and Piety in the Female Religious Communities of Renaissance Italy* (Cambridge: Cambridge University Press, 2003).

Thomas, Marie A., 'Muscovite Convents in the Seventeenth Century', *Russian History*, 10/2 (1983), 230–42.

Trexler, Richard C., 'Le Celibate à la fin du Moyen Âge: Les Religieuses de Florence', *Annales ESC* 27 (1972), 1329–50.

Turrill, Catherine, 'Compagnie and Discepole: The Presence of Other Women Artists at Santa Caterina da Siena', in Nelson (ed.), *Suor Plautilla Nelli*, 83–102.

Urbini, Silvia, 'Sul ruolo della donna "incisore" nella storia del libro illustrato', in Zarri (ed.), *Donna, disciplina*, 367–91.

Vacher, M., *Des régulières dans le siècle: Les Sœurs de Saint Joseph de Père Médaille aux xviie et xviiie siècles* (Paris: Clermont Ferrand, 1991).

Valone, Carolyn, 'Roman Matrons as Patrons: Various Views of the Cloister Wall', in Monson (ed.), *Crannied Wall*, 49–72.

—— 'Piety and Patronage: Women and the Early Jesuits', in Matter Coakley (eds.), *Creative Women*, 157–84.

van Boxel, Piet, 'Dowry and the Conversion of the Jews in Sixteenth-Century Rome: Competition between the Church and the Jewish Community', in Dean and Lowe (eds.), *Marriage in Italy*, 116–27.

Varano, Camilla Battista, *Le opere spirituali*, ed. G. Boccanegra (Jesi: Scuola Tipografica Francescana, 1958).

Vauchez, André, *The Laity in the Middle Ages: Religious Beliefs and Devotional Practices* (Notre Dame, Ind.: University of Notre Dame Press, 1993).

S. Veronica Giuliani, *Un resoro nascosto ossia il Diario di S. Veronica Giuliani*, ed. P. Pizzicaria (Prato: Tip. Giachetti, Figlio e c., 1895–1905).

Vigil, Mariló, *La vida de las mujeres en los siglos XVI y XVII* (Madrid: Siglo Veintiuno, 1986).

Vigri, Caterina, *Le sette armi spirituali*, ed. Cecilia Foletti (Padua: Antenore, 1985).

—— *Pregare con le immagini: IL Breviario di Caterina Vigri*, ed. Vera Fortunati and Claudio Leonaroli (Florence: Sismel Edizioni del Galluzzo, 2004).

Vincent de Paul and Louise de Marillac, *Rules, Conferences, and Writings*, ed. Frances Ryan and John E. Rybolt (New York: Paulist Press, 1995).

Walker, Claire, 'Combining Martha and Mary: Gender and Work in Seventeenth-Century English Cloisters', *Sixteenth Century Journal*, 30/2 (1999), 397–418.

—— *Gender and Politics in Early Modern Europe: English Convents in France and the Low Countries* (London: Palgrave Macmillan, 2003).

Warnke, Frank J. (ed.), *Three Women Poets, Renaissance and Baroque: Louise Labé, Gaspara Stampa, and Sor Juana Inés de la Cruz* (London and Toronto: Associated University Press, 1987).

Weaver, Elissa B., 'Spiritual Fun: A Study of Sixteenth-Century Tuscan Convent Theater', in Mary Beth Rose (ed.), *Women in the Middle Ages and Renaissance: Literary and Historical Perspectives* (Syracuse NY: Syracuse University Press, 1986), 173–205.

—— 'The Convent Wall in Tuscan Convent Drama', in Monson (ed.), *Crannied Wall*, 73–86.

—— 'Suor Maria Clemente Ruoti, Playwright and Academician', in Matter and Coakley (eds.), *Creative Women*, 281–96.

—— *Convent Theatre in Early Modern Italy: Spiritual Fun and Learning for Women* (Cambridge: Cambridge University Press, 2002).

Weber, Alison, *Teresa of Avila and the Rhetoric of Femininity* (Princeton: Princeton University Press, 1990).

—— 'Spiritual Administration: Gender and Discernment in the Carmelite Reform', *Sixteenth Century Journal*, 31/1 (2000), 123–46.

Wemple, S. Fonay, 'S. Salvatore/S. Giulia: A Case Study in the Endowment and Patronage of a Major Female Monastery in Northern Italy', in J. Kirshner and S. Fonay Wemple (eds.), *Women of the Medieval World* (Oxford: Oxford University Press, 1985), 85–102.

Wiesner, Merry E., 'Ideology Meets the Empire: Reformed Convents and the Reformation', in ead. (ed.), *Gender, Church, and State in Early Modern Germany* (London and New York: Longman, 1988), 47–62.

—— 'Nuns, Wives, and Mothers: Women and the Reformation in Germany', in Marshall (ed.), *Women in Reformation and Counter-Reformation Europe*, 8–28.

—— Merry, *Convents Confront the Reformation: Catholic and Protestant Nuns in Germany* (Milwaukee: Marquette University Press, 1996).

—— *Women and Gender in Early Modern Europe* (Cambridge: Cambridge University Press, 2000).

Wigley, George J., *St Charles Borromeo's 'Instructions on Ecclesiastical Buildings'* (London, 1857).

Wilson, Katharina M. (ed.), *The Dramas of Hrotsvit of Gandersheim* (Saskatoon: Peregrina, 1985).

Winkelmes, Mary-Ann, 'Taking Part: Benedictine Nuns as Patrons of Art and Architecture', in *Picturing Women in Renaissance and Baroque Italy* (Cambridge: Cambridge University Press, 1997), 91–110.

Wood, Jeryldene, 'Breaking the Silence: The Poor Clares and the Visual Arts in Fifteenth-Century Italy', *Renaissance Quarterly*, 48/2 (1995), 262–86.

—— *Women, Art, and Spirituality: The Poor Clares of Early Modern Italy* (Cambridge: Cambridge University Press, 1996).

Woodford, Charlotte, *Nuns as Historians in Early Modern Germany* (Oxford: Oxford University Press, 2002).

Woodward, W. H. (ed.), *Vittorino da Feltre and Other Humanist Educators* (Cambridge, 1905).

Worcester, Thomas, ' "Neither Married Nor Cloistered": Blessed Isabelle in Catholic Reformation', *Sixteenth Century Journal*, 30/2 (1999), 457–72.

Wright, Wendy M., *Bond of Perfection: Jeanne de Chantal and François de Sales* (New York: Paulist Press, 1985).

—— 'The Visitation of Holy Mary: The First Years (1610–1618)', in Richard L. De Molen (ed.), *Religious Orders of the Catholic Reformation* (New York: Fordham University Press, 1994).

Yardley, Anne Bagnall, 'The Marriage of Heaven and Earth: A Late Medieval Source of the Consecration Virginum', *Current Musicology*, 45–7 (Fall 1988), 305–24.

Zacchi, Alessandro, 'Giulio Morina al Corpus Domini: Nuove proposte per due problemi ancora irrisolti', in Fortunati (ed.), *Vita artistica nel monastero femminile*, 245–90.

Zanetti, Dante E., 'La demografia del patriziato Milanese nei secoli XVII, XVIII, XIX' *Annales cisalpines d'histoire sociale*, 2nd ser. 2 (1972), 83–5.

Zarri, Gabriella, *Le sante vive: Profezie di corte e devozione femminile tra '400 e '500* (Turin: Rosemberg & Sellier, 1990).

—— 'Recinti sacri: Sito e forma dei monasteri femminili a Bologna tra '500 e '600', in Gajano and Scaraffia (eds.), *Luoghi sacri*, 385–6.

—— 'Ursula and Catherine: The Marriage of Virgins in the Sixteenth Century', in Matter and Coackley (eds.), *Creative Women*, 431–54.

—— (ed.), *Donna, disciplina, creanza cristiana dal XV al XVII secolo: Studi e testi a stampa* (Rome: Edizioni di storia e letteratura, 1996).

—— 'Gender, Religious Institutions and Social Discipline: The Reform of the Regulars', in Brown and Davis (eds.), *Gender and Society in Renaissance Italy*, 193–212.

—— 'Monasteri feminili e città', in *Recinti: Donne, clausura e matrimonio nella prima età moderna* (Bologna: Il Mulino, 2000), 43–143.

PHOTOGRAPHIC ACKNOWLEDGEMENTS

Alinari Archives, Florence: 10, 14; Bayerische Staatsgemäldesammlungen: 2; Bayerische Staatsbibliothek, Munich: 20; Bibliothèque nationale de France, Paris: 13; The Bodleian Library, University of Oxford (G.A. Lond. 16° 32): 9; Bridgeman Art Library: 11; Bridgeman Art Library/Alinari Archives, Florence: 15; © The Collection of the Frick Art & Historical Center, Pittsburgh, Pennsylvania: 3: Denver Art Museum Collection: funds from the 1985 Trip Benefit and the Acquisition Challenge Grant, 1985.361: 12; Groeninge Museum, Musea Brugge, Belgium: 1; Hospitaalmuseum Sint-Janhospital, Musea Brugge, Belgium: 19; Lauros-Giraudon/Bridgeman Art Library: 6, 8; © Marghit Thøfner: 21; © Prado Museum, Madrid, all rights reserved: 7, 18

INDEX